ARNOLD AWOONOR-GORDON

REFLECTIONS ON MY LIFE

Edited by Winston Forde

ARNOLD AWOONOR-GORDON

Reflection on my life

Published by SONDIAT GLOBAL M in 2015

Copyright © Arnold Awoonor Gordon 2015

First Edition

The author asserts the moral right under the Copyright, Designs and Patents Act 1988 to be identified as the author of this work.

All Rights reserved. No part of this publication may be reproduced, stored in a retrieval system or transmitted, in any form or by any means without the prior consent of the author, nor be otherwise circulated in any form of binding or cover other than that in which it is published and without a similar condition being imposed on the subsequent purchases

www.songlome.com

Cover adapted by Khadi Mansaray

ARNOLD AWOONOR-GORDON

Reflection on my life

DEDICATION
This book is dedicated to the members
Of my immediate family who are no longer with us.
My grandmother
Mrs Emilie Awoonor-Williams (1866-
1960)
Mother Vera Fracess Awoonor-Gordon (nee Awoonor-
Williams)
(1901-1984)
Father Richard Onesimus Gordon (1905-
1978)
Brother Francis Awoonor-Gordon (1932-
1998)
Sister Dorothy Omodele Pyne (nee Awoonor-Gordon) (1928-
1994)
Her husband Charles Boisy Pyne (1926-
1991)
Brother William Richard Awoonor-Gordon (1930-
1977)
Nephew Richard Oluwasie Awoonor-Gordon (1957-
2010
Niece Allison Oluyemisi Pyne (1957-
2013)
Nephew Kenneth Magaji Pyne (1961-
1998)
Nephew Albert Akinwande
Pyne (1966-2002)
Grandniece Vera Awoonor-Pyne (1986-
2001)
May their souls rest in perfect peace.
My thanks to my good friend Syl Cheney-Coker, Sierra Leonean poet and writer (his latest book is entitled SACRED RIVER) for giving up his valuable time to read, edit, make suggestions and provide valuable assistance in order to bring this book to

ARNOLD AWOONOR-GORDON

publication.
The book cover was designed by P.A.W. Design, 158 Marrowbrook Lane, Farnborough. Hampshire GU14.0AD.

Table of Contents
1. THE START OF MY JOURNEY 9

2. ROOTS................................14

3. GROWING UP IN FREETOWN 20

4. THE OLD FAMILIES 27

5. OUR HOUSE 31

6. RHYTHM OF HOME LIFE................................ 37

7. FAMILY HIERARCHY IN CHURCH 41

8. SUNDAY AND OTHER PASTTIMES 46

9. THE MARK OF UNRIGHTIOUSNESS 50

10. SCHOOL DAYS 54

11. IN PRAISE OF THE OLD TEACHERS, AND A NEW LIFE................................62

12. LONDON AND OTHER DAYS 75

13. EXPANDING MY HORIZON 85

14. A REPORTER AT LARGE 89

15. THE VENICE OF WEST AFRICA, OLD DIVERSITIES, AND FABLED DJENNE 96

Reflection on my life

DEDICATION

This book is dedicated to the members of my immediate family who are no longer with us.
My grandmother
Mrs Emilie Awoonor-Williams (1866-1960)
Mother Vera Fracess Awoonor-Gordon (nee Awoonor-Williams) (1901-1984)
Father Richard Onesimus Gordon (1905-1978)
Brother Francis Awoonor-Gordon (1932-1998)
Sister Dorothy Omodele Pyne (nee Awoonor-Gordon) (1928-1994)
Her husband Charles Boisy Pyne (1926-1991)
Brother William Richard Awoonor-Gordon (1930-1977)
Nephew Richard Oluwasie Awoonor-Gordon (1957-2010
Niece Allison Oluyemisi Pyne (1957-2013)
Nephew Kenneth Magaji Pyne (1961-1998)
Nephew Albert Akinwande Pyne (1966-2002)
Grandniece Vera Awoonor-Pyne (1986-2001)
May their souls rest in perfect peace.
My thanks to my good friend Syl Cheney-Coker, Sierra Leonean poet and writer (his latest book is entitled SACRED RIVER) for giving up his valuable time to read, edit, make suggestions and provide valuable assistance in order to bring this book to

ARNOLD AWOONOR-GORDON

publication.
The book cover was designed by P.A.W. Design, 158 Marrowbrook Lane, Farnborough. Hampshire GU14.0AD.

Table of Contents
1. THE START OF MY JOURNEY 9
2. ROOTS................14
3. GROWING UP IN FREETOWN 20
4. THE OLD FAMILIES 27
5. OUR HOUSE 31
6. RHYTHM OF HOME LIFE................ 37
7. FAMILY HIERARCHY IN CHURCH 41
8. SUNDAY AND OTHER PASTTIMES 46
9. THE MARK OF UNRIGHTIOUSNESS 50
10. SCHOOL DAYS 54
11. IN PRAISE OF THE OLD TEACHERS, AND A NEW LIFE................62
12. LONDON AND OTHER DAYS 75
13. EXPANDING MY HORIZON 85
14. A REPORTER AT LARGE 89
15. THE VENICE OF WEST AFRICA, OLD DIVERSITIES, AND FABLED DJENNE 96

16. THE COMPLEX NARRATIVE THAT IS NIGERIA 99

17. A NEW DAWN 109

18. AT BUSH HOUSE, LONDON 125

19. MY EPIC HITCHHIKING FROM LONDON TO TOKYO 131

20. BACK IN LONDON..166

21. BERLINER WASSER, AND DROPPING MY PANTS FOR YOKO ONO! 171

22. FEAR OF HEIGHT; A MAN CALLED DIKKO, AND MEETING SIDNEY POITIER! 176

23. AN OLD TWISTER DINES WITH THE QUEEN, AND HOW I MET ENGELBERT HUMPERDINCK EARTHA KITT...180

24. TENANTS FROM HELL, A NIGHT AT THE BALLET, AND CHAMPAGNE WITH THE QUEEN MOTHER...188

25. BACK ON THE HOME TURF AND MY DUTCH DAYS 194

26. IN THE BELLY OF THE BEAST 217

27. GETTING TO KNOW UNCLE SAM'S PEOPLE IN FREETOWN 234

28. IN THE LAND OF BARBEQUE AND THE GRAND OLE OPERY..................244

29. IN THE SEASON OF LIFE AND DEATH 250

30. A BEND IN THE RIVER: MY LIFE GOES ON A NEW PATH..................260

31. HOW I BECAME AN INTERPRETER ....…….....274

32. A MAN WANTED BY HIS OLD PALS. ......…….......281

33. WE WERE ALWAYS IN THE DARK...……….....……...287

34. SOLICITORS AND ADJUDICATORS 291

35. THE GAINS (AND HEADACHE) OF BEING AN INTERPRETER 297

36. WHOSE STORY IS IT, ANYWAY? 301

37. A GLOBAL TEAM SOMETIMES MISINTERPRETS....307

38. THE ENIGMATIC HOME OFFICE, INTERPRETERS AND CASES 311

39. A TEST CASE ...…….........…………................318

40. THE WHISTLEBLOWER ....…….................320

41. KRIO, JAMAICAN PATOIS AND THOSE JUDGES AND COURTS 322

Reflection on my life

CHAPTER 1
THE START OF MY JOURNEY

My journey began on the 14th of October, 1933 in Freetown, capital of Sierra Leone. I was born, like many children in the City at that time, at the Dr. Jones Maternity home at Oxford Street, since renamed Lightfoot-Boston Street. My parents were Richard Onesimus Gordon and Vera Francess (Sissy) Gordon, nee Awoonor-Williams. When my father went to register my birth he was asked for my name, and not having thought of one, plucked the only name that came into his head, which was Palade, and that is the name I have on my birth certificate. I understand that on the day I was born, Governor Palade, governor of neighbouring Guinea, was visiting Freetown, and his name was in all the newspapers, hence my registered name. But later at my christening ceremony, I was given the names Arnold, after the popular Governor at the time, Arnold Hudson, Jeremiah, after my Godfather Jeremiah Williams and Matomije, a Yoruba name I later got to know meant ' nor fet wit me' (don't fight with me) Appropriate, I suspect, for a warring and possibly separating couple. I have never used any of my names except for Arnold, although a friend of mine insists on calling me Jeremiah, just to wind me up.

My father came from Gloucester, one of the mountain villages around Freetown, but his ancestry was quite fascinating. His grandfather was from Grenada in the West Indies, and was a member of the colonial West Indian army that the ruling British Government had brought over to help put down the so-called 'Hut Tax War.' This was a rebellion similar to the American Boston Tea rebellion, but in this case, Bai Bureh, the leader of the Temnes, one of the majority peoples in the country, had led them in opposing what they considered an unjust tax based on the ownership of huts.

ARNOLD AWOONOR-GORDON

My great- grandfather's regiment was stationed at the Tower Hill barracks, where the House of Parliament now stands, which was near the street that came to be known as Soldier Street because of its proximity to the barracks. Quite clearly, it was not uncommon to see soldiers on that street, either going on a date or just enjoying themselves.

Although the soldiers cooked their own food, their laundry was done by washer women who mostly came from the mountain villages of Leicester, Gloucester and Regent. One such lady from Gloucester became my great-grandmother. My great-grandfather fell in love with her during one of her visits with the other women to do the soldiers' laundry. When the regiment was demobbed, most of his compatriots returned to the West Indies, but he decided to stay behind. to marry his love and moved to Gloucester. Sadly, I have not been able to trace an ancestral tree in Grenada that flows from my great-grandfather.

My first few months were spent at 35 Wellington Street, in central Freetown, but my father and mother separated soon afterwards, and she and her four children moved back to live with her mother. As a result I grew up with my brother Francis, Sister Dorothy (Dele) brother William (Papaboy) with my grandmother at the family house at the corner of Waterloo street and Oxford, now Lightfoot-Boston street. It was a jolly and lively house, with cousins and aunties and uncles coming and going all the time.

Grandma Emilie, who, with her sister Annie had been educated in England from an early age, used to tell us stories about her time at school in London. They had both attended the Kilburn Priory College in London and one of the students, was the granddaughter of the founder of Madam Tussauds, situated at Marylebone Road. This created a special privilege for all the pupils at the school, who were given free tickets to visit the museum, and were often allowed to jump to the front of the queue that regularly stretched like a

Reflection on my life

crocodile file, from Kilburn to the museum.

The two girls, Emilie and Annie, were the daughters of the Reverend George Pompey Crowther-Nicol and Susan Crowther. Susan was one of the three daughters of Bishop Samuel Adjai Crowther and his wife Susan Asano Thompson.

MY GRANDMOTER, MRS EMILIE AWOONOR-WILLIAMS

ARNOLD AWOONOR-GORDON

My grandmother Emilie's father, was George Pompey Crowther-Nicol. His own father was called Pompey and came from the Temne people in the Protectorate. His mother named Sally, was a Susu woman. He had a sister called Hannah. George Pompey Nicol was born in December 1822 at Regent, baptised at Gloucester village, where his parents had moved when young, by the Rev Thomas of the Church Missionary Society (CMS) He entered Fourah Bay College on Good Friday in April 1838, when the Rev G.A. Kisling acted as the superintendent of the college. He trained as a priest and travelled to England for further instructions in June 1844, at the CMS College in Islington, whose Principal was the Rev. C. N .Childe. In 1848 he returned to England where he was ordained Deacon, and in June 1849 he was ordained as priest by the then Bishop of London, at St Pauls Cathedral. He served in various parishes in Freetown until 1869 when he was appointed Chaplain to the Forces in Bathurst, Gambia.

When we lived with my grandmother, she made us listen regularly to the BBC World Service over the Rediffusion radio box, which had been supplied by the colonial government. Amongst the presenters whose voices came over the air regularly were two that left the deepest impression on me, and I used to listen intently if they were on duty. One was Marjorie Anderson and the other Alexander Moyse. Even as young as I was then, I made up my mind that one day I too would become a broadcaster, and what's more work for the BBC. I did not realise then that my wish would come true one day.

My grandmother, as mentioned and her sister Annie, were educated in the UK. She told us that their guardians were the Barclays of the Barclays Bank family. She used to regale us with stories of visits to the ancestral manor house somewhere in Hampshire where they they were trained to ride horses. Although Grandma was never keen on riding, Annie on the other hand, became a very good horse rider. She also told us about the number of dogs they had, and how she

Reflection on my life

became very fond of dogs. She regretted that she was not able to keep dogs when she married, as her mother-in-law did not like them.

Her husband was Alfred Brigas Awuna-Williams, who was born in Keta, in the Gold Coast. His father was a carpenter from Waterloo a town east of Freetown who had been recruited to work in the timber trade in Keta and became a very wealthy timber merchant. He married a Keta princess of the Awuna people and the Awuna was attached to the Williams to form a distinctive surname. I have always wondered how the Awuna became Awoonor. I found out many years later that two of the Awuna-Williams brothers fell out, and so one changed the Awuna to Awoonor, but the other kept the Awuna. Even today there are family members in Ghana who spell it Awuna and those who use the Awoonor option.

After he became wealthy from the timber trade, Edward Williams, the founding father of the dynasty, sent for his two sisters from Waterloo to join him. One sister, Regina, married a Peter Renner creating the Awoonor-Renner branch of the family. The other sister, Vidawin, married a Moses Wilson, which led to the branch of the family which included the late Mrs Constance Cummings-John. Thus we have relatives in Nigeria, Ghana and the Gambia.

Chapter 2
ROOTS

The roots of my ancestry originated in the early 1800s with the founding father of the family on my great-grandmother Susan Crowther's side. Her father was Bishop Samuel Adjai Crowther, who was to become famous in Anglican Church history, as the first African to be consecrated a bishop of that establishment. His journey to that honour was quite a remarkable one. As a young boy he was captured in Nigeria, presumably in today's Abeokuta, the heartland of the Yoruba, and sold into slavery.

Born around 1809, he was named Adjai, meaning 'a child born face downwards'. He was about ten years old, when his village was attacked by slave raiders, and he and his family were captured and sold into slavery.

Separated from his family, he was bought by Portuguese slavers and put on a Portuguese slave ship, the ESPERANZ FELIX. Crowded into the ship's hold, with hundreds of men and boys, the ship sailed to the Caribbean. Luckily for him, slavery had been abolished in England by then, due to the great effort of William Wilberforce and his fellow Christians. The British then sent naval ships to patrol the seas along the coast of West Africa. Two such ships, the MYRMIDON and the IPHIGENIA, were on patrol, when they spotted the ship carrying Adjai and the other captives. The ship was stopped and the British Naval Patrol took it and its cargo of captives to Freetown, where they were released to start a new life.

By then, Freetown had become a British colony, where many of the freed slaves were settled. By the end of the eighteenth century, the Church Missionary Society (CMS) in the UK, had become concerned about the large number of receptive slave children, and so had built a home each at Regent and Bathurst, two villages in the

Reflection on my life

hills above Freetown where these children could be looked after and given a Christian education. Adjai was fortunate to be put in the care of two Missionary teachers, a Mr and Mrs Davey, who also

MY GREAT-GREAT GRANDFATHER, BISHOP SAMUEL ADJAI CROWTHER

ARNOLD AWOONOR-GORDON

took in a young slave girl called Asano. Adjai was very smart and quickly learned to read and write, including reading the bible. On the 11 December 1825, he was baptised into the Christian church, and took the names Samuel Adjai Crowther. The two English names were those of the names of the Reverend Samuel Crowther one of the founders of the CMS. He became the first student at Fourah Bay College, which was then a theological institute.

Afterwards, he went to England to train as a priest and eventually became the first African Bishop in the world. He was consecrated bishop on St Peter's day, 29th June 1864 by Charles Longley, Archbishop of Canterbury at Canterbury Cathedral. when Crowther was fifty-four. That same year he was also given a Doctorate of Divinity by the University of Oxford. He married Asano, the young slave girl with whom he had lived in the house of the missionaries. She had also been baptised and had taken the name Susan Asano Thompson. The one hundred and fiftieth anniversary of the consecration of Bishop Crowther was marked at a special service in June 2014, at Canterbury Cathedral, with the address being given by Archbishop Welby.

Amongst the guests at his consecration in 1864 were the first people who had looked after him, and the captain of one of the naval ships that had rescued him. Bishop Samuel Adjai Crowther lived a long and useful life, serving the church in Sierra Leone and Nigeria, where he was eventually reunited with his long lost mother and a sister. His eldest daughter Susan, as stated earlier married the Reverend George Pompey Crowther-Nicol, and they were the parents of my maternal grandmother. Another daughter married the Reverend T.B. Macaulay, the Principal of Lagos Grammar School. They were the parents of Herbert Macaulay, one of the prominent fighters for independence from the British in Nigeria. A third daughter, Juliana, also married a priest, the Reverend David Thompson.

Reflection on my life

Bishop Crowther had two sons. One son, Josiah, entered King's College in London to study medicine, but did not finish. The other, Dandeson, also became a priest and married into the Metzger family.

My grandmother was one of thirteen children, and one brother she remembered and spoke of fondly of was called Gurney. He went from Monkton Coombe School to Corpus Christie and was the first African to graduate from Cambridge University in 1879. He wanted to read law but his father insisted that he become a priest. Never a very robust person, according to my grandmother, he became a pastor in Bonthe and died suddenly in 1888. Grandma always said his death was due to a paralytic seizure, brought on by a bicycling accident when he was a student at Cambridge.

ANOTHER ANCESTOR, SALLY FORBES-BONETTA, THE ADOPTED DAUGHTER OF QUEEN VICTORIA

When we were living with grandma, she used to tell us the story of another ancestor, who she said was the adopted daughter of Queen Victoria. We never believed her and thought that it was an old woman talking. Several years later when I was living in London, I decided to find out whether the story was true or just the imagination of an old woman. I wrote to the Librarian at Windsor Castle, and I got a reply which said the story was indeed true.

This ancestor of mine was Sally Forbes Bonetta. She too had an interesting background and her story was published in a book entitled AT HER MAJESTY'S REQUEST. AN AFRICAN PRINCESS IN VICTORIAN ENGLAND by Walter Dean Myers and published by Scholastic Press. Her story would make an interesting movie. In October 1849, Queen Victoria sent the HMS Bonetta, under the command of thirty year old Commander Frederick Forbes, to King Gozo of Dahomey on the coast of West Africa, to entreat him to put an end to the slave trade. King Gozo played a major role in the capture and selling of slaves from the interior of the West African coast, and was notorious and much feared by the people. When Commander Forbes reached the palace of the King, he gave him the gifts that Queen Victoria had sent, and the message he had brought from the 'Great White Queen,' that he should put an end to the slave trade.

The King listened to the message and although he did not accede to Victoria's entreaty, he decided to send a present to the Queen instead. Just before Commander arrived at the palace, the King's raiding party had brought in the slaves they had captured, and amongst them was a little girl of about five or six. King Gozo then gave the girl to the Commander to bring to Queen Victoria as his gift to her. He could not do anything but accept the gift of the little girl, and brought her to England. He named her Sarah (Sally) Forbes after his mother and Bonetta after the name of his ship.

On the 9th of November 1850, in the presence of her son Edward Vll and her daughter Victoria, and other members of the Royal

Reflection on my life

family, Sarah was eventually presented to the Queen at Windsor castle. The Queen was very impressed by Sarah, who had by then learned English, and was able to relate what she knew about her story. The Queen adopted her and gave her an annuity. Sometime later, the Queen decided that the English weather was not suitable for the little girl, and, with the help of the Church Missionary Society, she was sent to Freetown to attend the Annie Walsh Memorial School, then under the Principalship of a Miss Sass. After her education in Freetown, Sally returned to England, and, at nineteen, received a marriage proposal from a Mr. James Pinson Labulo Davies, who was from Nigeria. The Queen gave her consent to the marriage took place on 14th August 1862, at St Nicholas Church in Brighton. Her trousseau was provided by Queen Victoria.

The newly married couple first went to live in Freetown but eventually settled in Nigeria. Their daughter was named Victoria, and the Queen consented to be the child's Godmother. We still have in the family the christening cup and plate made by the Royal Silversmiths, Garrards of London, presented by the Queen to her Goddaughter Victoria in 1864.

ARNOLD AWOONOR-GORDON

Chapter 3
GROWING UP IN FREETOWN

The house at the corner of Waterloo and Oxford Streets was always full of cousins, aunts and uncles. When any of the three Elder Dempster mail boats, the Apapa, Accra or Aureol docked in Freetown, sailing from down the coast to the UK, or the other way round, relatives would come ashore to meet the matriarch, grandma Emilie, and the rest of the family. They were often treated to a sumptuous meal of Mama's famous jollof rice. Over the years, we have been in touch with our extended family along the west coast of Africa. Many family members came from the Gambia, Ghana and Nigeria and stayed with us to attend school, and several stayed permanently after they had finished their education.

MY MOTHER, VERA AWOONOR-GORDON

My grandmother's best and oldest friend was Mrs Claribelle May,

Reflection on my life

fondly known to all as Grandma May. She was the widow of Mr Cornelius May, the Mayor of Freetown during the visit of the Prince of Wales in the 1920s. Grandma May lived at the eastern extreme of Oxford Street, now Lightfoot-Boston by the railway station, and we lived at the other end at Waterloo Street junction, just before descending into the area around Kroo Bay. Every Wednesday, for as long as I can remember, the two old friends would meet for afternoon tea using an alternating weekly logistics arrangement. One week I, or one of my brothers, usually it was me as I was the youngest, would walk grandma from our end of the street all the way to the other end, to deliver her to Grandma May's house; there were no cars then, or if they existed we did not have one. There, the two friends would have tea and gossip about their young days and their friends, children and grandchildren. At dusk, Tunji, granddaughter of Grandma May, would walk my grandmother back home. The following week, it would be Tunji's turn to bring her grandmother to our house, and as it became dusk, we would walk her back to hers. Tunji grew up, came to England and trained as a physiotherapist. She later married Dr Arthur Stuart and they had two children, David and Gwen.

MY SISTER DOROTHY AND HER HUSBAND CHARLES BOISY PYNE

ARNOLD AWOONOR-GORDON

MY BROTHER FRANCIS AWOONOR-GORDON

We children liked to eavesdrop on the conversation of the two old ladies, whilst gossiping, as we busied ourselves replenishing tea pots and cake holders. They both spoke beautiful English and were great snubs about other people. Alas, their Krio was not too good

Reflection on my life

and I remember my grandmother once asking what the house maid meant when she said that she had put something 'pantap' the table, which we knew as being on top of the table. One conversation I remember distinctly from all those years, was when they were talking about some young man, the grandson of one of their friends, who had gone away to study in England, and was bringing his English bride back home with him. I remember the conversation just as if it was yesterday; one of them remarked: 'She must have been a barmaid he met in a pub. No self-respecting Englishwoman of any class would marry an African.' And the other one concurred. I remember them also discussing another person who had married someone from the Gold Coast, and one saying 'I hope she is not a cloth woman' meaning she hoped she was someone who wore a dress and not the usual lappa. There's little doubt they really were big snubs.

Talking about the misunderstanding between English and Krio, I was told a story once, one of those urban myths perhaps, about the wife of a Colonial officer and her housemaid. After the housemaid returned from having a baby, she asked her mistress to let her off early so she could go home to give the new baby 'her bobby.' The mistress could not understand why she wanted to go and give her baby to a bobby because, as far as she knew, bobby was a policeman on the beat in England. It took a great deal of explaining before she realised that what the maid wanted to do was to go home early to breast feed her baby.

This business of misunderstanding between languages, or the way we pronounce words between languages, happened to me many years later when I first arrived in London. I was in central London looking for the Sierra Leone High Commission, which at that time was situated in Pall Mall. I had to stop several people to ask the way to Pall Mall, but no one understood what I was saying, until one person asked me to write it down. It was then I was informed that the place I was looking for was pronounced 'PELL MELL', and not PALL MALL, as it was spelt and as I was pronouncing it. Also on a bus going to what I was calling Bow, as it is spelt, the conductor, being a Cockney could not understand what I was saying until one of the passengers told him that I wanted to go to BAW and not BOW as it is spelt, and how I was pronouncing the name. I had to learn the hard way that in English, the spelling and the pronouncing of a word sometimes is not the same.

It is nostalgic to recall that Freetown had its own Oxford Street in those days, which sadly is now called Lightfoot-Boston Street. It was one of the longer streets in our small city, but I can still remember all the businesses and families who lived along the street. There was Grandma May's house at the beginning, followed by Aunty Beatrice Awoonor-Renner of Awoonor House at the corner of Wilberforce Street. After those houses, you came to the Bank of West Africa, now Standard Bank building, where my uncle Alfred Thompson-Clewry worked. Across from the bank was the Road Transport bus stop, which was always crowded, next to the Rawdon Street church at the corner of Rawdon Street. At that time, it was a lovely old building, which was pulled down to be replaced by what now looks like a bus shelter. At the other corner of Oxford and Rawdon Streets was J.T. Chanrai, an Indian shop. Across from the shop, on the other corner was the building which housed the Tea Shop upstairs and, downstairs, the famous Swissy Jewellery shop, run by a Mr Alami. The shop is still there. On the same side of the street, a block away from J.T. Chanrai, was Multi stores, which was the former French firm, the CFAO store, on the corner of Charlotte Street, and at the other corner of Charlotte Street, was the Bata shoe company, where we bought our shoes. I should add here that the Bata Shoe Company had branches all over West Africa, and the Yoruba word for shoes in Nigeria is BATA. Just thought I should add this here one of those useless bits of information I gathered on my journey.

Across Oxford Street, at the corner with Gloucester Street, was the

Reflection on my life

MY BROTHER, WILLIAM AWOONOR-GORDON

ARNOLD AWOONOR-GORDON

City Hotel, made famous by Graham Greene in his book 'the Heart of the Matter'. Sadly, many years later, I witnessed the hotel being pulled down, with tears in my eyes as I remembered all the regulars who patronised and drank at its famous bar, overseen by Freddie, the Swiss owner, and the equally famous waiter whom we called FLASH, with his trick of opening your bottle of Star beer, and flicking the stopper into the yard outside, through the window behind the bar. All now a fading memory. Opposite the hotel was, and still is, the building that originally was where another important girl institute, the Freetown Secondary School for Girls, (which I still call Oshora school,) and founded by the wife of a Nigerian called Mrs Oshora.

Chapter 3
THE OLD FAMILIES

Old Central Freetown, especially Oxford Street, had some other interesting buildings. There was the one that housed the CMS Bookshop, where we bought our school books. Sadly, the main business closed down a long time ago, although the building is still there.

On the same side of the road and at the corner with George Street was the home of the Williams family, mother, father, two daughters and one son. They were a very religious family who were nicknamed 'the Righteous Williams'. Next to them was a hotel which at one time was owned by Mrs Lerina Bright-Taylor, the sister of Dr Bankole-Bright, who was a good friend of my mother's and whom we knew as Aunty Lerina.

On the opposite side of Oxford Street, across from the hotel, was, and still is, the Secretariat building that served as the colonial administrative centre, operating the only internal passenger lift in Freetown. A stone's throw from it, and at the corner of Trelawney, now Lamina Sankoh street was, and still is, Wesley Methodist Church, which stretched from Trelawney, (now Lamina Sankor) to Walpole Street and is still being worshipped in by some of the oldest Creole Freetown families. Opposite the church was the Dr. Jones nursing home, where hundreds of Freetown babies were born. Further down the road is the George Ackland Masonic temple, next to Peters Brook market, named after Thomas Peters, one of the early Nova Scotian founders of the city.

Adding to Oxford Street's colourful atmosphere on the opposite side of the road was *Pa Armatey's* goldsmith shop. He was originally from the Gold Coast and soon became the premier goldsmith in Freetown. His clients were all the aristocratic ladies of

ARNOLD AWOONOR-GORDON

Freetown, and he served them extremely well. We saw his handiwork each Sunday at the Saint George's Cathedral, when the elegant ladies of this most esteemed first church, would parade proudly down the aisle to their pews, showing off their gold chains hanging halfway down to their waste lines, with beautifully crafted broaches clasped to their heaving bosoms, while large gold earrings peeped from under their most stylish hats. It was a sight to behold. I wonder what happened to all that gold jewellery when they passed on.

Next to Armatey's goldsmith shop, was the old Creole house belonging to the Samuel family. I mention this family because it was a house with beautiful daughters but no sons. You can imagine what that must have meant for adolescent boys at that time. The house, surprisingly, is still there although in a very dilapidated state, looking as if it will fall down any day now. On the same side, but further down at the corner of Pultney Street, lived Mr and Mrs Jaja Gooding. They had a beautiful niece who was married to a wealthy Nigerian lawyer, and they made frequent trips to Lagos to visit her. Mrs Gooding was a friend of my mother and I remember that she liked the fish we call *tennie*. It was a fish with very many small but strong bones and one needed patience to remove all the bones before cooking. As the Jaja Gooding's did not have a young person living with them, only an elderly house keeper, Ma Gooding would send the *tennie*, two or three at a time, for my mother to get one of us to clean and take out all the bones. This was a job we did not relish, but were forced to do by mother.

Opposite the Jaja Goodings, at the corner of the road that leads to Peters Brook Market, lived Mr and Mrs Lew- Ray. Mrs Lew-Ray was a well-respected midwife who brought many children into the world when she worked at the Princess Christian Maternity Hospital in the east end of Freetown. I remember having to interview her for a BBC radio programme while she was in London to attend a nurses' conference several years later. This was at the time when the Thalidomide scare was on. She was very upset at seeing the first children affected by the drug, and vouched that when she returned home she would see that the drug was never prescribed to mothers in the country.

Next to the Lew-Rays was a small shop which was owned by one of the most interesting characters in the cameo of Oxford Street. He was a shoemaker who had so many stories to tell that we would bring our shoes to him to mend, just to sit and listen to him tell one of his stories. The Connaught Hospital comprising a main building housing wards, a mortuary, medical administration block, dental department and the sanitary departments occupied an area that stretched from Percival Street to where the nurses' training school is now situated, next to the Masonic temple. The maternity wards of the hospital was on the Oxford street side, and people passing by would hear the women shouting and screaming as they brought another soul into the world. Being playful boys, if we were passing during one of these labour intensive occurrences would shout, 'quiet there you should have thought of the pain when you were enjoying yourself' or words to that effect. But I must say that we only did this under the cover of darkness at night.

Across from the hospital was a building that housed the Guardian newspaper, now no more; next to it was the home of the King family, and next to them, where the branch of the Commercial bank is now situated, was a building housing the nurses who were training at the Connaught hospital. Across the road was the home of the Patnelli family, with four boys who were friends of ours.....Johnny, the eldest, followed by the twins Khainde and Taiwo and the last Idowu. I remember the fun times we spent in that house.

And next to them lived Mama Spain, and at the corner with Bathurst lived Pa Clarkson the electrician. The house is still there but looks as it it also will fall down any day. Then you came to the massive Grammar school building with grounds filling up the whole block. After that, on the corner of Wellington street, lived our neighbour, the late Alex (Eku) Brown and his family, and then our family house on the corner of Waterloo street. On the other side of the road was, and still is, the Masonic temple, and next to them in what we called an '*adjoiney*,' which was really an extension of the house, lived Mammy Fatou and her family. At the tail end of Oxford Street, but opposite us was the house of the Renner-Lisk family, and next to them was Mama Joko Johnston-Taylor and her family. In the last house of the Oxford Street cameo lived Mama During and her daughter Miss Terris, facing Waterloo street, forming a cul-de-sac on Oxford Street, but with a steep incline for pedestrians to go down to the Kroo Bay. Cars now use the road to Kroo Bay, but then it was pedestrian only.

Reflection on my life

on Kroo Town Road, which was reached by walking up Waterloo Street, from our house, to Westmorland Street, which was then one of the main arteries of Freetown. Turning right on that street, you came to a 4-way junction at Jokey Bridge, with Brook Street at right angles on the left whilst the road ahead became Sanders Street and at an angle with Kroo Town Road leading off on the right. The Kroo men were mainly seafarers and many of them were recruited every time a ship needed a crew for its voyage down the coast to Liberia, the Gold Coast, Lagos and points further south, such as Lobito and Luanda We would know when they returned, as their wives would be rushing from Kroo bay shouting 'Muna Gee oh', which we assumed was Kroo for 'ships have returned', on their way to meet their men folk, and, we assumed, get their pay packets before the men spent them on what the women might consider frivolous, such as drink. And then later in the day, we would witness a procession of Kroo men and their wives returning to their abodes, carrying their distinctive beds used at sea made of canvas with folding wooden legs, and laden with what we assumed were presents for their families. Someone did mention later that the word 'Kroo' was a corruption of the word 'crew', as they were recruited as crew for the ships. Seems a little far-fetched to me, but who knows.

As our house was situated at the junction of two roads, for some unknown reason, the junction became a place where people would offer sacrifice with some form of fetish or juju in the middle of the night. Time and time again, we would wake up in the morning to see some fetish of cowry shells, red 'tafti' cloth and other ornaments that had been used and left there. What good it did them, I don't know. We never saw the people who used that junction for their juju magic as we were all fast asleep when they performed the sacrificial ritual. But one night, when all good people in the area were in their beds fast asleep, we heard a commotion taking place at that junction. Of course, it woke up the whole neighbourhood, and all windows flew open as we wanted to find out what the fuss was all about.

This was in the days when policemen did night time foot patrol in all areas of the city. That night, it happened that a policeman doing his rounds came across a lady stark naked dancing around the juju stuff she had placed at the junction of the road. He waited until she had finished her incantation and was preparing to return to her house when he tried to accost her. She ran into her house, which was opposite ours, but he chased her and caught and dragged her outside. The lady in question turned out to be a well-respected lady in the neighbourhood and a pillar of the Samaria Methodist Church up on Waterloo Street. By the time he caught her, she had covered herself up with a lappa avoiding any embarrassment.

With all of us hanging out of our windows, he then ordered her not only to clear the mess but also to wash the area where she had placed her juju fetish. Added to the hilarity of the situation, was that as she washed the road and swept it with a broom, the water ran down towards the front of the house of Mama During, who started to scream' Nor make da wata cam nar me compound' 'Don't let the water come onto my compound,' so that the obviously humiliated poor woman had to divert the water away from the front of the house of Mama During into the gutter. This happened about seventy years ago, and I cannot remember what happened to the shamed woman afterwards. I cannot remember seeing her around after the juju incident.

Living in an outhouse in the compound of a house next to ours, was a family who had a young child aged about three or four years, who had what we called 'dada' hair, but which nowadays is called 'rasta'. In those days, according to superstition, the hair of these children should not be cut until they were about ten years of age. And not before carrying out an elaborate ceremony, which involved

Reflection on my life

the cooking of black eyed beans, and lots of palm oil and then pouring the mixture over the head, before the hair cut. One day, the father of the child grew fed up with his 'dada' and decided to cut his hair without a ceremony. As soon as the scissors touched his head, the child fainted and went into a convulsive fit and fell to the ground foaming from the mouth.

There was great commotion in the compound, and the local witch doctor had to be summoned in order to pacify the child. I must say that after his usual mumbo jumbo with fly swish and cowry beads, the child recovered and did not look worse for his fainting fit. The mother, of course, was furious with father. He then had to dig deep into his pocket to have the traditional ceremony performed, before the child's hair was ceremonially cut. It is always difficult to believe these superstitions, but when one actually sees it happen, one gets confused and end up wondering, did it happen, or was it a dream?

Of course, as young children, money was very important to us. But apart from the daily money for school lunch, which went on *'patch granat'* (roasted groundnut) *akara* and *kanya*, we needed extra cash, as most young boys and girls around seemed to do. So we developed an audacious way of raising these extra funds, known as *'broke balance'*. We applied the practice whenever we had to do some of the shopping at the market. It was like this: Our mother would give us the exact amount to purchase pepper, fish, leaves and other ingredients necessary for making the stew of the day. Now, in order to *'broke balance'*, rather than spend, say six pence on buying peppers, we would spend five pence and the one penny was ours. If we did a 'broke balance' on every item, we would end up with quite a few pennies in our pocket. Wise to our ways, our mother, and I think the mothers of all young boys at the time, would complain that our purchase was not six pence worth of peppers. But we would explain that there were not many women selling peppers in the market that day. We would say peppers were scares owing to transportation problems, or whatever other excuse we could invent. I am sure our mothers knew that we were pinching their pennies as they complained occasionally about it, but did nothing. Obviously it wasn't regarded as a serious crime rather a case of boyhood prank!

Another way of making a bit of money on the side was that, on Good Friday, we would make an effigy of Judas and take it from house to house, singing '*Judas die don tiday, we go berr am tomarra*'. (Judas has died today, and we shall bury him tomorrow) and collect money from each house. It is like kids in the UK with their effigy of Guy Fawkes on Guy Fawkes' night.

At Christmas time, when the need for extra funds was much greater, we would go carolling in the neighbourhood. Moneys collected would be shared equally amongst those taking part. But I was put off going Carol singing again, when we were asked by some older boys to join their group. It was fun as we roamed far and wide and not just in our neighbourhood, and I know we collected much more money than usual. However, when it was time for us to get our share, the three older boys who had organised the singing, were nowhere to be seen. They had scuppered to Liberia with the money, which unexpectedly left us with no extra money for Christmas that year.

I must add here that the three older boys who had duped us did very well in Liberia, in later life, and one of them became a very successful banker. I got my own back; for when I saw him, many years later, I would demand my share of the proceeds of our Christmas carolling and attempt to riffle his pockets for some dollars. Even to this day when I telephone him in America I would jokingly ask him to send my share of those Christmas takings that he failed to share with us! I am always threatening to tell his children about the way he stole our money if he did not pay up, and he would beg and pay up. All in jest of course.

Reflection on my life

CHAPTER 6
RHYTHM OF HOME LIFE

Grandmother was an avid reader and apart from reading passages from the bible every day she subscribed to the Readers Digest and Women's Own magazine, both of which came from England when the mail boat arrived. She liked reading aloud, and I remember sitting on the floor or on her bed with other children, as she sat upright on her bed reading stories from the Readers Digest or Women's Own to us. The stories were normally about people and places and things outside Africa, which particularly fired our imagination and made us want to travel to these places.

She was also a keen gardener, and her specialities were roses and jasmine. She had both growing in the garden, and in pots on both sides of the steps leading to the house. As the boys' bedroom was on the side of the house facing the garden, I can still smell the fragrance of the jasmines especially at night. We also had two coconut trees and a tropical apple tree growing in the yard that produced pink apples. Every now and again the coconut man would come and climb the trees and pick the fruits, which were shared equally between us and the man. It was also a way of getting rid of the bats that made their home in the trees and kept us awake all night with their squeaking. When the apple was in full fruit, we could eat as many as we liked, and the rest would be sold. According to grandma the apple tree had been in the yard when she returned from Ghana early in the last century. Unfortunately it was recently chopped down by persons unknown, and the coconut trees had long disappeared.

We had a cupboard in the house which was full of Wedgwood crockery... soup tureens, large platters, serving dishes and much silverware. These were invaluable heirlooms, and were only used when we had important family gatherings such as weddings. These all disappeared after a relative came to the house, when most of us were away abroad, and helped herself to the lot. When asked why she did this, her reply was that as Grandma was getting old and alone in the house, she was afraid that thieves might break in and steal them. We never recovered them. One day her house caught fire and the flames consumed the attic where she had stored them. I consider this to be a case of poetic justice.

Sunday was regarded as the holiest day and no one could get out of going to church. If, for some unimaginable reason, we were not able to attend matins at the Cathedral with the rest of the household, we had to go to Evening service at Samaria Church up the road. Very little cooking was done on Sundays, and what we called Sunday Stew of meat or chicken, with hog (pig's)foot of course, was cooked on Saturday and locked in what we called a 'chop box'. There was a padlock on the box to stop anyone making a play for a piece of juicy meat or chicken during the night.

Also on Saturday, we would get our Sunday clothes ready, which could include ironing our shirts and suits. According to strict custom, the boys had short trousers until we reached 16 when we graduated to long trousers, whereas girls were given socks until they could use stockings when they reached 16. We would also have to iron the clothes of grandma and mother, and clean and polish all the shoes ready for church the following day. That evening we would be given our weekly allowances, which we called 'lunch money', and we would make for Kroo Town Road to buy peppermint, coconut cake, groundnut cake, and when in season, black tumbler, malombo, ditta, apple, plum and any other fruits we could find. Most of these would have all been consumed by the following evening.

I remember one friend of the family to whose house we would go each Saturday and he, without fail, would give us our 'lunch.' Surprisingly he lived to a ripe old age, and whenever I went to see him when I am in Freetown, to talk about the old days, and wanted

Reflection on my life

to give him some money, I would remind him that he used to give us our 'lunch' when we were young. Now it was my turn to give him his 'lunch.' As I put some Leones in his hands I would admonish him, as he used to admonish us, not to spend it frivolously. He would laugh at this, and say what a naughty boy I was, and had always been. He died at nearly 100 years of age.

Saturday was also the day that the washer woman, who did my grandmother's and my mother's clothes, would either come herself or send one of her children to bring the clean clothes, and collect the soiled linen. Grandma would inspect each clean item carefully before making payment, then the washerwoman or her child would leave with another bundle to be laundered during the following week. Many years later, I was admitted to a London hospital with of all things, tonsillitis, and the senior nurse on duty recognised me. She turned out to be one of the children of the washer woman who used to bring the clean laundry each Saturday. I was very pleased to see her and we reminisced about those days. One thing she told me was that they had fond memories of my grandmother as she was one of the few people they washed for, who paid on time and in full. Many others would squabble about the cleanliness of the clothes and not pay in full, or would delay payment until the following Saturday. She said that what we did not realise was that the money they collected for her mother doing the laundry, was the only income they had, and after delivering the laundry and collecting the payment, they would go to the market to purchase the food to last them for the week, to feed a household of eight. I asked her about her mother and siblings. Her mother had died, even before she came to the UK to study, and now being a nurse, she realised that the years of standing in a stream washing clothes, day in day out, must have shortened her life. All her brothers and sisters were doing well and some were now living in England. After she left, I had a little cry to myself, as meeting her brought back so many memories of my irretrievable childhood in Freetown.

ARNOLD AWOONOR-GORDON

We would get up early on Sunday morning and do our ablutions, which would include having a bath from a bucket in the outside wash house, with sapo (local sponge) and Lifebouy soap. As we washed ourselves we could hear the ringing voice of mother admonishing us not to forget to scrub behind our ears, under our arms and between our legs. Next door to our house lived Mama Maria and her two grandsons and a granddaughter called Sophia. They had the rooms at the top of the house, which also had several families living on the other two floors. Mama Maria would stand by the window and shout instructions and commands to the grandchildren in the compound below. One command I remember was to Sophia when she was having her bath in the washhouse. 'Sophia, nor forget for was yu fooooooooooot'. Sophia don't forget to wash your fooooooooot. Sophia was about sixteen. As Mama Maria strung out the word fooooooooot, we knew what instructions she was passing to Sophia. I leave you also to guess what she was telling her.

After we had scrubbed ourselves clean and got dressed in our Sunday best, it was time to walk to the St Georges Cathedral, which was about fifteen minutes away. Our Aunts and uncles, cousins and other friends, would walk down Waterloo Street and we would join them when they reached our house on the corner of the street. As we walked along Oxford Street, to church chatting to our cousins and friends, other families would join us so that by the time we arrived, we would be like about fifteen to twenty strong, all going to pray to the Lord.

Chapter 7
FAMILY HIERARCHY IN CHURCH

I must describe the hierarchy of the families who worshiped at St Georges Cathedral, the most fashionable church in town, where most of the prominent Creole families worshipped. Each family paid a fee for its own set of hard wooden pews on which they placed various cushions to make them more comfortable. Every family knew where they sat and no one, apart from strangers, would sit in a pew that did not belong to them. There was a central and two side aisles, and two other sets of pews on either side of the choir stalls. The set of pews near the aisle next to the organ was called the Aristocratic Corner. Only the very 'aristocratic' and old Creole families had their pews there!

More than seventy years later, I can close my eyes and still see the various Freetown Creole ladies of quality, as they sailed down the centre aisle to their pews like stately galleons, followed by the rest of the family. They really were stately, with their bosoms heaving with the family heirlooms of gold chain, stomachers, broaches, and ears drooping with earrings; a picture of poise completed with very slim folded umbrellas, held like walking sticks to help them along.

Some of the less affluent churchgoers found this a bit pretentious and, not surprisingly, gave them the *nom de guerre* treatment. There was Mama this and Mama that, Mrs This and Mrs That and so on: forming the 'cream' of Freetown Creole Society arriving to thank the Lord for his mercies.

Sometimes the service would run for hours, with long sermons, and when it was over the priest in charge would stand at the main door to greet and chat with his wealthy parishioners, all of whom he hoped, would have given generously in the gold plated collection plates as they were passed round. Here I must say something about the 'Sides -men' or wardens who ran the business of the church. Responsibility for the management of the service belonged to the Wardens and Sides-men and to be appointed as such was the ambition of every young man from the best families. It was indeed considered an honour to be called a 'Sides-man' of St Georges Cathedral. I don't know how they are elected or when, but a strict requirement to serve as one was that you should possess a British morning suit comprising a black tail coat with striped trousers, which did not always suit our local anatomical build. Some did look like penguins as the waddled from side to side.

On commemorative days such as Easter, Christmas and New Year Sunday, they were in their elements. They really felt there was no one like them. They strutted and waddled as they went about their duties, handing out hymn books, showing visitors to their pews and passing the collection plates round for the gifts that the congregation would give. They took their duties very seriously and would fight tooth and nail to be elected.

Reflection on my life

By tradition going back to Colonial days, the front row pew in the right side of the aisle under the pulpit was reserved for the Governor and his family. The front row pews on the left were reserved for the Bishop and his family. This was the accepted practice even after independence when we had an indigenous Governor- General. But likely as not the pew on the right was usually empty as the local person holding the post had his own church which he attended with his family, and only worshipped at what was regarded as the national cathedral on special occasions, when of course he occupied his 'special' pew. There were no special pews for the mayor of Freetown, but when Freetown was lucky to have a lady mayor, who was a regular member of the Cathedral, palaver ensued. The Lady Mayor insisted that the pews of the bishop and his family should rightly be allocated to her. And as she worshipped regularly at the Cathedral, as did the family of the bishop, you can imagine the shoving and pushing that took place between the lady mayor and the wife of the bishop, when both attended church at the same time. I don't remember how it was resolved, but the congregation had to look on aghast as these two very prominent Freetown ladies in society, dressed in all their Sunday fineries, jostled for position in the front row at the Cathedral.

For my part, I served as choir boy for some years and shared the enhanced view of the whole church and congregation enjoyed by choristers from the elevated choir stalls. An unfortunate incident took place on a particular Easter Sunday involving the last British Governor- General attending church with his wife, son in his early twenties, and two younger daughters. No sooner had the first family taken their seats along the front row, and before the service had even started, the son bent over and started to vomit. Pandemonium broke out. This continued until someone managed to find a bucket used by the cleaners, and with the help of his mother, using her white gloved hands, managed to scoop the vomit into the bucket and help to clean the floor. Disgraced first son was taken out by the side door of the church and, I suspect, to one long telling off by mama, the Lady Governor-General. While the poor, young boy was experiencing his discomfort, his father sat there stony faced, looking straight ahead as if nothing was happening around him. Later on, we learned that the young man had consumed much alcohol at a society party the night before waking up in a hung over state, obviously in no fit state to attend a church service. But his mother, a stickler for protocol, had insisted that he should accompany the family, as usual, with such a disastrous outcome.

Our choirmaster, old Pa Robin Rollings, proved a very strict disciplinarian with idiosyncrasies that left the boys rather petrified at times. Before any boy was accepted into the choir, he had to attend choir practice for several months as a 'probationer' to be trained up to the high standards the choirmaster espoused, before he was allowed to 'robe' by putting on the cassock and surplice and taking his place in the choir stalls. Before then he had to report outside the vestry door each Sunday morning in the hope of being invited in by Pa Rollings and given his robes. I hung around for nearly three months until that memorable Sunday when Pa Rollings took me by the ear and invited me in. I was so proud and could not stop talking about it for days.

When I joined the choir the lead soprano was Archie Taylor. He had a pure boy's soprano voice and was selected to sing all the soprano parts during the many anthems we sang each week, and also at all the fashionable weddings for which the Cathedral was held in high esteem. Then, in the middle of singing at a wedding one day, Archie's voice broke and although he struggled on, with all of us boys trying not to laugh, that was the end of his career as our soprano soloist. I cannot remember whether he stayed on as a tenor or not, but boys being boys, some had been envious of his exalted position and so were not too sorry to witness his downfall.

Reflection on my life

Chapter 8
SUNDAY AND OTHER PASTTIMES

By tradition, after church, we would all trips off to visit the homes of one family member or another, and spend some time with each before returning home. The only cooking that was done on a Sunday was that of rice and the heating up of the Sunday stew that would have been cooked the previous day. First, we had to change from our Sunday best to our regular weekly house clothes, and all of us would then sit down to lunch of rice and stew, which would be accompanied by what we called Creole salad. This concoction was made up of a large platter of lettuce, tinned salmon, sliced cucumber, onions, tomatoes, baked beans, tin potato salad, all drowned in Heinz salad cream. Salad cream yes, but never mayonnaise.

I can still hear the voice, ringing in my ears as grandma admonished us to chew our food properly and not swallow too soon. Food, she would sometimes say, should be chewed thirty-two times. What a hope with hungry boys around the table. I must here say what a naughty boy I was. If we had any unexpected guest whom we had to feed, and if we were short of some food item, I was told to say 'no thank you' politely as the youngest, when it came to my turn to serve, or be served. In protest I would threaten to add 'politely' after the 'no thank you'. So, all eyes would be on me at the table, holding their collective breaths waiting to see whether I would add the 'politely'. They need not have bothered as I never intended to do so. But, it made me feel good to make the threat and watch their apprehension.

After lunch, the person whose duty it was to do the washing up would gather all the plates, cutlery and pots, and take them outside to the yard, wash and pack them in a large basket. God help anyone who afterwards used one of the clean plates and did not wash and put them back immediately. He would bring the wrath of the

Reflection on my life

washer on his head before the day was over!.

On Sunday afternoons, my sister and any other young girl in the house, and also her friends from the neighbourhood, would gather to have their hair braided ready for school on Monday. They would also iron their uniforms, clean their shoes and in general get ready for the next day. My sister was also adept at hairdressing using the hot straightening comb, and would get some more pocket money by straightening the hair of the ladies of the night next door. Although grandma did not approve of their lifestyles, she allowed my sister to do their hair, as long as it was done in our compound, which they had to enter by the back gate. Never by the front gate.

All the children in the house had their rota of duties, which we had to perform regularly. These ranged from going shopping at the produce market, sweeping and cleaning the house, pounding rice, pounding and straining the chaff from foofoo, (a porridge meal made from cassava), plucking the leaves of various plants for the palaver sauce, washing our clothes and some of those of grandma and mother, and cooking the meal for the whole house. I think I can vouch that many boys of my generation can cook. African mothers are like Jewish mothers. They think that no woman is either good enough for their sons, or able to feed them like they would. So our mothers insisted that we should learn how to cook as a vital insurance, in case we might have a row with our wives in later life and they refuse to cook for us, then we will not starve, as we have been taught to cook for ourselves!'

A friend of mine told me that when he and his brothers complained that their mother was not so hard on their sister to do the cooking, the mother told them that if their sister did not learn to cook, she will either marry a man who could afford to hire a cook, or he would beat her until she learned to cook for him!

While on the subject of boys learning how to cook, I must here relate what happened many many years later in my life. The house that I had built was designed by a friend who was a government architect. I had paid him not only to design the house but also to help with the supervision of the building. When the house had reached a certain stage and he had not showed his face on the building site, I called to berate him about his lack of supervision of the work and he promised to come and collect me on the Saturday to take me to the site. He duly arrived while I was in the middle of cooking my Saturday plasass, and was surprised that I could cook. His mother, he told me, had not taught any of her children how to cook as they had an aunt who lived with them who did all the cooking. He then asked me whether I would like to do some cooking for him. It appears that his friends usually congregate at his house every Saturday to play cards, and they needed their Saturday plasass while there. His sister normally did the cooking, but as she was away on holiday, they did not have their usual Saturday foofoo chop. I teased him by saying 'why not ask one of your several girlfriends to cook for them while your sister is away'

He then told me that he would never eat anything cooked by any of his girlfriends, because, he once had lunch at one of their homes, but it turned out that the food had been cooked by her mother. My friend did not like to eat spicy food, and on that day the pepper in the soup was too much, but the soup was so delicious that he finished all that was put in front of him. Later on he had some doubts about what the mother could have put in the soup to make it so delicious, and he suspected that she could have put some juju in the soup to make him marry her daughter. It may not be true, and he was just being paranoid, but since then he had not eaten anything cooked by any of his various girlfriends!

I agreed to help him out until his sister returned. And so, every Saturday, his driver would come round to collect two different dishes of plassas: one the so-called draw soup of either crain crain or okra, or egusi (melon seeds) soup, and foofoo! Of course I

Reflection on my life

was handsomely compensated for my troubles.

ARNOLD AWOONOR-GORDON

Chapter 9
THE MARK OF UNRIGHTIOUSNESS

It was grandma who told us about what she called 'The Mark of Unrighteousness' in the family. It was not a mark really, but what would today be called a generic disorder. It went like this: Every now and again, children of the Nicol line of the family would be born with a very long thumb, which would curve at the end. In some children it was not too bad, but in others, it was so bad that they would find it difficult to write or even hold a knife properly. No one knew how it started or with whom, but grandma said that it came from the Nicol side of the family, as none of the Crowther side had it. But she did not tell us whether her father had the crooked thumb or not.

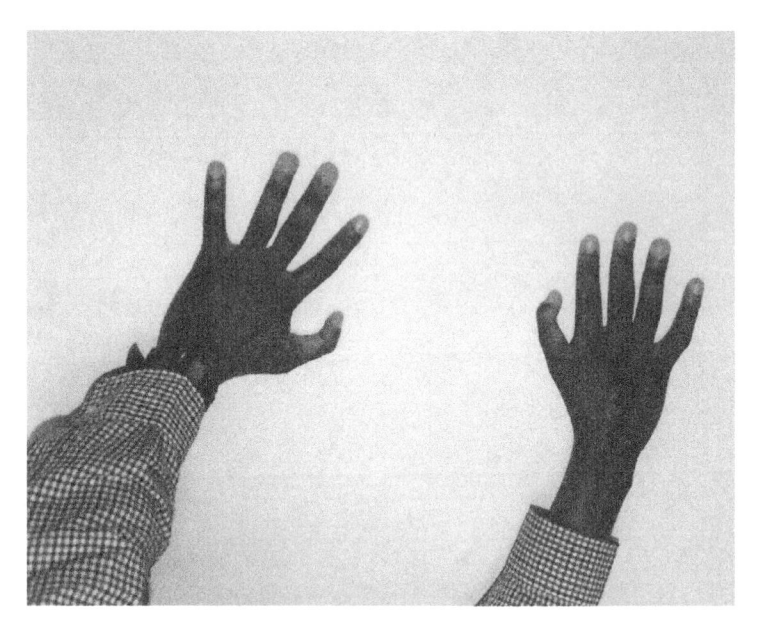

THE MARK OF UNRIGHTIOUSNESS

Reflection on my life

Grandma said it was a sign that if a young man of the family strayed and had a child before marriage, it would show him up and he could not deny the parenthood. She also told us the story about one of her brothers, who strayed and was caught out by the mark. By the way, her parents had eleven children, eight boys and three girls, and when her father was sent to the Gambia as Chaplain to the forces he took his family with him. He would from time to time go into the interior, to administer to the forces stationed there, and would take his eldest son, who was training for the priesthood with him. His visits were not too regular, and sometimes he would go every year to one station and at other times every two years.

On one such visit, he saw a little girl of about two with the unmistakable sign of the crooked thumb. Putting two and two together, he asked his son, as grandma put it, 'Did you go there?' The young man sheepishly, could not deny it and had to admit that two years earlier, on a visit, he had 'been there' with the mother of the little girl. I don't know what was said by father to son, but the outcome was that the girl was taken into the household of the Reverend George Pompey Crowther-Nicol, and was christened Harriet. Aunty Harriet eventually moved to Lagos with her father and became the matriarch of the Nigerian branch of the family. Her thumb was really bad, as I saw when I met her, and it was she who passed on 'the Nicol Mark' down through her children and grandchildren onto her great- grandchildren.

There was more to this story. One young man was found out when the new wife of his best friend gave birth to a baby girl with the unmistakably crooked thumb of 'the Nicol Mark'. Another young man from the Nicol side of the family went to study in one of the Scandinavian countries, met a girl there, but had to return home soon afterwards. Many, many years later, he decided to go and look for her, only to discover that, soon after he left the country, she had given birth to a girl, and she had the 'Nicol Mark.' The child's grand- parents, not knowing that the crooked thumb was hereditary, spent a lot of money on medical bills trying to straighten her thumb. The girl, now a grown woman with children of her own, was very glad to know when she met her biological father, that she was after all not a freak. But none of her children had the crooked thumb. Surprisingly none of my grandmother's children, grandchildren or great-grandchildren inherited the crooked thumb, although one of my sister's boys had a very long thumb, but it was not crooked at the end.

During World War II, the Freetown harbour, being the third largest natural harbour in the world, Allied convoys used it to assemble before crossing the treacherous Atlantic Ocean and as stopping off point for ships carrying troops to the Far Eastern war front. In addition to bunkering and replenishing of victuals, the soldiers and sailors were granted shore leave and could be seen perambulating the streets of Freetown in pairs and small groups in search of adventure and much needed 'jigi jigi,' as they called it. I can still see the harbour transformed by the grey and black silhouettes of hundreds of merchant vessels and ships of the Royal Navy anchored in the extensive Harbour embracing Destruction & Susan's Bays in the East, across Kroo Bay towards Whiteman's Bay in the West sometimes for weeks before they sailed.

Famously both Flagships, The Queen Mary and Queen Elizabeth took shelter in our Harbour at the same time once. There were several houses of ill repute in the City with one not far from our house. Grandma forbade us to look out of the windows on that side of the house, in case we got corrupted by what we saw. Not all the ladies of the night who entertained the soldiers and sailors came from lower class families. Some girls from some prominent Creole families also joined the brigades, and songs were composed about some of them. One that I clearly remember went like this:

Titi Ayo do ya go home you don put mamy to shame

Go home titi go home, go home titi go home, go home titi go

Reflection on my life

home you don put yu mammy to shame.

Two other sisters, who also became ladies of the night, were from what we thought at the time was a Lebanese family, but turned out later to be a Spanish family. They were very beautiful and as they had white skins, unlike their colleagues who were black, they were in great demand. As soon as they became pros, or as we called it 'Jomp nar treet' (Going on the street) they hired an open truck and, with the other girls, drove up and down the street where their family lived singing:

Mama do ya lef me make are fala man, when de bellego cam , nar me wan go tot am, mama do ya lef me make are falla man. (Mother, don't worry about me sleeping with men. If I get pregnant, I shall carry my burden alone) Surprisingly these two sisters lived to a ripe old age in the Kingtom area, across the bay from us, in a house they had built with their earnings. Who says selling your body does not pay? We used to call these girls *Sen Jagos* (Saint Jagos) a nickname that originated from the slave trade in Ghana where the European traders from Elmina Castle would go with the women in the local area known as Saint Jago point.

I did hear later that the city fathers had complained to the authorities not to let the visiting sailors ashore, as they feared for the safety of their wives and chastity of their daughters, who were regularly chased by the sex starved men wanting some jigi jigi. Their pleas must have worked because, many years later, sitting next to me on a London red bus, was an old man who, after learning where I came from, said that he did not have fond memories of his three weeks stay on the ship in the Freetown harbour. They were confined on board for that length of time, and all they wanted after weeks at sea, was to go ashore for some jigi jigi, which was denied them. I could only apologise to him that I was a young boy at the time, and was in no way able to help him.

ARNOLD AWOONOR-GORDON

Chapter 10
SCHOOL DAYS

I first attended the Bathurst Street School which was a junior school situated just a short walk from our house. At first I had to be accompanied until I turned seven when I could then start going to school on my own. I was about ten when, one day, walking home from school, I noticed that there was some movement in one of the Nissen huts that had been erected on the grounds of the old CMS Grammar School. Being curious I went to see what was happening, and noticed that there were lots of books in the hut with two ladies inside. I went home and told my grandmother and said that there was a notice on the hut, but I could not read what it said. She told me to go back and write it down. I did, and it said BRITISH COUNCIL. That was my first introduction to an organisation that was to play a very important part in my education.

The British Council was originally managed by two very influential local ladies, Mrs Nada Easmon-Metzger and Mrs Mary Edmondson. They took all young visitors to the Library under their wings and taught us the habit of reading and not just ordinary books, but titles such as Jane Austin, Shakespeare, Milton, Elizabeth Browning, the Bronte Sisters and many other English classics. They instilled in me, at least, the love of books and reading, which became the basis of my education. They would recommend the books we were to read, and would discuss with us what we had read, and make us understand what the meaning of words were. Both ladies are long departed this life, but I shall always be grateful to them for helping me with my education and the love of books, which has lasted all my life.

I later moved to the Government Model School on Circular Road, which encircles Freetown from its northern heart to a part of the central district. However, for some unexplained reasons, all my

Reflection on my life

friends were enrolled at the Cathedral Boys School near the Victoria Park in the heart of the city. After school we would all gather at Tower Hill, where the Parliament building now stands, and chew the fat for another hour or so, before dispersing to our various homes. Tower Hill, as I had mentioned, was where my fraternal great grandfather's West Indian regiment had been stationed. It was on that hill that we challenged each other to fight, and some of the fights were vicious.

I stayed at the Government Model School until I passed to standard six, and then moved to join my friends at the Cathedral Boys School. Our teacher was old Pa Scott, who was a strict master who did not spare the rod when necessary. I am not sure how effective he was as a teacher, but we must have learned something as we all passed the entrance examination that enabled us to enrol at the CMS Grammar school together as a tight group of friends.

I wonder how many of you reading this will remember what, as young boys and girls, we had to do before going into our classes. Let me remind you, just in case you might have forgotten. We all had to line up in the school compound and do our exercises. It went like this: Up (hands straight up above our heads), down (hands down by our sides), expand (hands outstretched by our sides), fold (hands across our chests), fists (make a fist and stretched in front of us) chest (hands back on our chests). After we had done our morning exercises, we would then march into our classrooms singing this ditty..

We are all going to our classes, With clean hands and faces, To pay great attention to what we are told, Or else we shall never be happy and clever, For learning is better than silver and gold.

A wag once said that as we were singing about '*learning being better than silver and gold*,' the colonial masters were siphoning our silver and gold and taking the lot to Britain.

ARNOLD AWOONOR-GORDON

I can still remember the games we played as children at home. This was long before the days of television and computers, and we had to make up our own games. One game we played regularly was hide and seek. With so many brothers, sisters and cousins, it was difficult to find a place to hide from the one doing the seeking. I also remember the song the seeker had to sing as we found our places to hide. *'Are coming oh? Yes oh.Go tel mama say, yes oh. Da soup way e cook,,,yes oh,,,,make e lef me yone,,,yes oh,,,kalaju kalaju,,,yes oh,,,are katch am nak am..yes oh,,,,are katch am nak am'* Which loosely translates as: I am coming after you, go and tell your mother; tell her I am coming for my share of the meal that she cooked. Tell her I shall catch and beat you up a bit. The idea being that once the seeker had found the hider, the victor was entitled to some reward; all in good fun of course! We would all try to hide under beds, behind doors and so on, until we were caught.

Another game, if you could call it that, was making a pact by shaking hands with these words...*from tiday we go kunt taytay we die'*; loosely translated as : Beginning today, we shall start counting the time until one of us dies." This meant that if you saw the other person with something you wanted, say a top or juicy akara, we would say *Ar kunt you dae*, and the person had to hand over whatever it was they had. But if they saw you coming they would say *Nor kunt, nor beg nor* cry for *half*..and the other person would not have to hand over whatever it was. One had to be very fast either to kunt or be kunted. I can assure you that fights used to take place as the person being 'kunted' would not want to give up what he had. Usually the 'kunting' bond would be broken nearly as soon as it was made. Another form of bonding was shaking hands with each other and saying *from tiday we go slap han*. This meant that if you saw someone with something you coveted, you could slap it out of his hands. These cult games should not be easily entered into as they could easily break up friendships over fierce arguments. It was also common that fist fights would occur when someone refused to hand over some priced possessions.

Reflection on my life

I am sure many of my old school friends will also remember the corporal punishments we received when we did not do our school or house work. Floggings on the bottom and on the palm of our hands were commonplace, both in school and at home. Recently, I was reminiscing with some young friends about such beatings, and one said, seriously, that all those beatings were nothing but 'child abuse'. We all laughed when one said 'why did you not tell that to your dad as he beat the hell out of you? Child abuse indeed' I think if we had even thought of that, or even said it, that would have increased the beatings even more. But, for some reason, we all agreed that it did not do us any harm. I was in a taxi in Freetown last year, when I overheard two women discussing punishing their children. I heard one say that today one cannot punish them as they will tell you that they all have 'woman (human) rights.' I had to laugh as we did not have 'woman or human rights' in my day.

Back then, whether at the elementary or secondary school stage, we had three streams of pupils, groups designed to break up large classes, but which I think was also to sift the clever from the not so clever. The very clever boys were those who, at exams time, came within the first ten, and the not so clever (I was in that group), came within the second lot from ten to twenty. The last lot, 'de fool man dem', as we called them, fell between twenty and last. We called them 'fool man', but today that group is known as people who are dyslexic. But whatever they are called today, they are still 'fool man dem' in our eyes.

Looking back now, I could pick out the clever ones, some of whom excelled and went on to great things later in life. They were clever and it showed even in those early school-days and we knew they were destined for greatness.

In those days, the school fees were not that much not like they are now in Sierra Leone. But, even so, many families could not afford to pay the fees, however little they were, and the children faced

ARNOLD AWOONOR-GORDON

having to be sent home until it was paid. I remember one very clever boy who always came first or second in class at the Grammar School. He dropped out of his education because his parents could not afford to pay his fees. That hurt me greatly and up to today, I can remember his name and the sadness I felt that here was someone destined for great things, but had to drop out of school because his parents could not afford the fees for him to carry on. I was glad when I saw him again many years later and he was working as a senior dispenser at the Connaught hospital. I embraced and hugged him, as I was so pleased that he had got a good and responsible job, despite not completing his secondary education.

Talking about not being able to pay school fees, one of the most senior bankers I know, who has now passed away, told me the story about how he got where he was today. His parents could not afford to pay his fees after Form Three, and a job was found for him at the locomotive section of the Railways Department. He had gone for his interview and already had his uniform to start work on the Monday. On Saturday, the Elder Dempster boat, the Aureol, arrived from England, and on board returning home was a cousin of his parents who had qualified as a medical doctor. On Sunday he and his parents went to pay their respects, after church and to welcome him home. While there, the cousin asked what he was up to, and he told him that he had left school because of school fees, and in fact he had to start work at the Railways Department the following day.

The cousin said 'No way. You are going back to school tomorrow, and I will pay your school fees'. He was as good as his word, and not only helped him to complete his secondary education, but also helped him through university, which brought him to where he was today as a banker of international standing. Here was one person who would have missed out to better himself and to contribute to the nation, just because his parents could not afford to pay his school fees. He told me his story when we met at the airport in Washington as he was returning home from attending a meeting of

Reflection on my life

the IMF. And you know what he told me? He was helping as many young people with their school fees as possible, because he could not forget the help he had received, which he would have missed by one day.

In those days we went to school bare footed (nak we ten toe nar gron), for even if our parents could afford shoes for us, it was not the 'done' thing to wear shoes to school. Shoes were reserved for wearing to church on Sundays. There were a couple of boys in our primary school whose parents were well of, and insisted that they went to school in shoes. But so as not to stand out from the rest of us, as soon as they turned the corner from their home, they would take off their shoes and socks and store them with the Fullah shopkeeper. On their way home after school they reclaimed their shoes and put them on again. Many years later, as grown men and in my presence, they confessed all to their mother who said that she used to worry at the time, when they returned from school in clean shoes but with filthy feet. She suspected what they were up to, but said nothing.

As we did not wear shoes to school our feet were susceptible to the ubiquitous dermatological phenomenon we called jigger, a scabies mite that got into and between our toes. We did not know what they were and whether they did any damage to our toes, but my sister was the best jigger puller there was. She could find the head, and after sterilising the needle over a candle flame, would get the bugger out in one piece and kill it over the flame. I still shudder when I think of it. I did ask recently whether children still get jigger in the toes, but was told that, because most children now wear shoes to school and there are more tarred roads, jigger has all but disappeared from the streets. I thank God for that.

We must have had some good teachers because some of what they taught us I remember till today. There was Pa Ballanta who taught music to us 'dander' heads. At the time I did not think I learned anything from him, but now I can still sing some of the classical songs he taught us, including 'Who is Sylvia?', 'Under the spreading chestnut tree' and 'Green-sleeves,' which he said was composed by Henry the Eighth (true, I found out much later) etc, so he must have made an impression on my brain at least. Pa Ballanta was in fact a fine composer in his own right; he wrote numerous songs, chamber music and an operetta entitled Afiwa. And I am happy to say that the only music academy in Freetown is justifiably named after him! Then there was the teacher, whose name I have forgotten, who tried to instil in us the love of poetry. I didn't think I learned anything, but today I can still recite 'Invictus' by William Ernest Henley: 'Out of the night that covers me, black as the pit from pole to pole, I thank whatever Gods may be, for my unconquerable soul'... or the funeral of Sir John Moore:' Not a sound was heard, but the funeral note, as he lay like a worrier taking his rest' etc. etc.

During that period, very few houses in Freetown had electricity supplies to the houses, and we had to do everything at night, including studying and doing our homework, by candles and kerosene lamps. This was very hard on us young people growing up, as we had to do all our homework by this method. Once I heard a prominent Sierra Leonean architect tell a story about his method of studying when he was a young boy. Just outside his house was a street lamp on a pole that cast its light into his house. He would sit on the ledge of the window and do his studying using the light from the street light. But many a time he would fall asleep and find himself on the grown outside his house. Lucky for him he was living on the ground floor of the house, so he did not have far to fall and so did not do himself any harm.

And talking about kerosene, reminds me that I was envious of the little boys like myself, who went round at nights selling small measures of kerosene. They used to shout kerosene ya. One coppor for pint kerosene. As their voices floated into our house from the

Reflection on my life

dark outside, I admired their entrepreneurship, as masters of their trade, and longed to be like them.

Chapter 11
IN PRAISE OF THE OLD TEACHERS, AND A NEW LIFE

I thank those teachers, long gone, for their efforts in shaping me. As was true with boys all over the world, we had nicknames for some of them, such as Vespere, which is Latin for evening. This teacher was always seen around town at night. And then there was Harpic. He was clean round the bend. I am also grateful to the teacher who tried to make us learn Latin, but without much success; for all I can remember is my first conjugation:

amo:	I love
amas:	You love
amat:	He, She, or It loves
amamus:	We love
amatis:	You (plural) love
amant:	They love

The person who taught us Religious Knowledge was the Reverend J.T.Anderson an old and scraggy man, who did not spare the rod, and used it at every opportunity he had. And as he beat us he would be heard to intone 'I taught your father' which was true as he had been at the school when the generation of our fathers were pupils there. Although the school was set up and run by the Anglican Church, and the ethics of the school was Christian, yet as it was situated at Bishop's Court at Fourah Bay, when I went there, which had one of the large Muslim community, we had several Muslim boys attending the school. Every morning as we filed into assembly for prayers, the Muslim boys would go into one

Reflection on my life

of the classrooms for their prayers. I was to learn much later from one of them, that they would say their prayers quickly and then spend the rest of the time talking until they were called to join us in the assembly hall for the notices for the day.

When I joined the Grammar school, the Principal was the Reverend E.D.C. Clarke, and when I left it was Frank Wood. He was the only expatriate principal in the long annals of the school who was not an ordained Minister of the Anglican Church. He was also the last expatriate to head the school, for thereafter all the principals since then have been Sierra Leoneans. Looking through the booklet that was published in 1989, of the schools register from its inception, makes interesting reading. I notice that I was registered as number 4440, and that I joined in January 1949. I notice that several of my contemporaries who joined the school at the same time, are no longer with us. I cannot understand how a school which was founded in 1845 could have educated only 4440 boys by the time I joined. I am convinced that some names may have been omitted.

I also now realise that I have lived long enough to be one of the few people who were around when the Grammar school celebrated its one hundred anniversaries in 1945. I remember it well as I lived in the family house which was a few houses from the old school at the corner of Wellington and Oxford (now Lightfoot-Boston) streets. I remember that we celebrated from the house of my Aunt Lina, whose house backed on to the wall of the school on Wellington Street. Several family and friends were invited to the house as we watched the flag of the school being raised and the school's song being sung lustily, by both the old and present boys of the school, followed by God Save the King, the British national anthem. As I was only twelve at the time I cannot remember what else took place, for all we children were interested in was the food and ginger beer which followed. But one thing I remember is that my brother, William secured one of the Centenary scholarships to attend the Grammar school, where amongst his other academic accomplishments, he became a very distinguished footballer, playing for the school and for Regents Olympics when he left school. What fun we had as children going to school, without a care in the world. As for playing truant, let's not go down that way. Let us place a blind eye on that part of our school escapade.

I remember what was then a great scandal, when, as the headlines in the papers reported, Moder marade (Nun marries). As I remember it, as told by my sister who was a border at St Joseph's Convent at the time, a new Irish nun, who was not much older than my sister and her classmates, arrived to join the other Holy sisters who were all much older. Opposite the Convent at Howe Street was the Swiss owned Freetown Cold Storage Company, run by some young Swiss bachelors, who were always making eyes at the convent girls across the road. It appears that one of the young men started to take too much interest in this newly arrived young Irish nun. The older nuns did not like it one bit, and the nun was soon packed off to one of their convents in what was then the Protectorate, to get her out of harm's way, until they could send her back to whence she came.

By some means she must have been in communications with the Cold Storage young man, because on her way back to Freetown by train, the young man intercepted the train at Waterloo, whisked her off to Freetown by car, and they got married at the Register Office before the Convent nuns knew what had hit them. So you can imagine the scandal of a married nun on a shocked city. Apparently the newly-weds were soon on the next mail boat out of Freetown, and back to Switzerland, I guess. Over the years, I have always wondered what ever happened to the young lovers. I will never know, but I still wonder all the same.

It was during that period that Freetown was in great excitement, when a film crew arrived to film external shots for the film of Graham Greene's book, The Heart of the Matter, which he set in

Reflection on my life

Freetown, where he was based as a spy during the Second World War. The people of Freetown were eager to set eyes on a real life film star in the person of Trevor Howard, the star of the film, for the first time. Many of us children went AWOL from school just to hang around in the hope of getting into the crowd scenes, as the shooting took place in various places in town, including the Law Courts and Cotton tree, Samba gutter and the old Government Wharf. Several years later, when I was Director of Television at the SLBS, I was able to obtain a copy of the film to show on television and to lend to friends to show in their homes. It brought back some nostalgia seeing parts of the Freetown that had disappeared during the intervening years.

In those days it was difficult to carry heavy goods from place to place as there were no lorries or taxis or omolanke as there are today. So if one had to transport, say a bag of rice from market to home, you had to hire someone to carry it for you. And there was no shortage of carriers. All you had to do was shout 'worok…worok' and several men would appear out of nowhere, and you will then have to haggle the price. And with brute strength, he would lift your load on to his head and away he will go with you following closely behind. Today you can hire an omolanke (hand push cart) or taxi to do it for you.

And while on the subject of omolanke, recently while visiting Freetown I witnessed an altercation between an omolanke and the driver of the Mercedes car in which I was travelling. There was the usual traffic jam and go slow on the Main Motor Road, and the car I was travelling in was stopping and starting, and stopping and starting much to the annoyance of the driver. Then an omolanke, piled high with bags of rice, tried to squeeze past, and in doing so, one of the bags of rice toppled over, and made a small scratch on the car I was in. I leave you to imagine the palaver that ensued between the car owner and the omolanke man. The driver got out of the car and in the altercation that followed, threatened to seize not only omolanke but the bags of rice as well, until the scratch was mended. There was much gesticulating and shouting and soon a crowd appeared and added their penny's worth to the mayhem. I stayed put in the car, but could not contain my laughter as I witnessed the drama that was unfolding before me.

Of course the omolanke man could not afford to pay for the repairs, nor could the owner of the rice, claiming that the accident was not her fault, and did not see why her rice should be impounded. By this time we were holding up traffic, which was building up behind us. I felt I had to do something, so I got out of the car, and after some calming of frayed nerves, agreed to pay for the damage, and that the omolanke man would repay me. This was eventually agreed to. I took the name and address of the man and gave him mine, where he was to meet me to find out the cost of the repairs and arrange the payment. The owner of the car was not too please at my intervention, and said that I would never see the man again. The cost of the repairs of the six inches long scratch was only Le100.000 which I was glad to pay.

The omolanke man did turn up two days later with Le5000 which he said was his days takings. But I did not have the heart to take his meagre days earnings. I let him off as I felt that the money was more use to his family than to me. I had to lie to the car owner that I had been paid when she asked me. It was while the commotion was taking place that I got to know that car owners in Freetown are referred to as 'MY CAR' especially by taxi drivers. It appears that if there is a collision between a taxi and a car owner, the car owner gets out of his car and says 'LOOK WHAT YOU HAVE DONE TO 'MY CAR'

When I was at the Grammar school, we used to attend afternoon dances sometimes at the Community Centre, Gooding's Hall, the old Grammar school building or Picket House in Charlotte Street. This was an innocent and friendly way of interacting with girls

Reflection on my life

from the main girl's school in Freetown. For some reason, which I still cannot fathom, I was the best dancer amongst my peers, and it fell to me to teach some of them how to dance. So after school we used to meet in one of the classrooms and I would go through the various steps with them. It was then I came to realise that some people do have two left feet, and cannot dance for love or money. Some were able to pick it quickly, some needed much coaching, and some, however much coaching they had never got the hang of it. They were the ones who when they asked a girl to dance would be politely refused.

One interesting aside. One day one of our young teachers found us at our dance lessons, and when we told him what we were up to, he asked me if I could teach him to dance. It appeared that he had a young girlfriend who liked to go dancing and he wanted to accompany her. So twice a week after school, we would go to his house and I would put him through his paces. He also had two left feet, and could not get the steps right, even with the jive. I gave up eventually and had to break the sad news to him that he would never make a good dancer however much he tried. Later I learned that he and the girlfriend had broken up, and I wondered whether it was because he could not dance.

We also used to organise outings to various seaside villages on public holidays, with girls providing the food and the boys the soft drinks like Vimto. This was in the days when Road Transport buses ran around the peninsular villages and it was easy to get from Freetown to York and back in one day. We had a song we sang as we sped along which went like this.

'Way down to Lumley I must go, for a Lumley lady wrote me a letter, to read last night, so way down to Lumley I must go."

We changed the location depending on where we were going, from Lumley to Goderich to Sussex and so on. I don't think we ever went further than Sussex. Recently I visited one of the friends with whom we used to go on these outings and he reminded me that it was at one of those outings that he first met the girl who was to become his wife ten years later. He was still married to her with a large family of children and grand and great- grandchildren. I had completely forgotten about it until he reminded me.

We were always teasing the girls from our sister school, the Annie Walsh Memorial School, especially writing love letters to them. I remember one love letter which we all seem to copy and it went like this. The heading read

Diamond City Golden Street Silver dated Madam, Having caught sight of your magnificent beauty etc.. etc.. etc..

I cannot remember the rest. What the girls thought of our innocent love letters I cannot imagine.

There was going the rounds of what I think was an urban myth story. It was sometimes reported that it was said by a girl from the Methodist Girls High School, and sometimes she was from Harford School, but never from Annie Walsh. They were too refined. The story goes that on being approached by a young man intent on becoming more acquainted with her, the girl is said to have told him 'Your betters have come I did not answer them, you tote your dorty sef and come, I will answer you tay.' Whether this actually happened I don't know, but it became something, which when said often enough, became as good as true.

When we joined the Grammar School we were allocated to various houses. I was allocated to Tertious House, and the only other house I can remember is Secondus, but cannot remember the others. But I think the houses were named after the Latin for One, Two, Three and Four, Secondus being two and Tertious being three. Each house specialised in a special sport, and as I was no good at football, I had to learn to run and specialised in the one hundred yards race, as it

Reflection on my life

was called then. And my only claim to fame while I was at the school, was when I beat the best one hundred yards runner at the school's sports day. His name was Arnold Nottige, or Ginger as he was known, and the only reason I beat him was this. As he was the best runner for his house, he had been made to run as many races as possible, and by the time he came to run the one hundred yards race, the poor lad was so knackered and exhausted that I was able to beat him easily. That not only put a feather in my cap, but also in that of our house as well. And Arnold Gordon beat Arnold Nottige at sports rang round the school for months afterwards. It was my one and only moment of fame while I was at the Grammar school.

When I was growing up in Freetown life was pleasant for us young people. We had constant electricity supply, good transportation with double decker buses running to time. But the only thing we did not have was constant water supply. This was before the Guma Valley Water Company constructed the dam at Guma Valley on the Peninsular. During the period I am referring to, very few, if any, houses had piped borne water supply to their compound, and we had to rely on the stand pipe in the street for our water supply. Because the water was rationed, and was supplied for a few hours each day, we had to get up very early in order to get the supply for the household from the street water stand which was situated at the corner of Wellington and Oxford (now Lightfoot-Boston) streets. This tap was conveniently situated by the house of our neighbour Alex Browne, whom we knew then by his house name of Eku. He had the advantage to get up earlier than us, to have several buckets lined up in place before we got there. I remember the fights we and the other boys had with him over the number of buckets he wanted to fill before ours. Little did we realise that one day, many many moons later, he would grow up to head the Guma Valley Water Company, and distribute water to all and sundry in Freetown and beyond. That's life for you.

During the forties and fifties the Rediffusion Service, with a radio listening box provided by the government, was our only link with the outside world and our only form of entertainment. We listened avidly to the BBC Overseas Service, as I have mentioned earlier, and the local news and entertainment programmes. One such programme was Variety Time with Ralph Wright and his band. The programme also showcased Calender and his Maringa band, the Cuban Swing Band with Lionel Millar and his sister Enid with her banjo, Michael Forde and his harmonica or mouth organ that he played sometimes with his younger brother Winston, the singer Roylene Rogers and Scrubbie. Scrubbie sang about when he had the scrubbie money, all the girls liked him, and called him Honey Scrubbie. But when the scrubbie money done, they called him Dorty Scrubbie. Nobody like Scrubbie when he had the scrubbie money. We listened avidly to the weekly Variety Time programme, with Ralph Wright the father of Handel Wright.

As a young boy growing up in Freetown there were no supermarkets and we did all our shopping for our provisions (groceries) from shops run by Indians and Lebanese traders. For the poorer people the corner shops run by Fullah traders were a lifeline. From these shops one could buy bread (Fullah bread) small packets of sugar, coffee, tea and single cigarettes and other necessities that made life easier. The Fullahs would purchase these commodities in bulk, decant them into small home-made packets to sell to the public. They were opened twenty-four hours a day, and I can recall hearing the knock knock on the door of the Fullah shop by our house after midnight, as someone wanted to buy something. The owner would open and make a sale, whatever the hour.

In those days to get to what we called 'farm' at Gbendembu Goderich, we had to take a Road Transport bus to Lumley, and then walk on the sand on the beach until we reached our destination. This was long before the peninsular road was constructed during the Second World War. Children residing in places like York and beyond, in order to come to school, had to get up very early in the morning, and using kerosene lamps, walk over the mountain to Waterloo, to join other school children, from Wellington and other villages on the Peninsular, to catch the train to Freetown. After school they had to do the reverse, five days a week. We were sorry for them as they had to be at the station at a certain time each day to catch the return train.

When I returned to live in Freetown in the seventies, I remembered that the mountain route they took to school must be there, and by trial and error, I found it. The path went from what was called grass field, just before Waterloo, climbed steeply to the top of the mountain, and dropped steeply to come out at a village called Black Water, the other side of York. I started to organise mountain walks from time to time, and gathered some twenty hardy walkers to do the walk. Half way down the other side of the mountain we came across the ruins of a court house and jail, and found out later that in the colonial days, the District Commissioner would be carried by hammock to this place, where the prisoners from the coastal villages would be brought for trial. After being sentenced the prisoners would be taken back to their villages in the care of the headman. The ruins of the court and cells where the prisoners were held, was still there when I was last there many years ago. I am sure the path is still there as it was used regularly by the men who went hunting in the area.

A Holiday

When I sat my Cambridge School Certificate examinations I went to Lagos for a holiday, to stay with my extended Nigerian family. But before I left I had to say goodbye to my sister Dorothy, who had obtained a government scholarship to study physical education in the UK. She did three years at the Coventry College of Physical Education. When she returned after qualifying, she became the first woman Physical Education Officer in the Ministry of Education, and worked in schools in the provinces, where she met, and married her husband Charles Boisy Pyne, a Plant Pathologist and a lecturer at Njala.

I was in Lagos when I received the results of my Cambridge examination, which was a little disappointing. I obtained credits in Geography, Religious Knowledge and English Language, and passes in Maths, Science and History. I know I was not good at maths and science, but I thought I was brilliant at history, so I was very disappointed that I only got a pass, but there was nothing I could do about it.

Soon after I arrived in Lagos I saw an advertisement for radio broadcasters in the papers. I applied and was granted an interview. The person who interviewed me was called Leslie Perowne, who had been seconded from the BBC in London, to help set up the Nigerian Broadcasting Service. He later became a lifelong friend when I met him in Freetown, several years later, where he had come to help the Sierra Leone Broadcasting Service. Leslie Perowne's claim to fame was that, when he was a producer at the BBC, he discovered Roy Plomley, and was the first producer of Desert Island Disc, the longest running programme on the BBC radio to date.

He gave me something to read as he said he wanted to see how I presented myself. I noticed that the piece contained the words 'embarrassment' several times. In fact the word came over and over as I read the scripts, and I could not understand why. It was much later that I found that Nigerians pronounced the word 'embarrassment' in a peculiar way and it was used to catch them out. I must say that I was able to pronounce the word in the correct manner and so I got the job as an announcer with the Nigerian Broadcasting Service. I only lasted one year when it was discovered that I was a 'Saro man,' a Sierra Leonean, and discrimination set it. By then Leslie Perowne had returned to the BBC in London. And so I decided to pack it in, and to go to London to train as a proper

Reflection on my life

journalist and broadcaster.

When I was living in Lagos I joined the Lagos Musical Society, which was made up of mostly of expatriates working in the city, with some locals. We put on several of Gilbert and Sullivan operettas including The Mikado, Pirates of Penzance's and Iolanthe. Although my voice was not very strong I was put amongst the altos and managed to hold my own amongst the stronger voices.

But I had to return to Freetown in order to work and save some more money for the passage to the UK and also to obtain a passport. In those days under colonial rule, Sierra Leoneans could travel between countries in West Africa on a West African Travel Certificate, but if we wanted to travel out of West Africa, we had to have a British Subject and Citizen of the Colonies passport.

While I waited, I got a job with the Sierra Leone Daily Mail, then under the veteran journalist, Sam Metzger. He was a good teacher, and I cut my teeth as a proper journalist covering the usual police cases, marriages, engagements and weddings, and started to save money for the passage to the UK. I also applied for my passport, and when it was ready, I had to go to the Immigration Office to be interviewed by a white Colonial Civil Servant. He questioned me about what I was going to study, who would support me while in the UK (my brother Francis who was by then in the UK as a student of Insurance) etc., etc.. Then he asked when I intended to travel. I said that I did not know as I needed another £10 in order to be able to purchase my ticket to the UK. Without another word, he opened his wallet, took out a £10 note, put it in the passport, handed it over to me and wished me good luck. I was flabbergasted and I must have thanked him. I cannot remember his name or what he looked like. But until today, I still think of that kind man who helped me to achieve my dream of coming to the UK to study.

Incidentally, I mentioned this incident on the BBC Radio 4 programme Saturday Live recently, in which people were asked to thank someone who had done them a good deed, but whom they had not thanked at the time. Some of my friends who heard it rang to urge me to try and find that Colonial Officer who had been so kind to me all those years ago. But I did not bother, as I am sure he must be dead by now. I was in my early twenties then and he must have been in his forties. As I am now in my eighties, surely he cannot still be alive. But wherever he is I still thank him for his generosity to the young man who he did not know. Incidentally the piece was included in a book of some of 'the thank you' letters published by the BBC.

Chapter 12
LONDON AND OTHER DAYS

I arrived in London in 1953 to train as a journalist at what was then the Regent Street Polytechnic, now the University of Westminster. As part of the course, visits were organised to theatres and concerts, and many parts of the United Kingdom, and to the continent, in order to give the students an exposure to as broad a cultural experience as possible. We were given free tickets to the theatre, which awakened my interest in the theatre, which has lasted all my life. I remember my very first visit to a theatre in the West End of London. It was to see a musical called Can Can. I must say I was very prudish in those days, and was very shocked when the ladies dancing the Can Can on the stage did the splits and showed their knickers and bottoms to the audience! But I soon got used to it.

When I first arrived in London I stayed with my brother Francis in his flat in Hampstead, not far from the pub where the nightclub hostess Ruth Ellis, the last woman to be executed in England, had only recently shot her boyfriend David Blakely. The pub, the Magadala, became a centre for tourists and rubberneckers, who gathered each day to look at the outside of the pub and the area on the pavement where he had been shot. The killing was the headline in all the papers for weeks, and started a debate about execution in the country, and in particular, the right to execute women. The hanging divided the country between those who said she should be executed, and those against corporal punishment per say. This was all new to me and I followed the discussion avidly. I think it was the execution of Ruth Ellis and the ground swell of public opinion that eventually led to the abolition of corporal punishment in England.

I am not sure how other people from Sierra Leone felt when they had to use an escalator for the first time. I was terrified, especially as no one had told me how to use this unfamiliar contraption. So when I was first confronted by one at Hampstead underground station, I stood there petrified for a long while, until a kindly person, realised that I was scared about getting on, took my arm and showed and helped me to navigate an escalator for the first time. I never looked back.

I was able to see several of the great actors and actresses of the time in some great plays, and although I could only afford the cheapest seats high up in the Gods of the theatre, I saw, amongst others, Lawrence Olivier, Alec Guinness, Ralph Richardson, John Gielgud, Michael Redgrave, his wife Rachel Kempson, Gladys Cooper, Flora Robson, Edith Evans, Martita Hunt and many others, in some of the great plays by some of the greatest English playwrights. Sadly all of these great Thespians have now gone to the great theatre upstairs.

We were taken to visit great country houses, cities in the north and in Scotland, Wales and Ireland, as part of our education. I remember the first time I saw ballet on stage, and became fascinated by the artistry of the dancers. The ballet was Swan Lake, in which the good overcame the bad, with the black swan Odile, and the white swan Odette, danced by the same dancer. It was at the Royal Opera House Covent Garden, and I was fortunate to see the Russian dancer Galina Ulanova, the Prima Ballerina Assoluta of the Russian Bolshoi Theatre, in the dual role, and I was hooked on ballet. Unfortunately as a student then, with very limited funds, I could only afford from time to time, the two shillings and six pence which allowed me to stand up way in the Gods to watch the action from afar? Not until many years later when I was working, was I able to indulge my love of ballet and opera, and the straight theatre. But today, with the cost of a theatre in the West End of London so prohibitive, and now retired I am only able to indulge myself from time to time.

Reflection on my life

One of the visits we made was to Paris in April of that year. It was an eye opener, and I shall never forget waking up in the hotel room I shared with another student from Nigeria, and opening the window to a beautiful spring morning, overlooking the tree lined boulevard, and watching the traffic below. It was magical. It was spring and it was April, and I could not help putting my thoughts in the notebook we all had to carry to write down our thoughts and feelings.

When we returned to London, I wrote a piece called 'April In Paris,' as part of my essay work. Even if I say so, it was a masterpiece, and I was congratulated by the lecturer, who read it in front of the class. I was so proud of what I had written that I sent it to the BBC African Service. The name of the producer, which I remembered from listening to the programme in Sierra Leone, was Sheila Stradling. I addressed it to her with a covering note to say I was a student of journalism and had just been to Paris, and if she liked it, could I record it for the Calling Sierra Leone programmes? I wondered.

I received a nice letter from Mrs Stradling saying she liked the piece and could I come to see her. Her office was in a building in Oxford Street, just where the GAP store is now, which was not far from the Polytechnic. I duly presented myself to her and we chatted for a while. I did not know until much later that she was testing me to see whether I had a suitable voice for broadcasting and whether I spoke enough good English. I must have passed as she asked me to return to record the piece I had written. In those days, recordings were done on large recording discs, and it had to be done in one take, with no mistakes. But before the start of the recording, I had to do several rehearsals and I must say that I sailed through without any hesitations or mistakes. And when it came to the actual recording, I did it in one go. This was my first ever recording which was broadcast all over West Africa, and was the start of my career in broadcasting.

ARNOLD AWOONOR-GORDON

Over the years, as I trained to become a journalist, I made many more broadcasts, all of which brought in extra funds, something much needed as a poor student. I don't know how it came about, but Mrs Stradling informed me that the producer of Woman's Hour on the domestic service had asked her to recommend an African student to write and broadcast a piece about an aspect of student life in London, and she had recommended me. I went to see the producer in Broadcasting House, just up the road from the Polytechnic. This was something different from making a recording in a small, cramped studio in which I had been making my recordings.

They were doing a series on landladies, especially landladies who took in students from abroad. Students from Africa today do not realise how lucky they are, for very few of them would arrive in the UK without having a relative or friend to stay with until they could stand on their own feet. In the fifties and sixties, when students from Africa began to arrive in the UK to study in large numbers, we had no relatives or friends to support us. The British Council was the only organisation that looked after us. When we arrived at Liverpool usually by one of the Elder Dempster mail boats, the MV Apapa, MV Accra or MV Aureol the British Council representatives were there to meet us, see us through immigration, provide rail tickets for us and see us comfortably settled in our train to London.

The trains would arrive at Euston station, where we would be met by another group of British Council representatives and escorted to our destinations. Mostly this would be one of the hostels they ran, or one run by the Methodist church in Bayswater. As we settled in they would find accommodations with landladies who had been vetted by them, and we would stay there until we could find our own accommodation. These landladies were a breed of Englishwomen that were never to be seen again after these times. They were like mothers to us and made us feel so welcome that

Reflection on my life

many of us became like their own family, and we kept up the link with them even after we had returned home. So when the producer of the programme asked me to write a piece about my landlady, and if it was good enough, it would be broadcast as part of the programmes they were doing, I did not hesitate, as I had the perfect landlady to write about.

I found Mrs. Murphy, or should I say, Mrs Murphy found me, through the accommodation section of the British Council at their offices in Spring Gardens just by Nelsons Column in Trafalgar Square. I had gone there to ask them to find me some other accommodation, as I was fed up staying at the British Council hostel in Hans Crescent just off Sloane Street and behind Harrods, which is now a county court. I and another student from Sierra Leone decided that it would be better if we moved into accommodation of our own, away from the petty restrictions of hostel life. I had to wait in the waiting room of the office of the placement section of the British Council, and as I was waiting a lady came in and was asked to also wait in the waiting room.

MY LANDLADY MRS MURPHY

ARNOLD AWOONOR-GORDON

She sat next to me and smiled and started talking to me. She asked where I came from and what I was doing and so on. She then told me that she was one of the registered landladies approved by the British Council to take in students, and as her daughter had got married and moved out of her house, she now had a room vacant, and that was why she was there to inform the students accommodation section about the vacancy. I told her that I was there to ask for them to find me and my friend a room as we were tired of living in a hostel. To cut a long story short, Mrs Murphy became my first landlady in London. And so began an association that lasted until she died many years later.

So I was able to write and broadcast a piece about my landlady Mrs Murphy, how I met her and how she looked after me and some of the other African students she had staying in her house in Wandsworth. In the piece I narrated how Mrs Murphy had shown much love and care to her charges, how she saw that our needs as students were met, and how she had become like a mother to us. The piece was broadcast on Women's Hour, and I received several congratulations from my student colleagues.

Money was tight for most students and we had to have some part time work to supplement our income. I first worked in a mental hospital in south London at weekends, but the money was not too good, and felt that if I stayed any longer, I too would become like the patients. Then I heard of a job in the kitchen of the nurses' home of a large teaching hospital in central London not far from the place where I was studying. It was a full time job, but I had to work from four in the afternoon until ten at night, which was good, as the latest our lectures finished was 3pm. I worked there for a year while still at the Polytechnic, and earned good money so that I could move out of my room at Mrs Murphy's and share a flat with three other students, who were all white. It is interesting to note that the notice I saw in the nurses home asking for a third person to share the flat, mentioned that the other three had no racial discrimination,

Reflection on my life

but educational discrimination. This was so refreshing when you considered that in those days rooms were being advertised openly stating that blacks, Irish and dogs were not welcomed. The flat was in Victoria and living there was one of the happiest years of my student life.

My new flat mates were all training to become dieticians, and one day they mentioned that the place where they were training was offering scholarships to anyone wishing to train as dieticians. It was not a popular profession then and so student enrolment did not meet the required number. As I had come to the end of my training as a journalist, and as the training allowance was good, I applied and was accepted. The programme was very rigorous academically, but as I was sharing a flat with three others who were in their final year, I was helped a lot by them. It was a four year course and I was at the end of my second year when, by chance, I changed careers: from becoming a dietician to becoming a full time journalist, that being the career for which I had come to train in Britain. More about that, later.

It was while I was living in the flat that I was invited to join some other students for a skiing trip to Norway. I had never skied before but had always wanted to go skiing. The trip was organised by the Youth Hostel Association, and we went to Hamremoen, a ski resort just outside of Oslo. Two factors influenced my choice; it was situated only half an hour away from Norefjel where the 1952 Winter Olympics were held, and only three hours away from the Holmenkollen Ski Jump, which is the focal point for the world-famous winter sports week. That year the week fell during our trip.

We arrived by boat from the UK to Oslo, but did not stay long there. We boarded a bus which winded its way up a hill and climbed to a height of about 4,000 feet, passing a 'Christmas card' countryside. On our left were mist-covered valleys with the mist swirling round and round like candy floss, and on our right the mountain rose sheer with snow covered pine trees that swayed every now and then in the light breeze sending sprays of silver snow on the road. By the time we reached the hostel the sun had come out and was displaying its glorious colours on the snow and trees. The hostel was situated at the top of a hill leading to a frozen lake. On either side, and in front of it, were three nursery slopes ranging from 100 yards to 500 yards long; just the thing for beginners, like me.

Amongst our party were six nurses, so we were in good company in case we broke a leg, which is what happened to me. But, more about that later. We were met by our ski instructor named Einer, who was a student of English at Oslo University and who spoke perfect English. Soon we were fitted with skis, boots and sticks and were out on the slopes getting our first taste of skiing, for which we had come so many miles. There were some Norwegian school children staying at the hostel, all experienced skiers, and they all gathered round to see how the first African they had come across in the flesh, would make out on skis. I did not let them down, but by the end of the day my bum was quite sore from falling down over and over again. In the evening we all gathered in the lounge, and being children they all started to ask me questions about Africa. It just happened that they had seen a film about wildlife in Africa the previous week, and I did my best to answer their questions. I must say I was impressed by their English, which they had to learn at school.

The next day our instructor took us to a hut situated at the back of the hostel in some woods. This entailed going through the trees on our skis, on a path that wound itself sometimes up steep slopes, and sometimes downhill; and what with the soft snow to contend with, we spent more time extracting each other out of it, and at the same time dodging the cascade of falling snow from the branches with every touch of the trees. It was hard work, but fun. The next day, although being a novice, I won my first diploma. I had practiced

Reflection on my life

earlier in the morning on a small ski jump built on one of the smaller slopes, and feeling very brave and confident I entered for the competition staged later in the day. I came in sixth after nearly knocking the wind out of myself twice. At a party that evening I was presented with the diploma inscribed 'for cleverness in skiing.'

The days passed quickly and took the same pattern each day. After breakfast, skiing until lunchtime, and then skiing again until sundown. After dinner we played cards and talked about our progress until bedtime. We spent one day at Norfjell and went on top of the mountain by ski lifts. From the top whole vistas of the snow covered range of pine trees stretched towards the horizon on our left, and on our right a series of valleys, with the Olympic slalom slope zigzagging down to a frozen lake, spanned by an ice-encrusted suspension bridge. It was indeed a breath taking sight.

Sunday was the day of the Holmenkollen jumping championship, but we all slept late and missed the early bus that was to take us to Oslo. But we needn't have worried as the weather was too misty for anyone to see what was going on in the jump. That day I won my second diploma for cross-country skiing, and fell and broke my ankle. It came about this way. Confidently, we had been doing some tricks on our skis and decided to go downhill three at a time holding on to each other. I was in front with the other two holding on to me from behind. We got downhill right enough but could not stop. I tried to make a plough, which was the way to stop, but as my skis were wedged between those of the others, I found my leg being pulled apart. So in order to stop I had to fall sideways on my left leg or I would have been torn in two. I did hear the crack as the bone in my ankle broke. I had to be carried piggy back up the slope back to the hostel. Luckily this all happened just two days before the end of the holiday so I did not miss much skiing.

My leg was soon encased in plaster and I had all the nurses in our party fussing and fetching and carrying me around. They were wonderful and so was everyone I met afterwards. From the bus conductor who brought us from the hostel in the mountain high above Oslo to catch our boat, the customs and immigration officers both there and in the UK, down to the porters at King's Cross station who produced a wheelchair from nowhere to wheel me to the taxi to take me home. They were all wonderful and very helpful, and I reached home with my leg plaster cast autographed by people I shall never meet again, and didn't. But I shall never forget the thrill of rushing downhill, the beauty of falling snow with the sun shining through, and above all the pleasure of meeting people from another country and interacting with them. The article for my skiing trip and accident appeared in the Sierra Leone Daily Mail of April 13, 1957.

Chapter 13
EXPANDING MY HORIZON

One day, early in 1957, I heard through the student's grapevine that the Russian Government was organising the Sixth Youth Festival in Moscow and were interested in having as many young people from Africa as possible to attend. I soon had my name down as it was one of those freebees that various governments organised to introduce students to their way of life. Of course, the British government did not want us to go for their own particular reasons, but go we did even without their blessing. I think the British government feared that by making such a visit we might turn communist. There were several Sierra Leoneans amongst the group that left London that July morning. We travelled by train from London through East Berlin to Moscow.

During the festival there were visits to collective farms, and long dreary debates with titles such as 'The effect of Imperialism and Colonisation in Black Africa'. I avoided such visits and debates but joined the visits to the cultural events that were organised to showcase the country. Heading the list was a visit to the Bolshoi Theatre, with its gold and scarlet furnishing, where I was fortunate again to see the great Russian ballerina, Galina Ulanova, dance the dual role of Odette-Odile in *Swan Lake*, the second time, the title role of *Giselle,* and the pas de deux from *Don Quixote*. I was also fortunate to obtain her signature on my programme after queuing with several others, outside the stage door.

One question I was asked over and over again, while in Moscow, was whether I thought that Communism would ever take hold in Africa. I hope I was able to convince them that, as the conditions under which Communism thrives does not exist in Africa, it was very unlikely that it would ever catch on. Furthermore Communism would have to contend with religion and tribal laws, which I assured them was very strong in Africa. With hindsight, how wrong I was when later, several African countries embraced the Communist ideology. But then, I was a young and naive young man talking. What did I know?

One thing that surprised me was how little the average Russian knew about their government's activities in the outside world. For example, they knew very little about the Hungarian uprising, which had then recently taken place, but which had been swiftly put down by the People's Army. Much of what they knew little as it was came from what they read in their newspapers, and that was very little about the truth. I tried to enlighten some of the hand-picked students, who were allowed to interact with us, much to the annoyance of some of the other delegates, who warned me that I was making myself a candidate for the Siberian salt mines.

I did tackle one of the officials, who was acting as a guide taking us around the Kremlin, about how news from the outside world reached the average Russian. He pointed out that there was a museum in Moscow where newspapers from all over the world are kept, and anyone can access them. Later I did find out that this was true, but at the time I was not able to convince him that people preferred that their news be brought to them by freely available newspapers, and also via the wireless and television, rather than having to go wading through newspapers in a museum. This lack of contact with the outside world, I think, left the Russian people with the impression that it was the West that was war-minded and not their Kremlin bosses.

But during my time in Moscow and meeting students outside our hotel, I sensed a rebellious feeling rising against the government. They were annoyed, and I thought then rightly so, at not being able to travel further than East Germany and Communist China on their

Reflection on my life

own initiative, unhindered by chaperones and regulations. Strangely, I discovered that the Russian people have a fondness for the British Royal Family, something that I found amusing, seeing that it was less than forty years since they assassinated their own royal family. Before leaving for Moscow, I had taken some photos of the Queen's coronation, and our Russian hosts fell over themselves to have copies. One royal fan even went so far as to have his enlarged and framed, and before we left, invited me to have dinner in his flat, just to show me the photo taking pride of place in his very tiny sitting room. All in all I found the Russian people very kind and generous who gave us many presents to take back with us. I came away from Russia with a good feeling and without a trace of Communism in me. That is except for the red blood transfusion I received in a hospital in East Berlin, where I spent a week with Asian flu on my way back to Britain. *Reader...please note that this was my impression of Russia in the fifties when I visited. Things have much changed since then.*

During the time that I lived in the flat at Victoria, the original three people who had invited me to share the flat with them moved on, and new people came and went. One of the new tenants was a young English graduate called Michael Crowder, and he arrived towards the end of my second year studying to become a dietician. He had only recently graduated from Hertford College, Oxford University, where he had gained a first class honours degree in Politics, Philosophy and Economics. He was interested in Africa, something that had begun while he was doing his National Service with the Nigerian Regiment. During his first vacation as a student he spent three months travelling in Portuguese Guinea, Gambia and Senegal. Soon after he moved into the flat Michael informed me that he was planning a much longer and wide ranging trip to West Africa, and although I did not realise it at first, he was trying to get me interested enough to make the trip with him. I must say he did succeed, because, as he unfolded his plans, I too became caught up in the excitement of making a journey and visiting countries in

ARNOLD AWOONOR-GORDON

West Africa I had never visited before and perhaps could never visit again. I did not need much persuasion.

So, without much arm-twisting, I jettisoned my studies, and on the nineteenth of September 1957, we left London together for an adventure that was to change my life. Michael had secured contracts to write about the journey from various parts of West Africa. He had also secured me contracts with the London owners of the three main newspapers in West Africa, the Sierra Leone Daily *Mail*, *the Ghana Graphic* and the *Nigerian Daily Times*, to write about our travels for them. We travelled by train to Portugal, and then by ship to Bissau, capital of what was then the capital of Portuguese Guinea, then to the Gambia, Senegal, Soudan, (now Mali) right across the whole of West Africa to Lagos and beyond. We went to Timbuktu, seat of learning, with its famous University of Sankore, when the Plantagenet were on the English throne; to the ancient walled city of Katsina in Northern Nigeria, and to Lagos, Onitsha in the east and west of the country. From Nigeria, we went to Cameroons, Ghana, Liberia, Sierra Leone and the Gambia. During our trip, during which all of these countries where still under colonial rule, we was struck by the differences produced by years of British, French and Portuguese rule between these countries, as we met and talked to both the governed and the governors wherever we went. We left the countries we visited convinced that the old ways will inevitably be lost and the Africa we had visited would increasingly be engulfed in the materialistic industrialised society of the West. These are findings that have become true over the forty and fifty years after our trip.

Chapter 14
A REPORTER AT LARGE

When we arrived in Guinea-Bissau, then a Portuguese colony, the missionaries we stayed with told us that there was a citizen of Sierra Leone in town. I was anxious to meet him, and he turned out to be Mr S.Z.O. Sogie Thomas, the Manager of Cable and Wireless. I had great difficulty in tracking him down as the Cable and Wireless office had closed down and no one knew where he was staying. I was eventually able to track him down, and he told me that had I not found him that day, I would have missed him. For he was waiting for a boat to take him to Portugal and then to London, to report to the Cable and Wireless headquarters, and after a holiday, he was returning to Freetown on retirement.

Mr Sogie Thomas came from a well-known Freetown Creole family of Andrew Street, in the western part of the city, but had lived most of his adult life working abroad. So after we had exchanged pleasantries and I had brought him up to date about happenings at home, I asked him how it was that he had joined the company. He told me that, in 1918, he had joined what was then called The Eastern Telegraph Company. The company recruited most of their staff in Sierra Leone as Sierra Leoneans at that time were the most educated of all the people in the British West African countries. In 1920 he had his first overseas appointment to Sao Tome and Mossamedes, where he stayed until 1923. Since then he had moved up and down the West coast of Africa. From 1926 to 1930 he was in Bissau for the first time, then on to the then Belgium Congo from 1930 to 1934, then Angola from 1937 to 1944, Accra from 1948 to 1951 finishing up in Bissau in 1952.

I asked Mr Thomas which territory, in all his travels up and down the coast, he had liked best. 'Portuguese Guinea' he replied without hesitation. 'Because,' he added, 'it is the only country without any racial discrimination, such as I found in Angola, and even in some British West African countries.' He said that nowhere in all of Africa had white and black learned to live more peacefully side-by-side than in Portuguese Guinea. He told me about the changes that had taken place within the company that he had worked for most of his adult life. The name, for a start, had changed and also mechanisation had been brought in. The latter had caught up with them in full, he said, and it now played an invaluable part in the quick despatch and delivery of cablegrams. With a machine like the Regenerator, he told me; cable messages could now be sent more quickly than before. Another most welcome change was that women had joined the company, and already did important work that only men did before. Salaries and conditions of service had improved over the years, and now that the company had been nationalised in countries of West Africa, the charge for sending a cable had been greatly reduced.

When I left Mr Thomas I could not help feeling sad about the closing of Cable and Wireless in Bissau. It was the last link between Sierra Leone and Portuguese Guinea. But Mr Thomas pointed me in another direction to meet the relations of another Sierra Leonean who had also worked for Cable and Wireless in the past. He was William Ellis Bull, who came to Portuguese Guinea in 1907. He eventually settled in Bissau when he retired, married a lady from Cape Verde and had three children. I met the eldest son James, who was one of the youngest first class administrators in Guinea-Bissau, and was in line for the post of Head of Administration. Though he could not speak any English or Krio, he was proud of his roots and considered himself a Sierra Leonean. One of the articles I wrote about my visit to Bissau, apart from my meeting with Mr. Sogie Thomas, and which was published in the Sierra Leone Daily Mail of November 7, 1957, was entitled *IN PORTUGUESE GUINEA THERE IS NO RACIAL DISCRIMINATION.*

Reflection on my life

When we were in Bathurst, Gambia, one of the persons I wanted to meet was an old friend of my grandmother. Grandma had spoken often about Lady Forster, the wife of the late Sir Samuel Forster, Barrister-at-Law. She was one of the leading citizens of Bathurst, and when I called on her, she was not in as she had left to attend a meeting of the Wesley Church Auxiliary, of which she was a staunch member. I left my name and the place where we were staying. Imagine my joy when I received a message inviting me to afternoon tea. She lived in a wooden house, with a small garden in front, and when I arrived I found her surrounded by her two lovely dogs, in a charming Victorian parlour.

She greeted me warmly and poured tea from a old fashioned teapot with a large tea cosy. She asked after my grandmother and said that they had not seen each other for some time, for as they got older, travelling between Freetown and Bathurst was getting too difficult. She told me that I had just missed a Wollof wedding party, and described how graceful the women were in their gowns of every hue and colour. She said that the Wollof women were the loveliest in Africa, vividly described their flowing gowns, and that she especially liked their outsize gold earrings which swung as they moved around. I asked whether all those clothes was not too hot in the tropics, but she assured me that the gowns were cool and not tight fitting.

She told me that personally she never wore such gowns, but instead dressed to suit her age and the climate. She used to wear cotton gloves, but now that they were made of nylon, she found them too hot. By this time, the smaller of the two dogs, the rude one as she called him, was getting restless and had to be taken out of the room. I told her that the name Forster was common in Freetown and asked whether her family had originally come from there. She said they did, and that her maiden name was Leopold, and though she was born in the Gambia she had been educated in Freetown. At the Annie Walsh School no doubt, I ventured to ask. But she pulled her small frame up and corrected me. 'I am an old girl of the Methodist Girls' High School'. But sadly, she added, she had only been back a few times to see the school, and did not think that she would go back now that she was too old.

She said Bathurst was now her home. She was happy there and had all her children, grand and great grandchildren there and would not feel happy parted from them. I said my grandmother was the same. I asked her what she did with herself, now that she had retired from active Bathurst society. She said she did not do much. She read a lot, sewed clothes for her grandchildren, wrote letters to those of her children and other family members living abroad, visited those of her friends still living and did some church work. Her grand and great grandchildren visit her often and keep her young and alive with their questioning. I was very sad to leave Lady Forster after spending over two hours with her, but I shall always remember her for the gracious manner in which she received me, and for her most inspiring conversation. Sadly she and my grandmother are no longer with us.

I wrote about my tea with Lady Forster which was published in the Sierra Leone Daily Mail of November 8, 1957. Other articles I wrote at the time, and which were published not only by the Daily Mail but also by the Ghana Graphic and the Nigerian Daily Times, during our six months trip throughout West Africa, had the titles..WHY NOT DEVELOP OUR NATURAL TALENTS? (about the arts in West Africa); TRAVELLING IS AN EDUCATION TOO (about how one can become enlightened through travelling like I was doing); FRENCH WEST AFRICA IS MORE POLITICALLY AWARE THESE DAYS; (about the movement for Independence that was on the move in French West Africa then);
DON'T INTEGRATE THE GAMBIA-GIVE HER PARTIAL AUTOMONY; (this was at a time the British and French were discussing whether to give the Gambia its independence or integrate

Reflection on my life

it with Senegal); THE GAMBIA'S BIG DELEMMA (about the cry for independence).

Of all the places we visited, Timbuktu left the strongest impression on me. But the fact that we reached this fabled city itself was by sheer luck. We had flown to a town called Goudam, a place we had never heard of, from where we had been assured we would be able to continue to Timbuktu by road as the transportation was excellent. But there was no transport leaving that night, nor it appeared was there any regular service between the two cities. Goudam was a lovely old town perched on top of a hill surmounted by a superb mosque, which reminded us of an early Gothic Cathedral, and which gleamed earth brown, reflecting its huge bulk in the muddy River Niger below. I understood then that the mosque stood as a symbol of the Muslim faith just as St Peter's Basilica in Rome stands as a symbol of the Catholic faith.

Fortunately for us, on the plane was the then Governor of the Soudan and his guest, the British Ambassador to France, who wanted to visit Timbuktu, and who had transport waiting to take them to the city. With great affront, Michael asked the governor whether he would give us a lift, and, reluctantly, he agreed. Soon we were all squeezed into a Landover and bumping along the sandy road on our way to this city which we had heard so much about. Along the way, we passed some real Tuaregs riding their aristocratic looking camels that rocked and rolled, making me nearly sick just to look at them. We then realised that we were indeed approaching the Sahara desert.

But expectation is better than realisation, because the ancient city was a great disappointment, as I wrote in the Sierra Leone Daily Mail published on 25th February 1958; a disappointment that most travellers felt when they reached the city. According to legend, Timbuktu was founded in the twelfth century by the Tuaregs and put in charge of a male slave called Buktu. Hence the name:

meaning 'the place of Buktu'. It was once a great centre of learning where, at the famed University of Sankore, research into astrology, astronomy, maths, philosophy and literature was carried out. There were hundreds of thousands of books in the city, and some of those have been preserved until this day. The great Arab Scholar and traveller Ibn Battuta, who visited it in its heyday, left a wonderful description of the city. Sadly, with the growth of the West African coastal slave trade, beginning in the sixteenth century, and due to internecine wars, Timbuktu fell into decline, a fate not helped by the encroaching Sahara desert. It changed hands many times until the French came in the nineteenth century.

The City that we saw had lost much of its ancient glory and presented nothing more than a view of some shabby looking houses built of earth. Its position as the gateway to the desert and to North Africa, through which all the caravans trading in salt and gold had passed, had by then declined. But as we explored it a bit more, we discovered some of the solidly-built houses in the old city, their heavy wooden doors embossed with brass, the great mosque tomb of Sidi Yaya, and the mosque of Sankore, which, as I had said, reminded us of Timbuktu's fabulous past, when it was an important commercial centre that flourished long before the advent of Europeans.

At the time, politically, the Mosque was of little importance, and the only other places of note from a western point of view, was the house of Major Gordon-Laing of the West Indian Army, the first European to reach the place, and those of the Explorers Barth and Rene Caille. But, we did not have much time to explore the City further as we had only two hours before the weekly river-boat left for Gao, our next stop.

We arrived in Goa, a town further down the Niger Bend, by a tramp steamer, which reminded us of an old Mississippi river boat. It was a floating market in itself, for whenever we stopped at each little

Reflection on my life

town on the river, loads of people came on board to shop and buy such delicacies as oranges, lime, cassava, tomato and bread. Not only the locals but also Europeans came on board as well, because, in such places, the weekly steamer was the highlight of the peoples' lives and the only link to the outside world.

ARNOLD AWOONOR-GORDON

Chapter 15
THE VENICE OF WEST AFRICA, OLD DIVERSITIES, AND FABLED DJENNE

If Timbuktu was a disappointment, for me the most beautiful town on the River Niger bend was Mopti, which was known as the Venice of West Africa, because of its situation on the numerous islands, just off the main stream of the river. The impression was also heightened by the beauty of its architecture, which included the sandy gold of its mosque, and the gondola-like canoes poling from island to island. Mopti had a bustling and colourful appearance pleasing to the eye. The men wore expensive looking heavy robes, and the women, their ears weighed down by huge heavy gold earrings, were dressed in brilliant bubas. The mosque at Mopti is a classic example of the many mosques we saw during our travels across the region, but the one in Djenne proved the largest. The town owed its prosperity to the dried-fish industry with fish mongers from all over West Africa travelling to the stinking fish market to trade, with bundles of this delicacy stacked high on their large lorries.

Two days later, after a long journey through some side streams and a five hour journey on the River Niger, we reached the fantastic city of Djenne. The first sight that the traveller sees is the spires of its mosques, which dominate the city and its island. I read later that its reputation as a centre of Islamic learning dates back to the thirteenth century. In the book I read entitled 'The Golden Trade of the Moors' by a Mr E.W. Bovill, he said that 'The fame of Timbuktu and the glamour surrounding it, have obscured the claims of Djenne as a commercial and intellectual centre of the first importance.'

Reflection on my life

I am not sure about it today, but when Michael and I visited, it was still populated by the Songhai, the founders of the great Songhai Empire, when King Sonni Ali, captured it after a siege of several years around 1473. Although he was a Muslim he also practiced several pagan rites, as Bovill put it in his book, 'like many Sudanese Muslims down the centuries.' But although the importance of Djenne has been replaced by the river-port of Mopti, then, and I suspect today, it was still a spiritual centre of immense importance as the Holy City of the then French West Africa, a lesser Mecca to which pilgrims from afar as Conakry and Senegal make the journey. In the centre of the city stood the mosque, reputed to be one of the finest of all the Sudanese mosques, built completely of red mud, but as Bovill writes, 'in proportion, concept and scale, it was like any of the Gothic Cathedrals of Europe, and a symbol of faith to Muslims in that part of the country'. I should add here that I learned later that it was designed by a French Administrator.

I would like to add here that one of the most memorable sights of travelling on the River Niger bend on the weekly boat happened one evening just as the sun was setting. I looked out across the vast expanse of the river and saw a man paddling his canoe upstream with the sun just setting behind him. The sight of that solitary figure is still vivid in my mind's eye after more than fifty years.

Everywhere we went in what was then French West Africa, we discovered that the Muslim religion was widespread, yet we found pockets of places that were still untouched. In one such place, not far from Djenne, the Holy City, and Mopti, the commercial centre, we came across what, at that time, must have been one of the most exotic pagan people.

We spent one day at a place called Bandiagara, which has a famous and impressive escarpment with a sheer 800 feet drop. At the bottom live the Dogon people, with whom the late French

Anthropologist Marcel Griaule spent most of his life studying them. Renowned for their unique architecture, the Dogon people live today, as they have done for centuries, in a series of villages built of mud into the cliffs, perched on the top position to guard both the approach to the summit and the plains below. The village we visited was called Sangha, and consisted of a collection of hamlets which extended in a series of weird arrangements of small turret-like huts, with paths snaking between them. There were also tiny mud houses that looked like granaries, but which we were assured were dwelling houses inhabited by people. It took about an hour for us to reach the lower village, and in this impregnable position, we could see how the Dogons were long able to resist and escape the slave-raiding Muslims and their religion. Slowly, but surely, the Dogons were giving up their ways of life and religion, and being converted by the advent of the Colonial administration, a process that I fear may now be complete.

That evening, as we travelled by the steamer to our next stop that would take us to Northern Nigeria, I could not help watching the sun set over the horizon, throwing up a red ball of light that made the tents of the nomads look like curious loaves of bread. As the dusk descended like a grey ghost, I had felt a sense of happiness and pride as I realised that I had done something that many of my West African generation had never done before.

Chapter 16
THE COMPLEX NARRATIVE THAT IS NIGERIA

From French Soudan, we travelled through Niamey, in French-speaking Niger, to Northern Nigeria, to the ancient walled city of Katsina, which was our first stop in the vast country of Nigeria. Michael had been given an introduction to the Emir by one of his sons who had studied with him at Oxford. I recall vividly that the white Colonial administrator delegated to take us to meet the Emir was rather tetchy and gave us all kinds of instructions about how to behave in front of such a lordly ruler of the vast region. He instructed us to be careful with the Emir, whom he said did not like visitors, or to be photographed and would prefer to speak to us in Hausa through an interpreter rather than in English.

In the palace courtyard, we met a small man dressed entirely in white robes and turban, and only the deference of the official indicated to us that he was the great Emir. He beckoned us into his council chamber, and speaking in perfect English asked Michael about his rascal of a son, whom he was trying to bring home to help him with his duties. He beckoned us into low armchairs, while his officials sat on the floor with their shoes by their sides. I was worried about where I would sit, as I am very uncomfortable sitting crossed leg on the floor. But the Emir, sensing my dilemma, and realising that I was not a Northerner, motioned me to one of the chairs. Michael told me later on that he saw I was looking very embarrassed throughout the meeting. I was embarrassed that these elderly and dignified men of the court had to sit on the floor while I, a young man sat on a chair.

Because of protocol, the conversation had to be in Hausa through an interpreter, and Michael asked some pointed political questions, which I thought would embarrass the Emir. Some of the court officials were quite worried and looked askance at Michael. But, he ignored them, including our Colonial administrator escort taking it all in his stride. The meeting ended with the Emir and Michael both squatting on the floor, speaking in a very educated English, looking through albums of photographs of the Emir in his polo playing days, and reminiscing about his father who had introduced polo to the Emirate. I understand it is still played in Katsina today. Meeting the Great Emir of Katsina was a most enjoyable experience.

Next day, he sent one of his officials who took us on a sight-seeing tour of the city in a sleek American car. We toured the vast mud city walls and passed through the gates through which Lord Lugard had entered the city on March 23, 1902, to conquer yet another of the great Fulani Emirate. A small plaque outside the gate commemorates this historic event.

At our next stop, Kano, Michael looked up an old Hausa friend, Amadu, with whom he had studied at Mill Hill School in London. I was introduced to him and when he realised that I was from Freetown, he said that I had to meet the Sariki of Sabon Gari. The title means Chief of the Strangers Quarter. This turned out to be Old Pa Barlatte-Hughes, a grandfatherly gentleman from an old Freetown Creole family. He greeted me with a warm embrace, saying he was glad to meet another Saro Man. He called for beer and regaled us with tales of his stay in Nigeria.

It turned out that Pa Barlatte-Hughes had come from Freetown to work as a clerk for Lord Lugard, and was with him at his headquarters at Jebba when he started his conquest of the north. He was very pleased to meet me and we reminisced about Freetown and several Creole families with whom he had lost touch. He was proud that Sierra Leoneans were the pioneers in the development of Nigeria, and was proud of his part in the

Reflection on my life

development of Northern Nigeria in the past fifty years. He said that he had known all the Emirs now ruling the country when they were little boys.

Pa Barlatte-Hughes was very outspoken and, many would say reactionary. He was critical of granting independence to a country that had only a handful of graduates and, at that time, did not think that the education of women was of much importance. He told us about once going to the Council of the Emir to plead the case of a young Hausa boy who wanted to become a lawyer. They disagreed and suggested that he become a Muslim teacher instead, even though his father was willing to pay for his education. But, he added joyfully,' I was able to get him a scholarship to train as a doctor in the UK instead, through the British Council'.

The old man was very well respected within and outside the walls of the city, by the Emir and his council of ministers and also the ordinary population of the city. Just before we met him, he had retired as President of the Mixed Court and Sariki, or chief of the Strangers' Quarters. Before we left Kano, Pa Barlatte-Hughes invited us to a wedding of an Ibo couple, and as we entered with the old man, the whole hall, which was full with about three hundred richly attired men and women, erupted with the cries of Sariki, Sariki, Chief, Chief. Turning to us, Pa Barlatte-Hughes, with a twinkle in his eyes said'You see my trouble? I cannot go anywhere without people calling me and wanting to meet me.' Of course, he was the guest of honour and was lead protesting, to the high table, next to the bride and groom. He later had to make a speech to the delight of the audience. I felt very sad when I heard later that he died soon after we left. He was 101 years old, and the last of his breed. Our journey through Northern Nigeria took us to Zaria, Kaduna, Jos and Makurdi, meeting and interacting with people of all classes: from Colonial administrators, tribal chiefs, rising politicians and taxi drivers, all looking forward to gaining independence from Britain.

ARNOLD AWOONOR-GORDON

We left Northern Nigeria and entered Eastern Nigeria at Onitsha where, as usual, Michael had brought a letter of introduction from an Oxford friend, to Dr Kalu Oje. Dr Oje was then the head of the General hospital and he welcomed us warmly. He had booked us into a small hotel called Evelyn's Guest House, whose owner turned out to be a distant relative of mine. Onitsha was a most intriguing place with a new market, one of the largest in Nigeria and elsewhere that had just been opened by the Princess Royal. It is said that you can buy anything, even a human being, in Onitsha market. Everything seemed to be packed into the three thousand stalls at a unit annual rent of £24. There was everything on sale from patent medicines to bicycle and car parts, jewellery, everything under the sun. As it was Christmas time, the market was festooned with Christmas decorations, and Christmas carols and songs blared from loudspeakers based at strategic points in the market. One thing I noticed while walking in the market as elsewhere I have visited, was that the hairdressing salons were full of women trying to look their best for the festive season. Whether they live in Mayfair, Manhattan, Soweto, Lagos, Nairobi, Freetown or Sydney, and however rich or poor, at Christmas time, any woman worth her salt, will visit her hairdresser to do her hair and try to look her best for the festive season.

While we were in Onitsha, Dr Oje arranged for us to call on the Obi of Onitsha, the most influential and important of all the Chiefs of the Eastern Region. When we arrived at the courtyard of the palace the red cap chiefs were already assembled in front of the throne. We were introduced to the senior chief, who held a fan in his right hand. When Michael held out his hand for a handshake, it was refused, for as we learned later, by tradition a chief never shakes anyone's hand. Then just after a young boy had covered the throne with a rush mat, the chiefs rose, and the Obi emerged from his palace. He was a tall, heavily built man with bloodshot eyes and the expression of a bloodhound. He wore a crown and from it protruded a number of white feathers. He sat heavily on his throne, and the first of the red cap chiefs, the aged ones as they were known, came forward to salute him. I thought it was a strange way to greet your king, thrusting their fists ceremoniously under his nose. Then followed the second group, who prostrated before him, and hitting their heads against a small whitewashed stone at his right feet. Dr Oje did the same, but Michael and I did a formal bow. I did not know whether mine was accepted or not as I was a young African, whilst Michael was a European. But as nothing was said, I assumed I had done the correct thing.

Conversation, as befits a king, was conducted through an interpreter, and from what I could gather, he was not too pleased that the colonial regime had usurped some of his powers. He was particularly incensed by the new Town Council over which he presided, but which was dominated by elected members who were non-Onitsha Ibos. He was very bitter about this, as we found out from most of the indigenous Ibos we met during our stay.

As it was Christmas, a lawyer friend of Dr. Oje invited us to his house for a traditional British Christmas lunch of turkey with stuffing, roast potatoes, followed by Christmas pudding, but downed with bottles and bottles of the local beer. Later on we sat on the balcony and watched the procession of people dressed in their Sunday best, followed by masquerades with some very frightening and grotesque face masks.

We left Onitsha on Boxing Day for Port Harcourt, where Michael, not surprisingly, had a university friend who was working as an anthropologist amongst the Kalabari of the Niger Delta. He was Robin Horton, today a well-respected and distinguished anthropologist of world renown. He is also a professor at the University of Port Harcourt, and a visiting professor at both Ife and Ibadan universities. But at that time he was just a young man trying to make his way as an Anthropologist, and was living and working in Abonima. Robin lectured us on the way Christianity and the belief in the existence of the supernatural existed side by side in Kalabari folk lore. He told us about the dilemma of people who were Christians and no longer believed in juju, but who were faced with the problem of resisting the temptations of performing rites which a Christian code forbids. According to tradition, the result of resisting those rites could sometimes bring death or some misfortune.

After the hospitality of Robin, we made a quick trip outside of Nigeria and went to Victoria in what was then Southern Cameroon, where we stayed with Raymond Snowsell, Principal of the Man-of-war Bay Training College, whom I knew from when I lived in Lagos. The college was set up to give young men self-discipline, self- reliance and initiative, as well as teach them to take orders without question. You have to remember that when we visited, the country was under colonial rule and was just getting ready for independence. So successful had been this College especially set up for Government administrative officers that big commercial firms enrolled their African staff members destined for executive position to be similarly trained.

We met old Chief Manga Williams, who was born in 1876 and became chief in 1908. His age caused him to stoop and he leaned heavily on a stick. He came to the college to talk to the students about the first century of Victoria, before the arrival of the Baptist Mission, when his people were worshippers of sea spirits and sacrificed humans to appease the spirits. He could attest to that, as, he said, as his own navel was removed and thrown to the sea to appease the spirits. As a politician, old Chief Manga was considered an old dodderer by the young politicians, and they winced when he claimed that the Cameroon was not yet ready for independence and that the people did not desire such a fundamental political change, which he did not think was a good move anyway. We learned that the political situation in the Cameroon was extremely complicated and best left alone.

Reflection on my life

We returned to Nigeria and took a lorry from Calabar, to Lagos, some 751 miles away. It was the longest and most tiring journey we made during our visit to West Africa. There were breakdowns, disputes, trouble with the police and at one time a fight broke out amongst the passengers over money. So it was with great relief that we arrived in Lagos at dusk, some thirty-six hours after leaving Calabar. Thankfully, when we reached our destination at 26 Bishop Street, the family home of my sister- in-law Mobi, we were given a most wonderful welcome. I was introduced to my latest nephew, Olu Richie Awoonor- Gordon, who later became one of the most radical journalists in Freetown, as the editor and owner of the PEEP newspaper. Sadly, he died a few years ago at the young age of fifty three.

After a wash and brush up, we had dinner and drank couple of bottles of the ubiquitous Star beer before we tucked in. Although Michael was used to eating African food and could eat anything put before him, he said that that stew was one of the hottest he had tasted.

Michael and I had agreed that if we ran out of money I would go ahead and wait for him in Freetown, so I did not stay long in Lagos. Although we were both writing articles, I for the Nigerian Daily Times, the Ghana Graphic and the Sierra Leone Daily Mail, and Michael for various newspapers and magazines in the UK, the payments were slow in coming and our London Bank accounts were running out of funds. So, I sailed on MV Aureol of the Elder Dempster line Aureol to Freetown ahead of Michael.

He stayed a few more days in Lagos meeting some of the rising politicians and interacting with some of the men who would later lead the country to independence. He then went to Accra where he did the same thing and was fortunate to meet Dr Kwame Nkrumah, the leader of the Convention Peoples Party, and the Head of the country. The air was full of talk of politics and the new independence. And the question on the lips of the last of the Colonial administrators was, Can democracy survive in Ghana? With hindsight, it did not, for a time.

Michael also visited the Ivory Coast and Liberia before our reunion in Freetown. As this was my home, I was keen to make him feel very welcome. Michael stayed with my brother Francis whom he had known in London, and I stayed at the family house at Oxford Street. Michael and my grandmother got on like a house on fire and although she was soon to celebrate her ninetieth birthday, he was very impressed at her knowledge of local politics and they spent many hours discussing Freetown politics and gossip. One person my grandmother recommended that I take Michael to meet was the veteran Creole politician, Dr Herbert Bankole-Bright. We visited him in his house on Garrison Street, known locally as the White House. He was recovering from a very serious illness, which local gossip said was the result of his bitter disappointment at the recent election in which, both he and the Creole cause he espoused, were defeated; he died in 1958.

Dr Bankole-Bright was very tired and a shell of the firebrand who had been a member of the Legislative council for twenty-one years, and a leader of the National Council of Sierra Leone. But from his tired old frame resounded a fierce and reasoning voice. He bitterly attacked the wholesale extension of the suffrage to what he called 'the natives,' which resulted in the 1951 constitution and the subsequent amendments. I am sure some people may not like me repeating what he told us, but that was his views at the time. He said 'We Creoles have been here for 180 years; whilst these natives have no education. I spoke to the Colonial Secretary, Oliver Lyttleton and told him he was being too autocratic. Why should he permit a minority to rule in East Africa and not here? Today the Legislative Council is a pantomime. I have been in it for twenty-one years, and I don't want to be there any longer. We Creoles have lost faith in the British. One day they will regret it.' He said a lot

Reflection on my life

more things that if he said them today would bring the political correct police on his case. So I shall say no more.

It is important, for those who are too young to know about him, that I say something about Herbert Bankole-Bright. Prior to Sierra Leone' independence, he was one of the most prominent Freetown politicians. Like most Creoles of his generation, he was the descendant of Liberated Africans. The story is that his grandfather had been liberated off a slave ship with his mother in 1823. As a young man Herbert studied medicine at Edinburgh University. I should point out that the first African to study at that institution was also a Sierra Leonean named Africanus Horton. It was while a student in Britain that Herbert Bankole-Bright became politically active, and was one of the founders of the West African Student's Union.

Returning home to Freetown, he set up practice, but politics was never far from his mind. In 1918 he founded a newspaper called Aurora, which he edited until 1925. This newspaper became an organ of his anti-colonial rhetoric against the British, and in 1925 he became one of the first Sierra Leoneans to be elected members of the Legislative Council of Sierra Leone. While there he used his position to campaign against racism and called for suffrage. In 1940 he founded his own political party, The National Council of Sierra Leone, which became the main opposition party at the 1951 general election. After spending the next six years attempting to obstruct all government activities, his party lost all its seats in the 1957 elections.

But not all Creoles at the time agreed with the views espoused by Dr. Bankole-Bright. One such Creole was the woman who defeated him at the election, Mrs Constance Cummings-John. She also came from one of the most distinguished aristocratic Creole families and believed firmly that the future of the country laid in the two communities going ahead as one. She must have been a tough person to brave the scorn of her own people to realise this ideal. When I took Michael to meet her she said that it amuses her that the more reactionary members of the Creole community called her by a native name, Fatu Cummings-John.

She told Michael, and I quote 'Although I am a Creole, I felt my place was in the Sierra Leone Peoples Party, which aims to bring the peoples of the protectorate and the Creole people living in the colony together.' She tried to put this into practice in her school, the Roosevelt Memorial School (now Vine Memorial School) where we met her. The school had some 643 girls, from both the colony and the protectorate. She told us that she was emulating the late Mrs Hannah Benka-Coker, wife of one of Sierra Leone's leading judges at the time, who founded the Freetown Secondary School for Girls in order to join Protectorate and Creole girls together in education. For she believed the saying by Dr Aggrey 'educate a man, you educate an individual, educate a woman and you educate a family.' In 1960, Mrs Constance Cummings-John was a member of the group who came to Lancaster House for the Sierra Leone independence talks. She became the first woman mayor of Freetown.

Chapter 17
A NEW DAWN

I must add here that all the people we met, from Emirs and chiefs, Government officials to rising politicians, are now dead, as is my travelling companion Michael Crowder. But I am grateful he persuaded me to abandon my studies and make the trip, which opened my eyes, for the very first time, to the diversity and cultures of my own Continent and its people and, at the time, their struggles for independence from colonial rule. I am glad to say their goal was achieved in all the countries we visited, within ten years of our visit. It is good that when I look back at the changes that took place in all those countries, I am glad I was a witness to some of them, thanks to that indefatigable Englishman, Michael Crowder who genuinely loved West Africa and asked me to come along on his journey of exploration. After the trip, we remained lifelong friends until he died in 1988. God bless his soul, where ever he is now up there.

But I can't end this homage to Michael without giving a brief summary of his illustrious career after he returned to London. As you might expect, he wrote a book about our travels entitled PAGANS AND POLITICIANS, which was published by Hutchinson's. He later wrote several books about Nigeria and West Africa, a list of which can be found at the end of these memoirs. Africa was in his blood, and so, after some years in the UK, he went back, this time to teach in Sierra Leone, where he became Dean of the Faculty of Economics and Social Studies at Fourah Bay College. After Sierra Leone, he moved to Nigeria as Professor and Director of African Studies at the University of Ife, and Executive Secretary of the International Congress of Africanists. At one time he was the editor of History Today.

While Michael and I were in Freetown after our long West African journey, I was offered a job as an Information Assistant at the Ministry of Information. I was in two minds about taking it as I had left undone several projects in London. But Michael persuaded me to take advantage of the opportunity and after a great deal of soul searching, I accepted the position. It was sad to leave Michael to finish the trip we had started over ten months earlier alone, as he went off to Guinea to complete the trip.

I am afraid that I did not last very long in the job as I did not get on at all with the colonial Government Information Officer. I think he was put off by having what he saw as this sophisticated Sierra Leonean from the UK, who seemed to know everything and everyone of note and importance in the city. He was also probably put off by the fact that the Financial Secretary, John Taylor, another colonial civil servant whom I had got to know when he entertained us in Jos in Northern Nigeria, before being seconded to the administration in Freetown, and his wife, would always invite me to official functions where I would rub shoulders with my boss on the same level. John and his wife Dorothy, found in me a like-minded soul, and would call on me if she needed any help navigating the Freetown social minefield. I used to help her with her sitting plan when she had to entertain local officials to dinner, as she did not know who was who, and who was married or not, or had a girlfriend he would bring to the dinner.

My Boss took his revenge on me, when he transferred me to Kenema, which at that time was not as developed as it is today. I found out that he had deliberately transferred the local Information assistant who had been there for years to Freetown, so he could send me there to be cut off from the bright lights of Freetown. It was a shock to the system, for when I arrived after many hours on a very slow train, I discovered that the family of my predecessor was still living in the house where I was supposed to stay. Luckily for me, a teacher at the school was an old friend who gave me

Reflection on my life

room in his house.

The official car that went with the job was a wreck, as it had been used by my predecessor to go to and from his farm, which was on a very bad road out of Kenema. It was not fit for purpose. I complained about the lack of housing and transportation to my boss in Freetown, but got no reply.

So one day, after only three months in the place, I packed up, boarded the very slow weekly train that took all day, and came to Freetown. Without telling anyone, I took the next Elder Dempster mail boat Accra, and was out of the country within a week. My resignation reached my Boss when I was on the high seas. I never saw or heard from him again.

But I must say that whilst working in the Ministry I was able to work with and learn from two of Sierra Leone's veteran and international respected journalists. The first was the veteran, journalist, poet and linguist Thomas Decker, who was then working in the Ministry of Information as Senior Information Officer. He was a passionate advocate of the Krio language and argued that Krio is not merely a patois, but a legitimate language. He even translated Shakespeare's Julius Caesar into Krio. He used to regale us young men about how he once tried to join the RAF in the UK, but was turned down because of poor eyesight. He then went into journalism, first working for the African Standard, owned by the veteran radical politician I.T.A. Wallace-Johnson, where his radical views were reflected in his writing. He later became editor of the Guardian where he was known for his skilled writing, which contributed to the national and political life in Sierra Leone.

He told us about his membership of the West African Youth League, founded by his mentor Wallace-Johnson, which had a strong anti-colonial message, which fought for equality and independence of Sierra Leone and its citizens. Tommy Decker, as he was fondly known, believed passionately in the unification of

Protectorate and Colony, and believed the Krio Language would have a large part to play in his dream of a United Sierra Leone. Sadly he died before he could realise his dream, but he left a great legacy not least in his writing.

The other person I worked with in the Ministry of Information was Bankole Timothy, a charismatic journalist and writer. Having worked in Britain for such respected newspapers as the Daily Express, where he was the Parliamentary reporter for the paper, he gained a great deal of international experience, and made several broadcasts for the BBC. His second journalist experience was when he was head hunted by the then head of the Mirror Group, Cecil King, who when he set-up the Ghana Daily Graphic at independence, recruited him as editor. He became a confident of Kwame Nkrumah, but as the political situation deteriorated, and as a result of his writing, he was deported, and returned to Freetown. He also used to regale us with stories of his travels and the people he had met and interviewed.

We were celebrating the christening of my niece in the house I was living in at Murray Town, when the people sitting on the veranda noticed a fire coming from somewhere in the centre of Freetown. Someone raced to town and came back with the news that the historic Wilberforce Memorial Hall, was burning. The historic building, named after the anti-slavery philanthropist William Wilberforce, was completed in 1887. There were many rumours circulating as to the cause of the fire, but nothing specific was offered officially as to the cause, and for years this remained a mystery. The North Koreans later built a new hall in the brutalism Communist style. It was an eyesore, and luckily this was destroyed during the rebel war, and the shell demolished ready for a new hall to rise in its place. I hope when it does, the name Wilberforce will still be its name.

When I joined the Ministry of Information I was put in charge of collecting material for the publication, Sierra Leone, Trade, Industry and travel, published by the Ministry. The magazine was printed in London by a charismatic South African Indian named Bobby Naidoo. I would collect all the material and photographs and send them to him in London. There it would be edited and printed and the publication sent to Freetown for free distribution to the public. I think we published three editions before the plug was pulled and we stopped publication. The reason being that government could not pay Bobby Naidoo for the work he had done to publish the magazine. During the time I spent gathering material for the magazine, I became friendly with Bobby Naidoo and his wife Sheila and their daughter Sheree. So when I returned to London, he gave me a job doing the same thing I had been doing in Freetown as his company was still doing the same kind of publication for Liberia. I worked for them for only three months before going to do some serious freelance work for the BBC. African Service

I used to chase stories all over the place, because the more stories I covered the more money I made. One story I covered soon after returning from Freetown, was the press conference at Australia House, next to Bush House, where the BBC Overseas Service was then based, to publicise the Commonwealth Games. This was to take place in Perth, Western Australia, in 1960. As I was the only black reporter there, I was surprised when I was singled out after the press conference, to have lunch with the Director of the Games, who was part of the delegation from Perth.

During the lunch, he asked me what I was doing and began to quiz me about what I intended to do in the future. I knew something was up but was surprised when he offered me a job in his department, and in Perth of all places. I had never heard of Perth and knew nothing about the Commonwealth Games, so said I would like to think about it. I then decided to do some research about the Commonwealth Games and about Perth. I liked what I found out and decided to throw in my lot and move Down Under.

In those days we had to travel to Australia by boat, which took six weeks. I think the boat I travelled on was the ORONTES, which was one of those ships that carried English migrants from UK to the other side of the world for only ten pounds. It was a very old ship and we were crowded six to a cabin. Although most of the passengers were families, there were many young Australians who had made the usual pilgrimage to the old country, to travel and work their way around the continent, and were returning home. They were a fun bunch and I soon made friends with a group that were up to all sorts of pranks on the boat, and I joined them. Amongst the group were two young students who were on their way to what was then Rhodesia, to work as volunteer teachers, and a young lady on her way to visit her sister in New Zealand. We became friends that was to last all our lives. The young lady met and married a New Zealander and had a large family. We meet every few years when they visit the UK and it is like old times again. Of the two students, one became a lawyer and today is heading one of the most prestigious law firms in the West of England, and also has a large family. Sadly we lost touch with the other student. But the others were friends that I made and have kept since meeting them on that ship to Down Under.

The dance craze at the time was the twist and I was a good twister. So every afternoon I organised twist lessons on deck, which was very well attended. On board was a TV producer who decided that when he got back to Sydney he would organise a twist competition on television, and wanted me to help him set it up. But unfortunately I could not take up his offer as I was getting off in Fremantle, the port of Perth, which was about a thousand miles from Sydney on the other side of the continent.

The ship stopped off in Gibraltar, and in Cape Town and Durban, South Africa. It was my first experience of apartheid, when I came face to face with it. I went ashore in a group of other passengers from the ship and saw for the first time notices of demarcation between blacks and white. I was not allowed to even walk on the same side of the street with my white friends, and we were followed everywhere we went by what I could only guess were plain clothes police in case we broke the law. So in order not to be arrested and locked up for breaking the laws of South Africa, I returned to the ship and waited for the others to return. They returned with a present of a Zulu shield made of cow skin. Sadly this was confiscated by the authorities when we reached Australia because of the fear that it may carry a disease that would decimate their cattle. Australia is very strict about bringing any fruit or other material that would endanger their cattle or fruit.

If I thought I had returned to the ship so as not to offend the sensibility of the white folk of apartheid South Africa, I did not leave it behind. Because we had taken on board some racist passengers from Rhodesia who were fleeing because of the threat of the country being taken over by the black majority. Thinking that they could bring their racist views on to a British ship they objected to my presence on the ship, and particularly to eating in the same dining room with me. I must say the captain was very firm with them and told them that as it was a ship sailing under the British flag they could either leave the ship at the next port, or put up with me being on board. We did not hear anything from them again until I left the ship in Fremantle, the port of Perth. But the story made headlines in the local newspaper and on radio, and as soon as I arrived was in demand for interviews by the news service in the other states of this vast country.

The City of Perth, where the 1962 Commonwealth Games were held, is the capital of Western Australia and is the most isolated capital city in the world. It is some thousand miles from the cities on the Eastern side of Australia. It was originally founded by Captain James Stirling in 1829, and gained city status in 1858. The city today is known worldwide as the 'City of Light' after the residents lit their house and street lights as American astronaut John Glenn passed overhead while orbiting earth on Friendship 7 in 1962.

BEING PHOTOGRAPHED AT THE TRAVELLING COMMONWEALTH GAMES EXHIBITION

Accommodation had been found for me with a professor and his wife who had a flat in town and a cottage up on the hills outside the city where they spent most of their time. As soon as I arrived and

Reflection on my life

had settled in, I was given the task of organising a travelling exhibition that would go on the road, state wide, to publicise the games to the people of the state. I had to wear my African robes, as it was felt that this would be in the spirit of the Commonwealth. The exhibition was designed by a Perth industrialist and made up of photographs, and telling the story of the Games and the Commonwealth. The exhibition took 1,200 square feet of display that could be folded and loaded on to a two-ton truck, and could be off-load and set-up within four hours.

The exhibition was a pictorial story of the games, with photographs showing some of the outstanding Commonwealth and Australian athletes in action, with progress pictures of the games village, the swimming pool, the stadium and the cycling track. There was also information about tickets and other items of interest, all accompanied by a continuously-running 16mm film of the previous games in Cardiff. The exhibition was opened in Perth by the Governor, Sir Charles Gardner, and was opened to the public for a week, before it started on its six months journey around the state of Western Australia.

THE UGANDA ATHLETES ARRIVING FOR THE COMMONWEALTH GAMES

Although there were two of us doing the driving, loading and unloading the exhibition, it was nonetheless a gruelling trip visiting the big and outback towns, where the interest was great, with people flocked to see the exhibition, and me, in my cotton *agbada*. We visited Banbury in the south then the legendary gold mining towns of Kalgoorlie and Coolgardie, Geraldton in the north of the state. I must say the people were very hospitable, especially the farmers and the farming community, into whose lives we brought a little bit of the world they never see close-up. The children too were very pleased to meet me and I cannot remember the number of schools I was invited to visit and talk about Africa, and Sierra Leone in particular.

It was not all work though. I was able to travel to other states and visit Adelaide, Melbourne and Sydney. The first time we drove across the Nullarbor Plain, which is the desert wasteland separating Western Australia from the other states, we returned the same way. The next time, we went by train and the last time by plane. I liked Melbourne and Sydney but preferred the old-fashioned quietness of Perth, with its old colonial buildings with verandas hanging over the road, and the old jail at the top of the main street. Unfortunately all this has now gone and Perth now looks like any other city in the world with tall skyscraper buildings reaching into the skies, with wide boulevards where there were once narrow quaint streets.

While in Perth I used to do the odd television programme for the Australian Broadcasting Service (ABC) station, including cooking such dishes as groundnut soup, pepper soup, couscous, jollof rice and anything I can concoct. When the games came to an end, I was offered a job in the production department of ABC in Perth but could not take up the job because of this reason. At that time, believe it or not, Australia had a White Australia policy, whereby only White people were allowed to settle there. My visa was for the

Reflection on my life

job I had gone to do, and when this was over I had to leave the country. An appeal was made to the Immigration Ministry in Canberra for an extension of my visa but this was not granted. And so, with a sad farewell, I had to leave Australia and return to London.

While I was living in Australia I learned a lesson that was to be with me all my life. That is never to make an of the cuff remark when journalists are present, and not to talk about things about which you know nothing. I had gone to Melbourne for the Australian Open Tennis Championship, and as usual, being a new black journalist around, the other journalists wanted to know about me, where I came from, what I was doing in Australia, how I liked Australia etc. etc. One of the journalists then asked what I thought of the Aborigines, and without thinking, I said they were lazy. My remark was published in the Melbourne Age, the most respected paper in the country, the equivalent to the Times of London, and the story was syndicated widely all over the country. Then all hell broke loose. The aborigines all over the country were angry at my remarks, and their leaders banded together and threatened to ask the Minister of Immigration to deport this upstart African. They wanted to know the basis of my claim that aborigines were lazy, and one prominent Aborigine leader even said that he had met many West Africans during World War II, and they were the laziest individuals he had ever met!

I was threatened with being horsewhipped, challenged to a debate on television and so on and so on. The story took on a life of its own and seemed not to want to die down, with the media playing it up for days on end. The journalists and photographers stalked me for days. It eventually did die down and I was thankful when it became stale news. It was my fault as I was just mouthing what I had heard from the White Australians I had been mixing with. And what was worse, I had by then not come in contact with any aborigines because, at the time, most of them did not live in the cities but in reservations. I should not have said something so stupid. I felt very sorry calling a whole community of people lazy, when in fact they had been marginalised by the white people for generations. Their anger at this upstart from Africa calling them lazy was justified. I learned a great lesson not to pass comments about things or people you know nothing about.

One of the most interesting programs I took part in was the school of the air. This was an educational programme unique to Australia, in order to bring education to children living in isolated farms far from any schools near them. From one central place in one of the big cities, using radio, school's curriculum go out to thousands of children who listened to the teacher as if in a classroom, and could interact with the teacher and ask and answer questions. I regularly took part in geography lessons talking about various African countries, the people and cultures. I enjoyed it very much as for the first time children scattered in the most remote part of the state, got to know something about a part of the world, which was alien to them.

When I lived in Perth two students from Sierra Leone came to study agriculture at the university. I took them under my wings and every Saturday I would collect them from their hostel for some home African cooking. In those days, I don't know about now, there was very little ingredients that I would use to make good Sierra Leonean food. But I was put in touch with someone in the Malaysian Consulate in Perth, and through him I was able to obtain four gallons of palm oil. Palm trees are grown extensively in Malaysia, but where we use it for cooking, there it is used for export to make soap and other domestic products. So I was able to cook some palm oil chop for them. I was also able to make groundnut soup and fish stew with rice and, when we could get it cassava. I lost touch with the two young students, to whom I gave the rest of the palm oil, when I left Perth. Many years later, when I was working in the American Embassy in Freetown, and I took an

Reflection on my life

exhibition to the Provinces, I ran into one of them, who recognised me from all that time ago. He was then a lecturer at Njala University. Unfortunately the other former student had died.

After I left Australia because my visa was not renewed, I did not return until 1999 in order to be one of the first to see in the millennium. I returned to Perth for a week to see some of the friends I had made the first time, and was sad about the changes that had taken place during the years I had been away. The nice old part of the city with old Colonial style houses, had been destroyed and new tall shinning buildings put in its place. The nice cobbled streets had now gone and tarred over and widened to take the ubiquitous car. I spent only one week in this my favourite city and caught the Trans Pacific Railway to Adelaide, some thousands of miles away on the other side of Australia.

The Trans Pacific Railway is the equivalent to the Trans Continental railway that used to go from London to Istanbul in the days of luxury railway travels. This Trans Pacific Railway runs from Perth all the way to Sydney on the other side of the Australian continent, passing through the gold mining towns of Kalgoolie and Coolgadie and hundreds of miles of deserts that had only kangaroo and wild camels. At some of the stops in this bleak place, lived people who make a living from keeping sheep in what I considered a hard living. Their only contact with the outside world was the weekly train at which they could receive discarded newspapers and whatever the cooks on the train could spare.

The train was the most comfortable I had ever travelled in, with luxurious cabins with all the modern facilities. There was a viewing coach where we could watch the desert go by, with the occasional herds of kangaroo and camels running away from the noise. The food was also excellent with breakfast, lunch and dinner served for the three days we were on the train. We got off in Adelaide in South Australia, and flew to the town of Alice Spring in the Northern

Territory. Our destination was what was originally called Ayres Rock, but which has now reversed to its original Aboriginal name of Uluru. Originally named Ayers Rock after Sir Henry Ayers, the Chief Secretary of South Australia by the white man who first saw

STANDING IN FRONT OF ULURU IN ALICE SPRINGS IN AUSTRALIA

Reflection on my life

it in 1873, even though for centuries the local Aborigine people have called it Uluru. It is a large sandstone rock formation near the town of Alice Springs, which is sacred to the Aborigines. In 1993 a dual naming policy was adopted that allowed the rock to be called by both the traditional Aboriginal name and the English name. It became the first official dual- names feature in Australia.

Uluru is one of the country's most recognised natural landmarks. This sandstone formation stands 348 metres (1,142 inches high, rising 863 metres (2,831 feet) above sea level. Uluru is notable for appearing to change colours at different times of the day and year, and I noticed it glowing red when we were there at sunset. When I visited people were allowed to climb the rock to the top, but I understand that has now be discontinued on the instructions of the Aborigines, who guard this place which is sacred to them.

From Alice Springs and Uluru, we moved to stay with old friends in Melbourne, where we saw the Millennium in, in great style, with food, champagne and balloons and some good company. We were glued to the television and watched the first rays of the sun rise over the island of Nauru, which was the first place to see in the new millennium, and from then on we watched the sun as it rose over other Pacific islands, until it reached Australia, and the new century was brought in with the most spectacular fireworks display over the Sydney Harbour bridge. Then Melbourne, then Perth in the west. Between drinks and food, we were glued to the television watching as the sun rose in country after country from Asia to the Middle East to Europe, but by the time it reached the Americas we were fast asleep as it was early morning in Australia.

As soon as we saw in the new century I started to telephone friends in London, where it was still day, and wishing them a happy New Year. They found it strange, as it was not yet the New Year. I had to convince them that where I was, it was the New Year. Lots of laughter. There were lots of sore heads on New Year's Day, but it was worth seeing in the new century which I will never see again.

Reflection on my life

Chapter 18
AT BUSH HOUSE, LONDON

After five years in Perth and the Commonwealth Games, I returned to London and resumed working freelance for the BBC African Service. By then my mentor Sheila Stradling had retired to her home in South Africa where she died. But I had new mentors who included Veronica Manoukian, Roger Ketskemety, Johnny Wilkinson, the deputy head of the service, Dick Clemens (later co-writer of The Likely Lads, Dorothy Grenfell-Williams who later became head of the service, Bill Everingham and Frank Barber. The programmes I worked on mainly was Calling Sierra Leone, but contributed from time to time to Focus on Africa, and Goodmorning Africa, the forerunner of Network Africa, hosted by the incomparable Pete Myers, whose wakeup call was GOOOOOOD MORNING AFRICA. From time to time I was roped in as a 'voice' when recording the plays broadcast to Africa.

By then I was joined by a host of broadcasters, all from Sierra Leone; Veronica Wilson, Eddie Williams, Hannah Neale nee Bright-Taylor, John Sorbar-Greene, Tonie French nee Tucker, John Bankole-Jones, Rosetta Nwanzoke, Eric James, and the irrepressible Glenna Forster-Jones. We were known as the Sierra Leonean mafia, ruling the third floor at Bush House, where the African Service was located.. The grandfather of us all was the Reverend M.G.M.Cole known fondly among us as Metro Goldwyn Myer. Rev MGM had a weekly spot on the Calling Sierra Leone programme, in which he talked about the Sierra Leoneans he had met and what they were doing in London. As he had his own church many Sierra Leoneans worshipped there, and so he had lots of stories to tell each week. He always started his talk saying 'Well, well, well here we are again'. His talks were so popular that even when he became blind, I would go to his house with a recorder to record his piece. He did it until he got too frail to continue, and we lost a great broadcaster.

I found out later that in his younger days in Freetown, he was one of the top football referees in Freetown. His nickname was 'give me my ball'. Apparently when there was a dispute between the two teams, and a fight broke out between the players, he would wade into the crowd saying 'Give me my ball' and he would take the ball before blowing his whistle to stop the game. We had the time of our lives making interesting programmes for broadcast when Sierra Leone celebrated its independence from Britain in 1961.

We all spent many hours sourcing programme ideas, and one idea I put up was interviewing West Africans about the records they liked and bought. I found a record store called Stern in Tottenham Court Road, which the only shop that sold records was made by African musicians and singers at that time. It was run by a nice old man who always had the most up-to-date recordings from all over West Africa. After an interview I did with him, I asked if I could come on Saturday mornings, when most of his African customers came to shop, to interview them on their choice of records giving them the opportunity to send a message to their families and friends back home and he agreed.

So every Saturday morning I would turn up with my recorder and interview the people who were there to buy records, and ask them to send messages to their folks back home. They would give me their addresses and we would write and tell them when the programme would be broadcast. The shop owner would lend me the record which the customer had just purchased, and I would return them after the broadcast. The spot on the programme, whether Calling Sierra Leone, Calling Nigeria or Calling Ghana was very popular as it brought those in these countries in touch with their loved ones in the UK.

Reflection on my life

I am usually game for anything either to make money or to gather material for a radio programme. So when I saw an advert for volunteers to take part in a research programme on the common cold, I was up for it and volunteered. The research was being carried by the Common Cold Research unit at Salisbury in Wiltshire set up by the British government in 1946 to undertake laboratory and epidemiological research into the common cold, with a view to reducing its human and economic costs. At that time, the common cold accounted for a third of all respiratory infections and the economic costs were substantial in terms of days taken off work.

We were thirty volunteers recruited through newspaper advertisings, and we were paid a small sum for our troubles. We were infected with a preparation of cold viruses, and typically during a stay of ten days were housed in groups of two to three, with each group isolated from the others during the course of the stay. We were allowed to go out for walks in the countryside, but the residential areas of the town were out of bounds. During my stay I caught one hell of a cold which stayed with me for about a week after my ten days stay at the unit. But I was able to make a programme about my stay, which I put down to a quiet holiday break. But I don't think I will do it again, even though I understand that these days the tests are run as a Flu Camp by private companies who pay volunteers the sum of £3000 for a fortnight's stay in a hotel style laboratory.

Like me, everyone remembers where they were in November 1963 when the announcement came that President Kennedy had been assassinated. I remember it clearly as though it were yesterday. I had gone with a friend to the National Theatre in the Old Vic at Waterloo to see Hamlet by Shakespeare with the actor Peter O'toole making one of his rare stage appearances. As we had to catch the overnight train to Glasgow, where we were to spend the weekend with friends, we left the theatre as the curtain came down in order to reach Euston before midnight, so we missed the announcement to the audience from the stage. But when we got to the outside of the theatre there was a newspaper man hawking the early edition of the Times, with the headline PRESIDENT KENNEDY ASSASINATED.

To say I was shocked would be putting it mildly. I cancelled my trip to Scotland and rushed to Bush House, knowing that they would need all the assistance in whatever programme they would be putting out. I was right, and for the next few hours we worked like the proverbial slave putting out hour on hour bulletins, jointly with the other services, in the various languages. We did not finish until eight the next morning, when it was decided that we should go home for a rest and come back later in the day. I had not reached my flat in Notting Hill Gate and was just about to get into bed, when the phone rang. Kennedy's alleged killer, Lee Harvey Oswald had been shot by Jack Ruby, and we were required to return to Bush House to start all over again.

The next twenty-four hours was a blur, and with the passage of time I cannot remember what we did or what programmes we put out. But it was a joint effort when all the services got together and pulled all the manpower resources at their disposal to do a twenty-four hour round the clock service for listeners overseas. The next few days and weeks were also hectic as the drama unfolded in the United States, with the swearing-in of Johnson the Vice-President, and the funeral service for Kennedy. We were up on our feet twenty-four seven, and it was several months before things got back to normal and we were able to continue with our usual programming.

I mentioned earlier that the assassination of President Kennedy put paid to a visit I was to make to Glasgow in Scotland. But I was able to make the trip later on in the year, and spend New Year's with a friend and his family. They lived in an attractive cul-de-sac

Reflection on my life

of six Georgian houses, and I got involved with the little known Scottish tradition of first footing. On New Year's Day, the first person to set foot in the house should be a dark person, or a Caucasian carrying a lump of coal.

So who better to enter a Scottish house than a black man. Soon as the word got round that I was staying with people in the cul-de-sac, the invitations kept coming inviting me to call on them after midnight. I agreed, but what I did not realise was that as you entered the house, you were given, and had to drink, what they called 'a wee dram.' A wee dram in Scottish is 'a drop of whisky'. Well, I don't drink or like whisky either, but as it was offered, and it is the custom, I had no choice but to drink it. So as you can imagine, by the time I had been the first person to set foot in five houses, and had a wee dram in each house, I was completely plastered, so much so that when I finally returned to where I was staying, I was sick and had to be put to bed. So be warned. If you are African or a dark person, keep clear of Scotland on New Year's Eve.

Soon we were again getting frantic in Bush House, as the time for Olympic Games in Tokyo was upon us. The Games were to take place in October, 1964, and I was dying to be included in the team that was going to cover the games. I was told that there were no plans to send someone specifically from the African service to cover the games, and in fact there were no funds to do so. Anyway, the BBC was sending a large contingent to cover the games, and it will be broadcast by the African Service. I remember pleading at one of our daily meetings for me to be included in the BBC team that was going to Tokyo. This was dismissed as not possible.

Then I remember one of the producers, looking at my cast fallen face, jokingly said 'Why don't you hitch-hike to Tokyo, then you can cover the games for us.' He said it as a joke, but the head of the service then said 'What a good idea. Why not do it Arnold, then you can send reports back to us for a fee as you progress.' This sounded like a good idea, for as I was then doing freelance work, I could hitch-hike and at the same time get paid which would finance the trip. Once the seeds were sown, everyone rallied round to make suggestions and to help me plan my route. When that was done, the Head then wrote to radio stations along the way to say I would be in their area, and could they give me as much assistance as possible to make recordings, which they could send back to Bush House for broadcasting to Africa.

Reflection on my life

Chapter 19
MY EPIC HITCHHIKING FROM LONDON TO TOKYO

Armed with letters of introduction, I flew to Paris to begin my epic adventure. I reckoned that, as I would be roughing it along the way, I may as well start with some luxury. I met up with some friends who were from Munich and were visiting France, and so for three weeks we toured France, Switzerland and northern Germany, taking in Cologne, where I learned about Au de Cologne, water of Cologne, the city that gave its name to the scent that women wear all over the world, before we eventually we reached their home in Munich.

One of the German friends I met up with in Paris, in his young days was one of Hitler Youth, and acted as a guard, stationed in the building which housed the office of Adolf Hitler. I asked him whether he did meet Hitler and what he was like. He said that he had great charisma, which made all who came in contact with him, fall under his spell. He said that the building was very large, and he was sometimes stationed in a remote part, away from the front. He told me that even in that remote part of the building, he and the other guards would sense when Hitler was not in the building. And when he returned they could sense he had returned, even if they did not see or hear him. So great was the aura around him. He also told me that, with hindsight, if Hitler had put all that charisma into doing good, he would have been a great person.

My friend also told me that as a teenage boy, he witnessed a group of Jewish prisoners being marched through his village, when a rabbit ran out before them. They fell on it and devoured it raw. He remembered turning to his father and saying, 'You see, Herr

Hitler is right. They are barbarians eating a raw rabbit'. He said 'No son. They are not barbarians, they are hungry'. He admonished his father for what he said, and wanted to argue with him, but his father clamped up and did not say anything more. He said that looking back now, he realised why his father did not argue with him. For children then had been schooled to report their parents to the authority for anything they did or said that was out of place.

The highlight of my visit to Munich was to visit the famous beer halls, to drink huge glasses of beer, whilst sitting on long tables, linking arms with your neighbour, singing German songs and eating large sausages. The surprising thing was that however much beer we drank, we never seemed to get drunk. I suspect the alcohol content was not very strong.

From Munich I hitch lifts to Salzburg, then to Innsbruck, finally to Milan in Italy. Here I must tell you about the cult of hitch-hiking, with its own laws and dos and don't s, which I soon learned. In the first place try not to link up with another hitch-hiker, if you can help it. People picking up strangers will never pick up two people, especially ones with backpacks looking a little worse for wear. They are frightened of being mugged. If you have to link up with another person, do so with a woman as women drivers are more likely to pick up a man and woman than a man alone. Never stand too near another hitch-hiker, leave some distance between yourself and the other person so that if a driver stops for you, the other will not think it is for them and rush to take the lift that is rightly yours. Always stand in a position where the driver can stop without holding up other traffic. And the best place to put yourself is at the beginning of the motorway, just by the access road to the motorway. For motorists are not allowed to stop on the motorway itself.

And one thing I learned by myself was to try and dress decently, as

Reflection on my life

people will not stop if you look scruffy like a tramp. Lorry drivers are some of the friendliest people I came across. They do long distance driving and are happy for the company, and although the language can be a problem, we can converse in that strange way that people do when they cannot understand each other. They are also the most generous people on the road, and time and time again, when they pull up for rest and food, will pay for your meal and allow you to bunk in their bunk beds if they have to stop overnight at a rest stop.

I did have one scary moment with a lorry driver in Greece, but this was due to miscommunication. I was travelling with an Australian girl I had met in a youth hostel, and we were picked up by a lorry driver. We both sat in the cab with him and as it got dark, he motioned to us that he would have to stop for the night. He motioned that I could sleep at the back of the lorry and the girl could have his bunk for the night. The girl interpreted this to mean that he wanted me to sleep at the back while she slept with him. She started to protest, and not knowing why she was protesting, he got upset and stopped the lorry and told us to get out, which we did. It was pitch black and there was nothing in sight but a small hut. We crept into the hut and went to sleep as we were very tired, having travelled all day.

Imagine our surprise the next morning to be awakened by the snorting of pigs trying to lick us. For unknown to us, we had spent the night near a pigsty. The farmer was very understanding and as we smelt of pig's shit he took us to his house, where we had a bath and change of clothes. His wife prepared a smashing breakfast of homemade bread and cheese and yoghurt. It was one of the best breakfasts I had had for a long time. Home cooking is the best. Later on he took us to a spot on the motorway where we could get a lift.

People were very kind and generous when giving lifts to complete strangers, including to a black person. I don't think it happens like that these days, what with all the violence that one encounters on the road today. Some people did not only offer me lifts, they paid for my meals and sometimes invited me to stay with them and their families.

From Milan I hitched a ride to Florence. I wanted to go to Florence particularly to see the statue of David, but I was very disappointed as it was all boarded up because it was being cleaned. The marble statue of David by Michelangelo is one of the most famous statues in the world and represents the biblical hero David and was created between 1501 and 1504. Originally it stood outside in a public square until 1873, when it was moved into the Academia Gallery. The one outside in the square is a replica. But although I was not able to see the original David, I was able to visit some of the great churches and museums in Florence such as the Uffizi gallery, one of the top art museums in the world, housing works by Leonardo da Vinci, Botticelli and Greek and Roman statues, before finding my way to Rome, the Eternal city.

I did not stay too long in Rome but vowed to return one day to savour the atmosphere. So it was a whirlwind tour of the Vatican, St Peters basilica, the Coliseum and the most famous of all, the Sistine Chapel, with the ceiling of the Last Judgement painted by Michelangelo, which he took four years to paint laying mostly on his back. Oh, I forgot that, like most young people who visit the city, I spent some time lounging on the Spanish Steps and threw coins in the Trevi fountain, like every other greenhorn tourist. Two things that stood out from my visit was seeing the statue of the Pieta, Mary with Jesus on her lap, in St Peters, and the statue of Moses in another church, St Peter Ad Avuncular. In those days there were not as many tourists as there are today, so it was easy to get into these places. After getting a cultural fix that would last for a long time, I left Rome. I was waiting at the beginning of the highway for a lift to the south when a large black official looking car, complete with chauffeur, stopped and the person in the back seat, rolled down the window and asked me where I was heading for. I told him I was going to Naples, and he said they were not going that far but would take me part of the way.

He turned out to be an Italian politician who was on his way to his constituency where his aunt lived. As we chatted about where I came from and why I was hitch hiking he was very interested in my background and said that if I was not in a hurry, perhaps I would like to visit his village and stay the weekend. He would like to introduce me to his old aunt, whom he said, he was sure, had never met a black person before, and he would like to see her reaction.

I accepted his invitation and when we arrived the whole town, led by the Mayor turned out to meet him. I must have looked strange in this milieu, and as I could not speak Italian he had to translate for me. At the end of the formalities, he took me to his aunt's house where most of his extended family had gathered. His aunt was very old but she embraced me and, speaking in Italian, said that now she had seen a black person in the flesh, rather than on television and the newspaper, she could die happily. As usual in houses with extended families, there were quite a number of children who all wanted to meet me, shake my hands and rub my skin to see whether the black would come off. They were disappointed. I later learned that one smart little fellow was charging his friends a few pennies in order for them to come to the house and shake and rub my hand. I am sure he grew up to be a smart entrepreneur!

There was feasting with lots of pasta and the local wines consumed right into the night, and I slept very well that night. The next day, as he was returning to Rome, he gave me a lift to the nearest auto route and dropped me off at a place where I was likely to get a lift.

I forgot all about the politician and his kindness of taking me to meet his aunt, until some years later when I read that the Prime Minister of Italy, one Aldo Moro, had been kidnapped by the Red

ARNOLD AWOONOR-GORDON

Brigade and murdered. I was shocked when I heard this, and saw his photo, as he was the very man who had given me a lift as a hitch-hiker, and had taken me to meet his aunt. I can only hope that by then the lovely old lady had died and was saved the trauma of the dreadful passing of her Prime Minister nephew. I still think of him often and pray for his soul.

I was anxious to reach Naples as I had arranged to link up with two young American twin brothers whom I had met at the Spanish steps. They had wealthy parents who had bought them Euro rail passes which gave them unlimited travel on railways all over Europe. They were both very enterprising and in order to make some extra money, they had sold one of the rail passes cheaply to some British students. But they were still able to use the other pass to travel using an ingenious method. When they took their seats in the railway carriage, one would sit near the door and the other by the window. The one seating by the door would have the jacket of the other one hanging by the hook near him. When the conductor came into the carriage checking tickets, (this was in the days when trains had compartment carriages) the one by the door would show his ticket and as the conductor went down the carriage, he would slip the ticket into the pocket of the jacket near him. The other brother, sitting by the window would pretend to be asleep, and when the conductor woke him up he would ask his brother to pass him his jacket and show the ticket to the conductor. As they were twins the photo on the ticket would be the same, and the conductor was none the wiser.

They were staying in Naples in the villa of friends of their parents, who were back in the States and had said they could stay there. So they invited me and some other casual friends they had made during their travels, to stay with them. It was a good time for me as there was food galore, a swimming pool, a car which we used to visit Pompeii to see the destruction that Mount Vesuvius did to this ancient city in AD 79, when it erupted covering everything,

Reflection on my life

including humans, with stones, volcanic ash and fumes. Vesuvius has erupted many times since then, and is the only volcano on the European mainland to have erupted within the last 100 years. Today it is regarded as one of the most dangerous volcanoes in the world because of the population of some 3 million people living nearby.

On The Road Again

Although I was living in the lap of luxury I had not forgotten that the reason for my trip was to get to Japan before the Olympic Games started. So after nearly three weeks I said goodbye to my hosts and took to the road again. I hitched from Naples on the Mediterranean coast of Italy to Brindisi on the Adriatic Sea off Italy. I wanted to reach Athens to stay with the family of a Greek girl I knew in London and, also to make some recordings of my Italian trip to send to the BBC at Bush House as part of the deal.

The last recording I had made was in Rome, so I was anxious to reach Athens to make another couple. For the more recordings I made, the more money went into my bank account, and the more money I would be able to spend. I had left some signed bank cheques with one of the secretaries at Bush House, and from time to time, as I was running out of money, I would contact her and she would cash the amount and send it to me at my next destination.

Most hitch-hikers and backpackers would use the services of American Express, a company with offices in cities all over the world. Their section that dealt with mail that has been sent to them for collection by travelling customers proved a very useful facility. So, when you turn up at an American Express office, with an identity, the lady handling mail will find yours, if it is there. One of the largest mail collection points that I found was just by the Spanish Steps in Rome.

I was really anxious to reach Athens not only to pick up my mail but to make some recordings to send back to Bush House. So I took the ferry from Brindisi to Corfu and then to the mainland. I was lucky as I found out that, in Greece, even long distance bus and coach drivers will stop and give a lift to a hitch-hiker if he has a free seat. So although I wanted to visit Olympia, where the Olympic touch is normally lit, I was lucky to obtain several bus lifts which took me directly to the centre of the Greek capital, Athens.

Unfortunately it took me a long time to find the house of my local host family. I thought they lived in Athens, but found out that they lived in port of Piraeus. I did finally find the family and they welcomed me with open arms. They had not seen their daughter, my friend in London, for some years as she was now married and had a family. So they were pleased that I had brought some news of her and wanted to know as much as I could tell them. The father was a captain on one of the many ferries that went back and forth, from Piraeus on the mainland to the many islands that dot the seas around Greece.

They lived in a very tiny one bedroom flat, and as there was only the two of them, I had to sleep in the living room, which had a sofa bed. They were very hospitable people, and plied me with food and the local drink of retsina, which I got to like very much. During the day, I would take the local bus into Athens to visit the Acropolis and other museums and watch the Greek guards outside the Royal palace, in their unusual uniforms which included a flared skirt, as they changed guards. I also visited the Acropolis on top of the hill overlooking the City.

The captain invited me to join his ferry, free of charge, on a visit to one of the most popular islands called Mykonos. This island had the most spectacular views, as we approached, of white and blue houses. We did not stay overnight but I was able to wonder around narrow steep streets and savour something of the way of life of the people who lived there.

Another time, he took me on a longer trip to the island of Crete,

Reflection on my life

where we stayed overnight. I was fortunate to be there when they were filming what became one of the most popular Greek films ever, Zorba *the Greek*, with Anthony Quinn and Alan Badel. I was able to rubberneck as they filmed scenes at the cafés on the waterfront, and hoped that I would be included in one of the crowd scenes. But I think a black face amongst Greek faces would have spoilt the scene.

While in Athens, I went to the radio station and presented my letter of introduction with the BBC letterhead showing prominently. As usual I was surprised at how the name BBC, apart from being well-known in every country I visited, opened doors for me. Some of the broadcasters I met on my journey were in awe that I was actually working for that great institution. Many times I was asked how they could get a job there if they got to London, and I was able to tell them as much as I could.

It was at the radio station in Athens that I recorded one of my pieces that I still remember, and which caused much hilarity when they heard it back at Bush House. I remember that it had to do with not understanding the language. For then I could rightly say the expression 'It's all Greek to me' and really mean it.

On my way back from Crete I met two French journalists and as we got talking, they told me that they were on their way to visit the monasteries at Mount Atos. I had never heard about this place before and decided that as it was on my way I should pay it a visit. Mount Atos is on an island off the mainland of Greece and houses some twenty Byzantine monasteries of the Eastern Orthodox Faith. Only men are allowed to visit them, for which one needed a permit for a limited period. It is a self-governed region and houses a community of monastic Christian monks, living in monasteries, where they worshipped in comparative solitude, while allowing them a level of mutual practical support and security.

Legend has it that Mary, the mother of Jesus walked on Mount

Atos. The scene approaching the island by ferry from the mainland was spectacular, and when we reached we were met by the Tourist Master who booked us in for a week.

There are no cars on the island, and I understand only male animals are allowed. There is a prohibition on the entry of women on the island, for it is felt that the presence of women would alter the social dynamics of the community and therefore slow its path towards spiritual enlightenment. I understand that the ban on women was officially proclaimed by the Byzantine Emperor Constantine in 1046. It is related that one Serbian Emperor brought his wife to Mount Atos to protect her from a plague but she did not defile the ground during her entire visit, as she was carried in a hand carriage all the time she was there. In 1920 a woman writer entered Mount Atos disguised as a sailor and later wrote about the escapade. In another incident, in 1930, the woman who won the Miss Greek beauty pageant shocked the world when, dressed as a man, she sneaked onto the island.

Not to be daunted, in 1953, an American Fulbright Programme teacher from Athens, Ohio, landed on the island briefly with two other women, which stirred up a controversy among the local monks. The European Parliament passed a resolution in 2003 requesting a lifting of the ban for violating what it termed 'the universally recognised principle of gender equality' I don't know whether they succeeded or not. In the time I was allowed on the island, I visited three monasteries: Agrias Anna (St. Ann); Agrias Andre (St Andrew), and Zogratou, sleeping in a cell and joining the monks in their daily rounds of prayer, chanting and worship, and having meals with them. Although most of the ceremonies was conducted in silence, the monks were allowed to converse with the various tourists who visit them during meal times. I found that not all of them were Greeks, and they came from as far away as the United States of America, all drawn to a place of prayer and solitude, and away from their women folks. It was an eye opener seeing how contented they were in their new roles.

A Spy in Their Midst?

I must here recount how I nearly got arrested in Greece because I was suspected of being a spy. I was sitting by the roadside waiting for a lift and I decided to make some notes about my visit to Mount Atos, when suddenly a convoy of military vehicles came trundling by. I took no notice and continued to make notes, as truck after truck went by. Suddenly an army jeep pulled up and three men with guns jumped out. They pointed their guns and frightened the hell out of me. They asked me in Greek what I was doing, and as they realised I did not understand what they were saying they called the driver, who spoke some English, to come over. They wanted to know what I was writing, as they thought I was recording their troop movement. I showed him my note book and although his English was not too good, he was able to explain that I was a hitch hiker and the notes I was making was about my trip rather than recording their movements. It was rather scary, but they let me go with the warning that I put my note book away and not make any notes while they were about. It was a close shave, as I did not relish the thought of spending time in a Military jail in a far off country, where no one would know where I was.

I suddenly realised that I had been on the road for far too long, and so I began to hurry to reach my destination as soon as possible. From Greece I crossed over to Turkey and made for Istanbul, getting lifts on long distance buses and lorries all the way. I reached that fabulous city at dusk and had a hard time finding the youth hostel where I was to stay. Someone pointed me to what turned out to be a hostel for migrant workers, and so I spent the night amongst construction and dock workers. They all looked so fierce that I could not sleep for fear that I would be robbed of the few possessions I had in my backpack, or perhaps even killed for the money I had in my money belt. But I should not have worried, as they were all so exhausted after their hard day's work that all they wanted was to sleep and rest their weary bones.

I did find the youth hostel the following day. Here, I should tell you something about youth hostels, which were, and still are, the cleanest and cheapest places dotted all over Europe, where hitch-hikers like me could stay for just a few pounds per night.

The history of youth hostels is a fascinating one. In 1912, over 100 years ago, a German called Richard Schirrmann created the first permanent Youth Hostel in Germany. These first hostels were the version of the German Youth Movement, to let poor city youngsters breathe outdoor air. The movement soon grew all over Europe and today they can be found in countries all over the world. These Hostels tend to be budget orientated, with considerable low rates, and have shared rooms and bunk beds, communal showers and toilets, and, at that time, no food was served. When I stayed in them they were very basic, but I understand that they are now more upscale, with private rooms with showers and canteens and tennis courts and other facilities. But they catered for my needs when I was travelling in remote places where I needed just a bed to lay my head and have a shower. It was at these youth hostels that one met other hitch-hikers and swapped stories about the best places to hitch a lift and so on.

Staying in youth hostels one builds up a comradeship with the other hitch-hikers one meets along the way, and pick up information as to which county was best for obtaining lifts, which country to avoid because of the local police, which hostel is best and so on. When I was in Turkey I picked up the information that in order to get some money, one could sell one's blood. Sell my blood? I was a little horrified. But I was persuaded that it was easy money and did not affect one in any way. So with a group of about five of us, we trooped down to the blood bank, and sold our blood.

Reflection on my life

As I was told, it was easy with no questions asked as to one's blood group or whether one had any illnesses lurking in one's blood. I thought I would feel faint, but nothing happened and the whole business lasted only fifteen minutes. After resting for about another fifteen minutes I was given some strong coffee and some biscuits, paid the equivalent of five pounds sterling, and I was on my way.

I learned later that in more civilised countries, one had to wait for a month before giving another blood, but in Turkey, you can give as much blood as is available in your body, so long as you do not go to the same centre. After my first experience, I did not do it again although many of the hitch-hikers staying at the hostel gave blood every day for a week. Good for them, but not for me.

It was at one such hostel, can't remember where, that amongst the hustle and bustle of the shared dormitory, that I saw an America chap who was slightly older than us, kneel down by his bed, saying his prayers. I was very impressed that he could do that without flinching or waiting for the room to quieten down. It must have taken some courage for which I admired him greatly.

I was glad to be in Istanbul, a city I had heard so much about. It was previously known as Constantinople, after Emperor Constantine the Great, who founded the city in 1324. In the 14th century the country was conquered by Sultan Mohammed 11, who renamed it Istanbul. One of the great Byzantine Churches in the city known as Hagia Sophia, was turned into a mosque and four minarets constructed. Today it is a museum visited by thousands of tourists from around the world. I read somewhere recently that there is a movement to turn it back into a mosque, which will be a great pity if it goes ahead. The place is worth a visit and can be seen from every direction of the city. Istanbul is a city that sits astride Europe and Asia, and is separated by the Bosporus, the Sea of Marmara and the Dardanelles. It is a cosmopolitan city that is reflected in this dichotomy of straddling two continents, looking towards both east and west.

Apart from the Sophia museum, I visited the Topkapi Palace, now also a museum. One thing I was told I should do when in Istanbul was to go and eat freshly grilled fish under the Galata Bridge, which spans the Golden Horn. Every evening, the fishermen would come to a place under the bridge and grill their catch, which one eats with flat bread. It seems as if every tourist visiting Istanbul has been told about this, and when I arrived the place was packed with people from all over the world, tucking into the most delicious grilled fish you ever had. I must say that I visited the bridge each evening I was in Istanbul. I understand that the place is still as popular with tourists as it was then.

As I mentioned earlier, I was getting side-tracked with many such visits and realised that if I wanted to be in Tokyo before the games started, I had to hurry. I was then very lucky to be given a lift by two American construction workers who were on their way to Iran, to join a construction group building a road from Tehran to the border with Afghanistan. They had one of those camper van type of vehicle, which could sleep six and had all the comforts of home, including cooking facilities, toilets and shower and a small fridge. They had already picked up two young New Zealanders who had got the idea of travelling in Europe by bicycle. One had had his bicycle stolen in Athens, and the other fellow had strapped his to the roof of the camper van, with the intention of selling it in Tehran.

It was one of the most interesting rides I ever had and it took two weeks in total. First of all our hosts wanted to visit the black sea on the north of the country, to see whether the sea was really black or was it just a name. Typical Americans! We travelled north to the black sea town of Samsun, and followed the coast by the sea to Trabzon. Disappointedly, for my American friends, the sea was not black, but the same colour as most seas, but the scenery was spectacular. Sometimes we travelled through towns close to the sea and sometimes we went high into the mountains overlooking the sea from afar. It was interesting to realise that on the other side of this expanse of water was the Soviet Union, as it was at that time. Although we had cooking facilities in the vehicle, yet apart from making coffee, which the Americans drank in large quantities, we mostly ate street side food of kebab, flat bread and rice. Surprisingly for Americans, they enjoyed the local food as they had been working on various construction sites in Greece and Turkey so they were used to the food. It took us over two weeks to reach Tehran where the Americans had the headquarters of the construction company. The company was constructing a road from just outside Teheran towards the Afghan border, whilst the Russians were constructing one from just outside Kabul. So it was a race to see which country finished first. What I did not realise at the time was that it would be the last time I would be able to hitch-hike because, from Teheran onwards, I would have to pay to travel!

In those days, people did not travel long distances by car in that part of the world, only lorries and buses plied the routes. Moreover, it was dangerous to travel alone as there were brigands and cut throats all along the way, just waiting to pounce on the lone traveller. I hope it has changed since then.

By the time we arrived in Tehran, the road being built by the Americans was a quarter of the way completed and they were working night and day in order to beat the Russians. Our friends dropped us off at the headquarters, and promised that if we needed another ride the company trucks going and coming with goods and materials would help us. At that time Iran was ruled by the Shah, and although things were more relaxed then, than when the Ayatollah took over, it was still not easy to find somewhere selling liquor. But putting our noses to the ground we were able to find a place where beer was sold, and during the time we spent there we patronised this place regularly. The bicycle was sold at a huge profit, and in dollars. So the owner was able to buy us some beer with the proceeds.

But I was anxious to push on as time was getting short before the games started. So we hitched a lift on one of the construction vehicles, which took us to the camp site near where the road had reached. Unfortunately our friends were not there as they were at the front of the construction, but we were made welcome and for two days we tucked into real American hamburgers and fries and drank gallons of real American Coco Cola, as hard drinks were not allowed in the camp-site. After two days, our friends returned, but the American camp cook fell ill with stomach problem and had to be airlifted to Tehran.

Although he had some local Iranians to help him, none of them knew how to make American food. Without thinking I offered to help in order to repay their kindness of letting us stay at the camp. I did not know what I was letting myself in for. Because I had to get up at five in the morning to prepare breakfast for the team leaving for the site, and prepare the same for those returning from the night shift. I must say the food was plentiful as everything was flown in on a regular basis. Steaks, hamburgers, chips already cut up and only needed to be fried, fresh fruit, vegetables, and greens, eggs by the case load, racks and racks of bacon, and bread and rolls that only needed to be heated up. I did have help to cut things up and fetch and carry, but I had to do most of the cooking. Never knew there was so many ways to fry eggs, as everyone seemed to know the way they wanted their eggs...sunny side up, flipped over, only one side, both sides etc., etc. I must say that within a week I had learned the ropes of American cooking. I learned about hash brown, how to cook a rare and medium rare steak and how to make a mixed salad. I also learned that Americans liked their bacon fried to destruction, black and hard.

But after a week when the replacement cook had not arrived, I was

Reflection on my life

in the process of throwing in the towel. But they begged me to stay and even offered to pay me $1000 a week to stay. I must say I was tempted. And since then I have looked back over the years and wonder whether leaving was the biggest mistake I ever made in my life. I would have come away with loads of American greenbacks, which would have lasted me for a long time. But I would have missed the Olympic Games in Tokyo. Also the two New Zealand young men, who had travelled with us from Turkey, were anxious to move on, and I did not relish the idea of travelling alone. It is no good saying 'what if' at this distance of time. I did stay another week during which time I tried to teach one of the local staff who helped in the kitchen. I don't think I succeeded, but when I left I had an envelope stuffed with $3000, which was most welcomed. So we said a reluctant goodbye to the luxury of the American camp-site and hit the road.

As there was no possibility of hitching a lift as people did not travel by cars in Iran, we had to pay on one of the long distances Afghanistan buses, decorated with fringes and bells and packed with passengers inside and on top, with loads that looks as though they would topple over at any moment, but didn't. I understand that these kinds of buses have long disappeared and there are now sleek Western type buses plying the routes. By changing three or four buses we reached Kabul in three days. The Kabul I visited then was not the same as Kabul today, which after being in the centre of a war with the Taliban, first with the Russians, and latterly between the Coalition forces, led from the front by the American, has changed beyond all recognition Then it was a dusty and neglected looking place, with very few hotels or guest houses, and we found it very difficult to find somewhere to stay. We eventually found a room in the house of the bus driver who had brought us on the last leg of our journey to the City.

I had heard about a huge ancient Buddhist statue carved into mountains in the north of the country, and was determined to visit the site. But this proved very difficult as it was situated in a very remote part of the country where bandits roamed. So I never saw what was to become a UNESCO World Heritage site and which, I was sad to read much later, had been blown up by the Taliban. But although there was consternation and justified anger around the world at what was considered a sacrilege when this happened, if one knows anything about the history of this troubled country, the British also did something similar when, in 1879, they blew up one of the most famous mosques in Kabul, in retaliation for the killing of their envoy.

Here, a little history is called for. In the 1830s, the British Empire, firmly entrenched in India, feared that Russia would invade India through Afghanistan, an encroachment which would be fatal to the British company and interests in India. They sent an envoy to the ruler of Kabul, to form an alliance against the Russians. The alliance was rebuffed, and in retaliation, the British attacked Kabul on the duplicitous excuse that they were merely supporting the legitimate government against foreign interference. How many times have we heard that?

The troops pillaged the countryside, defeated all opposition, demolished the city's main bazaar and withdrew through the Khyber Pass. Many voices in Britain, including those of Lord Aberdeen and Benjamin Disraeli, criticized the war as rash. The perceived threat from Russia did not really exist. But in 1878 the British again invaded Afghanistan, a move which historically has been called the second Anglo-Afghan war. But this time the British army was massacred, and only one survivor was able to make his way to the British outpost.

We did not stay long in Kabul but found a long distance bus that was going to Pakistan and so we were on our way. The journey was also one of the most interesting of my trip, as it took us to the North West Frontier and down the Khyber Pass, both

Reflection on my life

famous in British colonial history, then on to Peshawar in Pakistan.

The Khyber Pass connects Afghanistan to Pakistan, cutting through the north-western part of the Spin Ghar Mountain. It is an integral part of the ancient Silk Road and is one of the oldest passes in the world. Throughout history it has been an important trade route between Central and South Asia. It is also a strategic military location, as the Americans have found to their costs as they use it to transport goods and arms from Pakistan to Afghanistan.

Long before the Americans came to the country, the Khyber Pass was used by Alexander the Great and Genghis Khan, Muslim invaders of South Asia. The Sikhs also captured the pass in 1798. So going through the Khyber Pass was a most thrilling experience in the footsteps of all those historical figures, and the many British soldiers who lost their lives in what was a fruitless war. How history can repeat itself is a salutary reminder of the futility of war, as it is happening today in that part of the world.

As we were in a hurry we did not linger in Peshawar, but caught a train to Punjab and thence to India. I must say that one of the legacies of the British Colonial rule in India is the excellent train network they left when they pulled out. The network has been maintained by the Indians until today and is a testament to the British Raj. We crossed India from the north going south, changing trains until we reached Punjab and Amritsar. Amritsar is a holy place for the Sikhs as it contains the Golden Temple, known to the Sikhs as The Abode of God. This golden edifice gleaming in its reflection in the lake on which it is situated is the most beautiful sight to behold. It was built in the 16th century, and inside is the holy scripture of Sikhism. Known to Sikhs as the Gurdwara, it has four doors symbolising the openness of the Sikhs towards all peoples, and today it is visited by millions of Sikhs from around the world.

ARNOLD AWOONOR-GORDON

In the early nineteenth century, the Sikh Maharaja, Ranjit Singh, secured the Punjab from outside attack and covered the upper floors of the Gurdwara with gold, which now gives it its distinctive gold appearance and the English name of Golden Temple. Many years later, I learned that the temple, the Sikhs most Holy Temple, had been attacked on the orders of the Prime Minister, Indira Ghandi, to get rid of a rebel and political revolutionary Sikh leader by the name of Jarnail Singh Bhindranwale, who was the thorn in Mrs. Ghandi's side. He and his followers had holed up in the temple. The operation was carried out with tanks, artillery, helicopters and armoured vehicles; the rebel and his followers were killed and the temple destroyed. But I understand that it has been rebuilt to its former glory. Four months after the operation, Mrs Ghandi was assassinated by two of her Sikh guards, in what has been called an act of vengeance.

Our next stop was, of course, Delhi where we arrived in the middle of the monsoon season. The main square, known as Connaught Square, was inches deep in water, and we had to walk under the awnings of the shops that surrounded the square. We found lodgings in the YMCA hostel, one of the most up to date hostels we stayed in during our travels in that part of the world. Of course one could not go to Delhi without visiting nearby Agra and the Taj Mahal. They say the Taj is best seen at moonlight, but I say the Taj is best seen when it has rained. The marble was shining and glistening from the rain, and the whole edifice was something breath-taking to behold, when I saw it.

I think most people know the love story behind the building of this temple dedicated to love. Well, if you don't, then here it is. The Taj Mahal is a white marble mausoleum built by the Emperor Shah Jahan, in memory of his beloved third wife Mumtaz Mahal. Today it is a UNESCO world heritage site and is recognised as the jewel of Muslim art in India. The construction was begun around 1632 and completed around 1653. If there is one

Reflection on my life

thing you should put on your bucket list, it must be a visit to the Taj Mahal.

At the YMCA hostel, we met several young Australians, Brits, Americans and New Zealanders, all on what was then called the 'Hippie trail', a spiritual journey to find themselves. Without exception they told us not to venture across the Indian continent as it was full of dangers to foreign back packers, and many have been robbed and some even killed. I said that I was trying to reach Japan, and the suggestion was that I should go to Bombay, now Mumbai, and try to get a ship that would take me directly to Tokyo. One should remember that, at that time, the war in Vietnam was still raging and it would have been impossible to go through Burma and Thailand, or Cambodia, let alone through Vietnam. I took their advice and boarded the train to Bombay, hoping to get a boat to Japan. The two New Zealanders I had been travelling with since Turkey decided that they would risk it and try to go through this troubled region. So sadly we parted company and although we exchanged addresses, we never kept in touch.

My train to Bombay was very crowded with people sitting on top of carriages, dodging electric wires as we passed under them. I could not get a seat, even in the first class section, and had to stand for a few hours, squeezed between what must have been the whole mass of the world's unwashed, all trying to get to their destination. What was surprising was that amongst all that herd of humanity, the most smartly dressed ticket inspector made his way, checking tickets. He seemed to enjoy his work, especially when throwing people without tickets off the train. But I must say he did save my life, for when he reached me and I asked if he could find me a seat, or a sleeping compartment, he willingly took me to his own small sleeping compartment and said I could stay there as he hardly ever used it.

He was too busy checking people without tickets, and I never got his name or thanked him, but for the next 72 hours I was able to curl up in the rather tight compartment and have some sleep. When we reached Bombay, I could not find him amongst what must be the whole of humanity cramped into the station. It made me even more aware that India had the second largest population in the world!

I did find the YMCA hostel after some searching and was able to rest my weary bones after the cramped condition of the ticket inspector's quarters. When I was there the place was known as Bombay but is now called Mumbai, after Mumbai, the Kola Goddess. Today the city is the most populous in India, the second most populous metropolitan area in India and the fifth most populous city in the world, with an estimated population of 18.4millions. It is also the financial and entertainment capital of India, and is the wealthiest city in India with, the highest GDP of any city in South, West or Central Asia. This is now, but when I was there I did not have time to linger and take all this in, but to find a ship that would take me to Japan.

After visiting several shipping companies, I eventually found out that a French ship of the Messageries Maritime Line, which was based in Marseilles, made regular month long voyages to the Middle and Far East. They had three liners in the fleet, the *Vietnam*, *Laos* and *Cambodia*, and the one that was leaving within a week was the *Cambodia*. I was able to get a space in the third class section of the ship, which, although I would have to share a large room with six other passengers, I had to take as it was cheap and would get me to Japan.

The ship was indeed a luxury liner full of French people going to the Olympic Games. It also carried some of the rowing and gymnastic French teams. They had on board their rowing boats and gymnastic equipment and they spent most of the days practising. Although I was worried about sharing with six other passengers I

Reflection on my life

need not have worried, as they all turned out to be young people like me, some of whom were also going to Tokyo for the games. I shared the cabin with a young Cambodian, returning home after studying in France, two Americans, one Australian and one New Zealander. I must say it was one long party on the boat and our cabin soon became the centre of activities. So much so that even some of the French athletes on board would sneak in from the first class section where they were staying and, visit us in our steerage section to party. After a night of revelry we would sneak into the kitchen and raid the fridge for food. Oh youth! The person who said that youth is wasted on the young must have been an old man who had forgotten his youth.

Our first stop was in Ceylon, now Sri Lanka. A lady I worked with at the BBC was from Colombo, and had given me an introduction to her family. She came from a wealthy family and their family house stood on its own extensive grounds. They had about five cars, including two Rolls Royce's parked in the garage. I had lunch with them, which was a God send as the food on the ship, despite being French, left much to be desired. The family consisted of a father, who was a retired dentist, the mother still practising as a physiotherapist, two sons, both doctors and their wives and children, all living in this sprawling bungalow type house, with a luxurious garden looked after by two gardeners. My friend in London, who was working as a producer, was their only daughter and unmarried. The mother pulled me aside after lunch and wanted to know whether her daughter had a boyfriend, who he was and whether there was a possibility of her getting married? I was not able to tell her anything about the private life of her daughter as I only knew her as a colleague at work.

Our next port of call was Singapore. Here the Australian with us had a brother who was working for an Australian bank. He met us off the ship and gave us a whirlwind tour of this city-state, including a visit and drink at the famous Raffles Hotel. It was there I had my first Singapore Sling, a cocktail for which the hotel is famous. The Raffles hotel is one of the most famous hotels in the world and was built in 1887 in the Colonial style, and named after Sir Stamford Raffles, the founder of Singapore. It has still retained the colonial atmosphere and, sitting in the bar, one can imagine the Malayan planters sitting there reading the papers sent from London, and drinking their Singapore sling.

The Singapore sling is a South-East Asian cocktail. This long drink was developed, sometime early in the last century, by a bartender working in the long bar of the hotel. I understand it was originally called gin sling. The original recipe consisted of gin, cherry brandy, orange, pineapple and lime juice. Again, I recommend a visit to the Raffles Hotel in Singapore on your bucket list; you must sit in the long bar with a tall glass of Singapore Sling, and relax!

Next port of call was Saigon, now Ho Chi Minh City. The captain did not recommend that we go ashore because of the Vietnamese war with the Americans that was raging not far from the city. But, many of his passengers disregarded his advice and decided to take the risk anyway. Although the name was changed after the Communists won the war, I shall call it Saigon, for that was what it was called when I visited.

Under French colonial rule, Saigon was the capital of French Indochina, and when I visited the city it still had the air of a French city, with cafés and bars and wide boulevards. But for its tropical air, one could have been in Marseilles. But there was also an air of tension in the city, as if it was waiting for something to happen. Because of the war against the Communist North Vietnam and the Viet Cong, in which the Americans were heavily involved, their presence was everywhere. I remember sitting with the others in an outside café when a car backfired. Everyone, except for us, dived for cover. It showed that everyone was on edge waiting for

Reflection on my life

the Viet Cong to arrive in the city at any time. They did arrive eventually, and we all know what happened when they did. The photo of the helicopter on the roof of the American embassy evacuating some of the long line of people wanting to leave the city is etched in our collective memories until today.

From Saigon we stopped off in Hong Kong, but I was not able to go ashore as I was down with severe diarrhoea. I suspected it was something I had eaten in Saigon. I could only stand on the ship's rail and look at this city, which was still then under the British. I did vow to return, and did so some sixty years later.

After a final day at sea, we reached our destination, Yokohama, the port of Tokyo. And that was where the fun began!

IN THE LAND OF SHINTO

I was collected in great style by the Australian Consul-General in Yokohama, who was a friend of my uncle Ivor Cummings. I had been introduced to him when he was in London sometime earlier, when he was then the Australian High Commissioner in Ghana. So when I decided on the madcap adventure of hitch-hiking from London to Tokyo for the games, I wrote to him and he invited me to stay with him when I arrived. So here he was collecting me in his chauffeur driven official car. My other companions, with whom I had spent such a happy time on the ship, were very envious of my good fortune, but I agreed that we would meet up again in Tokyo, which we did.

My host was living in one of those typical Japanese houses, with mat floors and sliding bamboo partitions. It also had a small lake stocked with golden Carp. There was also a small pool which was most welcome in that intense heat. My host had a Japanese housekeeper known as Mamasan, who prepared the most delicious Japanese meals.

ARNOLD AWOONOR-GORDON

After a day of rest in such luxurious surroundings, the driver took me to the BBC Olympic office located in the NHK (Japanese equivalent of the BBC) radio building in the centre of Tokyo. They were not expecting me as in all the confusion of my leaving London, Bush House had not informed them of my arrival as they'd hoped I would cover the games on a freelance bases. I was lucky to be identified by the person in charge, who had worked in the Japanese section at Bush House and knew I had been connected with the African service. Unfortunately it was too late for me to obtain accreditation as this had been done a year earlier. All they could do for me was to give me a job as a general dogsbody, to help in the office, and perhaps later I would be able to be passed off as one of their officials. This never happened and it seemed as if I had travelled half way round the world for nothing.

The 1964 Summer Olympic Games, officially known as The Games of the XV111 Olympiad, had been awarded to Tokyo by the International Olympic Committee six years earlier. It was the second time the games had been awarded to the city. The first time was in 1940, but it was cancelled when Japan invaded China, and the honour was switched to Helsinki. The 1964 games were the first to be held in an Asian city, and the first time South Africa was barred from taking part due to its apartheid system, though they were allowed to compete in the Summer Paralympics Games. It was also the first time the games were broadcast internationally without the need for tapes to be flown overseas as before. The games were scheduled to take place in mid-October to avoid the midsummer heat of Tokyo. (The 2020 games are to take place in Japan for the second time.)

The highlight of the games for me was watching the Ethiopian Abebe Bikila winning the marathon for the second time, and looking as fresh as when he started. He died a few years later but he had set the record and opened the way for all the other Ethiopian men and women who became world champion marathon runners in

Reflection on my life

later years.

I stayed in Yokohama for about three weeks before moving to Tokyo. I had found it difficult to commute each day from Yokohama to Tokyo, as the trains were always very crowded, and as one can see when films about Japanese railway stations are shown on television, it is no joke to be pushed into the coach by hired thugs, as they were known. And pushed, they did, and one was squashed between the Japanese masses going to work each morning, and the same rush going back home each evening.

A few of the young people who worked in the BBC offices were also foreigners from Britain, Australia, New Zealand, America, Belgium and Holland. They had also come to Tokyo with the hope of getting jobs and to be able to see the games. So six of us got together and rented a typical Japanese house in an area called Shimbuku, which was not too far from the centre of town. It had mat floors, on which we slept with our sleeping bags, with bamboo partitions, a small kitchen but no bath or wash room. The public bath was just down the road, which we were able to use.

The Japanese do not get into a bath and wash themselves like Westerners do. You undress and hang up your clothes. You then put on your kimono and go into a communal area where you hang up your kimono, then sit on a small stool and scrub and wash yourself. You then clean yourself bailing water from a pool, using a bamboo like cup with handles to bale the water and clean yourself. You then swim in a communal hot bath to refresh yourself in the heated pool. As you have already washed and cleaned yourself, the water is clean and it is just there to refresh yourself. No one is self-conscious about exposing themselves in such a place full of naked bodies. But I must say that every time I used the communal bath, I could see the other men giving my private parts surreptitious glances. But this is no different to when I visit a gym in London, and change in the communal area, or in the shower. I think every man looks to see how big the other man is, especially when the other person is a black man!

Our house was not too far from the athletes' village and it soon became a hub for a meeting of all the athletes who wanted to escape from the restriction of the village. The Australians were the first to find that our house was available as a place for escape, and they soon brought some of the others. And so long as they brought their own booze, they were welcome. Of course, the neighbours, being respectable Japanese families, objected to the carrying on next door and would bang on the door to complain about the noise. They got fed up with us and one day got the police involved. Unfortunately it happened on the night when the Australians had dressed some of the Russian athletes in the Aussie outfits, and smuggled them to the party. Half way into the full swing of the merry making the police arrived. We were able to pacify them, but the Russians, coming from a police state, took one look at the uniforms and freaked out. I remember them scaling the fence as they made their exit as hurriedly as they could. I never knew what happened to them or how they got back to the village wearing Australian athletes' uniforms.

Almost every night we would gather at a club called Manos, run by a Russian who, it was rumoured, was in the pay of the Japanese secret service. The place was situated in the heart of the city at Shinjuku, which was full of nightclubs, bars and hotels. The hotels put on cabaret with some of the big international stars, and after they had finished their performances after midnight, they would all gather at Manos, where we would drink, dance and party until morning.

At the time I was there Judy Garland was performing at one of the hotels, and one evening, she turned up at Manos with her entourage, who included one Peter Allen, an Australian singer and dancer, who sometime later married her daughter, Lisa Minnelli.

Reflection on my life

During the course of the night, the DJ started to play Judy's recording of her singing 'Somewhere Over the Rainbow'. The music had not gone very far when Judy got up from her table, went to the DJs booth, grabbed the disc and threw it on the ground, saying, 'THAT'S A LOUSY RECORDING. I CAN SING BETTER THAN THAT.' She then sat at the piano and, opening her mouth, sang the song as she had never done before. The whole club went silent as we listened to this woman, who was well past her prime, singing as she recalled her youth. When she had finished, there were some moist eyes amongst her listeners, including mine, and silence for a few minutes. We all then broke into a wild applause, which she bowed and acknowledged, as if we were applauding her at one of her concerts at Carnegie Hall. It was a moment I shall never forget.

Some of the people, who visited Manos after their performances in various nightclubs in the area, were some drag queens, mostly from America. Some were so good that they could pass for real women, and some did. But we, the regulars, knew who was a drag queen and who was a real woman. Not so a drunken American soldier, who did not know his drag queen from a real woman, and insulted a beautiful Japanese woman by calling her a drag queen. I shall never forget the scene as she pulled herself to her full height, pull down her knickers and showed, for all the world that she was indeed a real woman. He was very apologetic and started to beg forgiveness for his mistake. Of course we all edged him on, shouting for him to get down on his knees and lick it. He didn't of course, and the situation was calmed by the owner who offered the woman a drink on the house.

While I was working, and playing, in Tokyo, I was able to send back a few stories about the African athletes who were taking part. As I did not have an accreditation I could not get into the stadium or any of the other venues, but I managed to waylay some of the African athletes as they went in and out of the village and got their stories, which I sent back to Bush House.

Amongst some of the people we came across were some of the black American soldiers stationed just outside Tokyo. We met them at various bars and they would come to our house with their Japanese girlfriends, when they had a weekend off. Once, I was taken to the base and passed off as one of them. The guards were Japanese and they could not differentiate one black person from another. I spent some time stocking up on goods at the PX and we had some American grub for a while at the house.

But, one day, one of them overstayed his time away from base, and the military police were at our door early the following day. When I opened the door they mistook me for one of theirs and started to read the riot act to me. I soon enlightened them that I was a Brit, and not an American soldier. They got their man and took him away. Never saw or heard from him again. I suspect he was put straight into the guard room for going AWOL.

As the time of the closing Ceremony of Games drew near, the six tenants in our house decided that we should do something spectacular to end the games. We decided that we would dress up as athletes and gate crash the closing ceremony. We borrowed some athletic vests and shorts and on the day of the closing ceremony, one of us was able to get a van, from where I do not know. We started drinking the local Sapporo local beer at about noon, and by the time the closing ceremony drew near we were all so drunk that we did not know what we were doing. One had to be drunk to pull of such a stunt.

Surprisingly, we were able to get the van past several of the Japanese guards, and, I suspect that, seeing us in running gear, they thought we were athletes. But the van was stopped at the final gate and as the guards started to question the driver, I got out and slipped past them and, hey presto, I was on the track with the athletes enjoying themselves at the closing ceremony. I ran

Reflection on my life

round the track waving to the thousand strong crowd, who waved back urging me on and the newspapers referred to me the next day, as 'the last runner'. I stopped and bowed to the Emperor as all Japanese do, and ran off enjoying myself with the crowds urging me on. I think the officials must have been stung into doing nothing as I am sure they must have thought that indeed, I was the last runner enjoying myself like the other athletes were doing. Anyway, they soon caught on that I was an interloper and chased me off the field, much to the annoyance of the crowd who urged them to leave me alone. They didn't, and I was caught and frogmarched out of the stadium, still waving and blowing kisses to the crowd.

ARNOLD AWOONOR-GORDON

THE LAST RUNNER...MAKING A FOOL OF MYSELF AT THE CLOSING CEREMONY OF THE OLYMPIC GAMES IN TOKYO.

For the life of me, I cannot remember what happened after that, or how I got home in my drunken state. I remember some of the journalists wanting to know who I was, but I was tight-lipped and did not divulge my identity. But all my friends at the BBC and in Australia, who saw the closing ceremony on television, recognised me, and it took many years for me to live down this escapade of my youth. You can see the photo of me making a fool of myself in my young days, in this book.

When in Japan I was asked whether I would like to teach English to young Japanese students, who were very keen to learn the language. It was mostly teaching them to speak correctly, and correcting their grammar. I found out that this was a very lucrative way of earning some extra cash for foreigners living in the country. I did my best two evenings a week, trying to teach them to pronounce 'L' which always came out as 'R'. The letter 'L' is not in the Japanese language, so they could not get their tongue around the letter. For example if I asked them what they were studying, they would say they were studying 'Raw' instead of 'Law'. I must have been good at it, because by teaching at a language school, I had some students coming to our house for extra tuition. In fact I was offered a job by

Reflection on my life

the owner of the school, to stay on in a permanent position, to teach the wives of Japanese Foreign Service officials who were being posted abroad. But turned it down as I was then keen to return to London.

One of the people who used to visit our house, and who was also a regular at Manos, was a slightly older Belgium who seemed to have more money than any of us. We knew he stayed in one of the top hotels, but as he was always free and easy with his money we did not question him too closely. I kept in touch with him after I returned from Tokyo, and one day when I was in Brussels I called him and he invited me to his apartment. What I did not realise until then, was that he was the son of one of the wealthiest banking families in Belgium, and had a title. He lived in a very expensive penthouse at the top of the family bank. It appears that he had had a very nasty and expensive divorce from his wife, and that is why he had gone to the Games to get over it.

I was in awe as I took the private lift to the penthouse. When the door opened, I was met by the butler who bowed and took me down a long corridor to meet my host in the living room. But what threw me was that lining this long corridor must have been at least twenty of those skeletal bronze figures by Giacometti. I recognised them, and he spoke about his love and his passion for collecting them, and how he went about sourcing them, most of which were in private collections. I realise people are rich, but it was the very first time I had come in contact with someone who was really very rich. We spent the evening chatting about what we had got up to in Tokyo, and eating some delicious food, and drinking some good wine, served by his butler. I never saw him again, and was sad when I read sometime later that he had died of AIDS. I wonder who got all those Giacometti.

Also amongst the group of people who came and went and used our house as a meeting place, was an Australian and his American girlfriend. One day they announced that they were getting married at a Japanese Shinto wedding and all the hangers on trooped to the Shinto shrine for the wedding. This was quite an elaborate affair conducted by the Shinto priest and his acolytes. At the end he gave them a certificate, but told them, in the hearing of all present, that although a Shinto wedding was legal in Japan, and in the United States, it was not legal in Australia. He suggested that they go to the Australian Embassy to find out about the legality of the marriage. I don't think they did something that was to have consequences later on in life.

Here I must divert from Japan to Australia. Many years later while visiting Perth in Western Australia, I decided to look up the young man who had married his American girlfriend at the Shinto wedding. He was not too difficult to trace as he had an unusual double barrelled name and the family was well known in Perth. Unfortunately he had died, but I was told that his sister had an art gallery in the centre of town, and so I visited her. She was very pleased to see someone who had known her brother in his young days, and invited me to dinner to meet his mother who was in her early nineties. The old lady was very pleased to see me and wanted to know what her son had been up to in Japan. I told her that I was at the Shinto wedding, and casually mentioned that the Shinto priest had said that the wedding was not legal in Australia, and wondered whether they had taken his advice to go to the Australian embassy to have it legalised. When I said that I did not realise that I was opening a can of worms. For it appears that the couple had returned to Perth after leaving Japan, but the wife did not get on with the family and soon returned to America.

When he died, and as he was heir to the family fortune, which was considerable, she had tried to claim a sizeable portion of the fortune as his wife. I then asked whether the marriage had been legalised at the Australian embassy, and was told that they did not know, and they could not tell me then. But the following day the family lawyer

Reflection on my life

got in touch with me, as he wanted first-hand information about what had taken place in Tokyo all those years ago. The long and short of it was that I had to appear before a judge, to make a sworn statement that the Shinto priest had informed them categorically in my presence, that although he was giving them the certificate of marriage, that the marriage was not legal in Australia and that they should go to the Australian embassy to have it legalised.

The joy on the face of the old aristocratic lady when I did this, was something to behold. They wanted me to stay on for the case, as they were disputing her claim, but as it was not to take place for another six months, I said I would return if they needed me. I was not needed, for in the light of the evidence I had given, the wife dropped her claim and agreed a cash sum for her troubles. I must say that a few years later, when the old lady died just short of her one hundred birthday, she left me something in her will for my testimony, which saved the family from carving up the estate for a greedy American woman.

Back to Tokyo. I was hoping to return to the UK after the Games, on the Trans-Siberian Railway. This would have meant taking a ship from Yokohama to Vladivostok in Russia, from where I would have been able to find my way to the train. But the shipping between Japan and Russia then was not too frequent, and by the time I found one, the Siberian winter had set in and the port at Vladivostok had been closed. So I had no option but to take a ship to Marseilles and from there take a train back to London. The name Vladivostok by the way, means RULE THE EAST in the Russian language. Another useless information I pickup during my travels.

Chapter 20
BACK IN LONDON

When I got back to London I rented a flat in Notting Hill Gate, then not as fashionable as it is now. I had arrived back at the beginning of the so-called 'Swinging London' period, and soon got into the swing of things. I had a group of friends both men and women from all parts of the world, who on Saturday mornings would congregate in my flat and we would then make a pilgrimage to the antique market on Portobello Road, which was just round the corner. After parading up and down and meeting and greeting friends, we would then go to a pub on Portobello Road for the first drink or two, then make our way to Kings Road, Chelsea, for another round of parading up and down, meeting friends, going in and out of the trendy shops, buying trendy gear and just hanging out. Some of the shops we visited had such strange names like Grannie Takes a Trip, Hung On You, Biba, the Pheantry, Michael John, Bus Stop, Sex and Mary Quant. One shop on Kings Road, outside which American visitors liked to be photographed was Thomas Crapper & Sons, Sanitary makers. They made and sold bathroom equipment and fittings such as lavatory bowls, wash basins, baths and showers, all in various colours. I understand that the word 'crap' came from Thomas Crapper and Sons. (another useless information.)

Sometimes we would go to Carnaby Street which runs parallel to Regent Street, but we felt that only tourists went there. At some point during the day we would stop at our favourite eating place, the Chelsea Potter, for lunch, where we would meet other friends and again just hang out. All this hanging around would be fuelled with lots of drink, mine was gin and tonic, which I would quaff in great quantities.

Reflection on my life

In the afternoon we would repair to the flat of one of us for tea, after which we would all disperse to our various abodes. But, that was when the evening part of our fun began. For we would put on our trendy clothes and meet either to go to the theatre or cinema, followed by dinner at one of the many restaurants that had sprung up in London at that time. The ones I remember that we visited regularly were Bruno One, near Earls Court, Giano, La Capanina in Soho, which is still there and run by the same couple, Linda and Giano. After dinner it was time for dancing either at one or the other of our usual hangouts, the Bag of Nails, behind Hamlyn's, off Regent Street or the Cromwellian on Cromwell Road. We particularly liked the Cromwellian because they showcased some of the up and coming pop groups and singers. That was where we saw Ike and Tina Turner up close as we danced around them. We also saw the Animals whose song WE GOT TO GET OUT OF THIS PLACE became quite popular and is still my favourite song to this day, and Procole Haram, whose drummer went out with a member of our group. The song, Whiter Shade of Pale by Procol Haram is still regarded as one of the most popular song of the sixties. The Beatles and the Rolling Stones were by then too famous to play in such places, so we never saw them up close.

We often danced until morning when we would stagger home. And that was not the end of our weekend. For on Sunday we would meet at someone's flat for brunch then go to one or other of our favourite pubs for drinks. In those days the pubs had to close at 2pm, but there were many small clubs that had licences to stay open past that time. One such was in Archer Street in Soho, where we would scramble to find a taxi to take us there. The day would end with afternoon tea. By then we would have all been too exhausted to do anything else. I must confess that this was our regular pattern every weekend for many years until I went to work in Holland.

Amongst the group that I hung out with at the time was someone called Michael Fish. Michael who used to work for an upmarket and posh shop called Turnbull and Asser, operating from a shop in Jermyn Street in Central London. They sold very expensive men's shirt and ties and were patronised by the great and good of the land, including Members of Parliament and film stars. But, what Michael wanted was to have a shop of his own that would attract a much younger crowd. One of his clients agreed to back him financially. And so what was to become one of the most fashionable men's shop in London at the time, came into being in a street just round the corner from Seville Row in central London. Called simply MR FISH, it specialised in suits with wide lapels, shirts with unusually high collars, silk rolled neck shirts and, the most famous of all, the Kipper Tie. This was a large tie which when tied looked like a kipper. And when that was featured in all the fashion magazines around at the time, it took off, and no self-respecting swinger in London would be seen without one round his neck. The photographers used to hang outside the shop just to photograph the famous men and celebrities going in and out to shop. And the Sunday magazines used to be full of stories about Mr Fish each Sunday. This was great publicity for the shop, and it attracted every man who thought he was fashionable and a swinger, to the shop.

The shop soon became a magnet for all the most fashionable men in London including Michael Caine, Lord Snowdon previously Antony Armstrong-Jones Husband of Princess Margaret, Lord Leitchfield the fashion photographer and the Queen's cousin, Lord Montague, Roger Moore, before OO7, Sean Connery, then OO7, David Bailey, the fashion photographer, who used to arrive with a bevy of fashion models, Albert Finney, David Frost, the pop groups the Beatles with their various girlfriend, Rolling Stones, the Animals and many more. Some days, the shop looked like a bazaar with all the most fashionable men in London trying on suits and buying armfuls of shirts and ties.

Reflection on my life

In those days credit cards had not been invented and you either paid by cash, which most did not have on them as the beau monde never carried cash, or by cheque. Michael used to frame the cheques of Lord Snowdon, the Beatles and the Rolling Stones, and hang them on the walls of the shop. As some of the cheapest products cost not less than £100, and some men spent over £1,000 each time they visited the shop, you can imagine the loss this made. Then again the sponsor of the shop would sweep in on Saturday afternoon, clear all the cash in the till and fly in his private jet to his house in Tangier, a place which was fashionable at the time, and spend the weekend there with his friends. He would return sometimes during the week with armful of brightly coloured caftans for sale in the shop, which would all be snapped up by the end of the week.

It was no wonder that the shop failed within two years because no one took any notice of the financial side of the business. To them it was something to do, which was fashionable at the time, and making money, which they would have done, was not the priority. But I too was able to purchase some of the most fashionable and expensive suits, shirts and ties, at a discount of course. I remember going to Freetown on holiday during that time and turning up at the Red Feather Ball at the Paramount Hotel. I was wearing a white jacket with black trousers with one of Mr. Fish's roll neck white silk shirt. It gave the great and good people of Freetown something to talk about, until they realised that what I was wearing was the height of fashion in London. I understand many of the younger lawyers soon followed my lead and started to wear roll neck shirts.

Mixing with such people who came to the shop, where I helped out from time to time when I was free, we got invited to all the best parties in town. One I remember well, and will not forget in a hurry, was given by a lord at his ancestral castle. It was a Kings and Queens party. Not knowing what to wear a friend of mine, Paul Danquah, suggested that I could borrow his Kente cloth outfit which had been given to him by his father, Dr Danquah, the great politician in Ghana. So I went as the Ashanti king wrapped in yards and yards of the most fabulous Kente cloth you have ever seen. I won fifth prize as the great African chief. After the judging, as the Kente cloth being very heavy to wear all the time, I took it off, folded it and left it in the room where we hung our coats and changed. At the end of the party, which went on till morning, when breakfast was served, I looked for the Kente cloth and could not find it. We searched everywhere, but it soon dawned on us that it had been nicked. Paul was also at the party dressed as an Arab Sheik, and he also helped me look, but we did not find it. What made matters worse, the Kente cloth was an heirloom which had been handed down from generation to generation and now it had been stolen. Paul was good about it, especially when the lord, whose party it was, claimed the loss on his insurance and Paul got £25,000 for it. I never borrow anything else from then on.

Although many of the fashionable girls about town did visit Mr Fish to buy clothes for their boyfriends, the fashionable shop for girls then was Mary Quant in the Kings Road and Biba in Church Street, Kensington. Biba was started by a young lady named Barbara Hulaniki, who designed a smock like mini dress, something like what was won by Bridget Bardot, which was published in the Daily Mirror. She received 4,000 requests in the first week, and eventually sold 17,000. For the first time young girls could buy clothes that were affordable. Her store also became a favourite place for young celebrities such as Cilla Black, Julie Christie, Marian Faithful and Lulu. It also came to look like a bazaar, with girls stripping down to their bras and knickers as they tried on clothes after clothes in the middle of the store, without batting an eyelid. The names Biba, Mary Quant and Michael Fish epitomised all that was good and fashionable about swinging London in the sixties, which attracted people from all over the world. Mary Quant was famous for the Mary Quant hairstyle which set the style for every young girl in the UK.

Chapter 21
BERLINER WASSER, AND DROPPING MY PANTS FOR YOKO ONO!

We had some German friends who would come over to London from Berlin from time to time to take part in the swinging London scene. And from time to time we would all fly to Berlin to visit them. This was at the height of the cold war and planes flying over East Germany to reach West Berlin, could not deviate from a given route, and even when the weather was bad, planes had to fly in a straight path. I cannot tell you the number of bumps we had, going through bad weather as we headed for West Berlin. There, our favourite haunt was a place called Ellie's Beer Bar. It was not really a bar but a night club in a dingy basement in a building next to a church. It must have been the only building standing after the Allies bombed Berlin during the war, so old was it.

The place was run by an old crow known as Billy, who wore black lace tights and short pants, gold top with an old black wig that had seen better days. He sat at the bar all the time smoking a cigarette from a long black holder. Billy claimed that the place had been there in the twenties and thirties, was the favourite haunt of Christopher Isherwood, and was the original in his book of *Berlin I Am A Camera*, which was later made into the film *Cabaret* starring Lisa Minnelli. Of course we didn't believe him until I saw the film many years later. Billy produced a cabaret made up of the boys dressed as girls, and girls dressed as boys, and the place was full of old time Berliners who all seemed to have been there since the thirties. The atmosphere was decadent but fun, and we danced and drank and imbibed an atmosphere of thirties Berlin. I remember one Sunday morning, leaving the bar, when it was daylight and bumping into the little old ladies going to mass in the church next door. The looks they gave us could have been from my mother whom I know would equally have disapproved of such goings on.

During the day we would go to a lake called the Wansee, where we would swim and drink the speciality called *Berliner Wasser (Berlin Water)* a long refreshing drink made of beer in a large round glass bowl, with something added to it.

I wonder why I did not go off the rails what with the drinking, drugs and free love that epitomised the time. But then, I had just celebrated a memorable thirtieth birthday and was old enough to know right from wrong.

So, although I indulged in the free love and drink, I never smoked pot nor take any of the hard drugs that were freely available. When I attended parties where everyone was smoking pot and passing the joint from person to person to take a puff, I would accept the joint without taking a puff then pass it on to the next person. As they were all stoned out of their minds they did not notice that I had not taken a puff of the joint. I must say that all the people in my circle of friends at the time also did not smoke pot, and we are still here today, fit and strong. And I thank God for that and a long life.

But I was once caught out when at a party I drank a lot of a Caribbean punch, which I was told contained only vodka. But I was not told that the punch had been laced with LSD. Because of this I went on an LSD trip for two days, during which time I thought I was a Jumbo jet, which had just made its maiden flight and was in the news. When I came out of the trip I was so strung out that I went to see my Nigerian doctor. Being an older man, he cautioned me about the dangers of drugs, and warned me against drinking anything that was mixed without my knowledge. He said I was lucky as when under the influence of the drug, and being a Jumbo jet, I could have jumped out of the window pretending to fly. If that had happened I would not be here today. I have never drunk another punch since.

Reflection on my life

I remember my thirtieth birthday party which I held in my ground floor flat in Notting Hill Gate. I swore that it would be the last birthday I would celebrate, and the next would be when I was sixty. The small flat was full of people, some I knew and had invited, and some I did not know. But as they all brought a bottle, they were admitted. The neighbours complained about the noise, especially the old lady who lived in the basement flat. The police were called twice and asked us to keep the noise down each time. We did, but as soon as they left the music was turned up again. At about six in the morning, when the party was in full swing, the police turned up yet again, marched in, turned off the music, and as I was the host, I was arrested for disturbing the peace. I spent the rest of what was left of the night in a police cell, and was released later in the day with a caution. It was the last birthday I celebrated. By the time I turned sixty, I had gone off the idea of celebrating my birthdays, and have not celebrated one with a party since then. What was surprising was the door to my flat was wide open and there were bodies laying all over the place, when I returned to my flat.

But I did start a tradition of a pancake party on Shrove Tuesday, which is known as Pancake Day. I would invite friends round; make a large bowl of pancake mix, and trays of fillings such as cheese, honey, sugar, lemon, prawns and many other fillings. The idea was that everyone would make and toss their own pancake, and fill them with what took their fancy, whether sweet or savoury. I can recommend it as a good, easy and fun way to have a party. I even had several when I returned to Freetown.

An interesting incident happened which I must here relate. We had spent the New Year's evening at our favourite restaurant called La Capanina in Soho, where Linda and Giana, the owners had put on a New Year's party for their regular customers, to which I wore an agbada. After the party, as is usual on New Year's Eve in central London, getting a taxi is like looking for gold. We walked up Regent Street trying to hail a passing taxi. I was left behind as the others had walked on ahead, and I was struggling behind wrapped in my agbada to keep off the rain. Suddenly a car pulled up, and without asking I jumped in to find a rather startled man. He had stopped because he thought I was a woman wearing robes, and was hoping to get a catch to see in the New Year. When he realised that I was a man, he saw the funny side of it and offered to drop me off home. Whether he had offered or not, I was not going to get out of his car in the rain. He was good as his word and dropped me off at my flat. He went off laughing and I am sure he dined on it for a long time afterwards. The others were furious when they heard I had got a free lift home, while they had to walk home in the rain.

As for the drinks, I am surprised that I never became an alcoholic, because I did like my gin and tonic, and drank gallons of it. Our group of close friends all drank, except for Malik, who was a Muslim from Indonesia. His faith must have been very strong for him to resist all the temptations of drink and drugs that were all around him. He did take part in all the parties and travels but shied away from the demon drink.

People always ask me what were some of the most memorable interviews I had done during my broadcasting career, and I remember four as the most memorable. At one of the daily meetings we had, at which ideas for interviews were discussed, I mentioned that I had heard on the Today Programme, on Radio 4, that a lady had arrived in London from America to make a film about people's bottoms, and I would like to go and interview her. I was given the go ahead to do so. I eventually found this lady, who turned out to be Yoko Ono, and who eventually met and married John Lennon of the Beatles, and who is rumoured to have split up the Fab Four. At the time she had not yet met John Lennon.

She was willing to be interviewed about her film but told me that first, I had to audition to take part in it and had to drop my pants to do so. There was no way I was going to show my bottom to this

Reflection on my life

strange Japanese woman, and so I declined. She said no audition no interview. So I left. When I returned to Bush House and told the producer about my encounter with Yoko Ono, that she wanted me to audition for her film before she could do the interview, and how I had declined to show my bottom to her, I remember what the producer said: 'You will never be a good broadcaster by turning down what is the story... taking part in the film is the story.' I was ordered to go back and do the audition.

With my tail between my legs, so to speak, I went back to confront this strange lady in her very strange studios, and told her I had changed my mind and would like to audition for a part in the film. Shamefacedly, I stripped and had to walk on a treadmill, while she looked at my bottom through the lens of her camera. As I got dressed, hoping to now get the interview, you can imagine how deflated I was, when she told me that I had failed the audition. Because, she said, my bottom lacked expression. I could not get out of her studio fast enough. My humiliation was compounded when the producer asked me to recount my encounter with the strange lady, and my expressionless bottom, on the programme, which was broadcast not only to Africa but to the whole world. I knew this, because for months afterwards, I received letters from places as far away as Australia and the United States of America commiserating with me for a bottom which lacked expression. This was not all: the story appeared in the London Evening Standard, with a cartoon of a series of white bottoms and one black bottom amongst them. I must say I did dine on the story for many months afterwards, but always refused to show this expressionless bottom of mine to the public again. She did make the film, but thankfully, without the starring role of my bottom.

Chapter 22
FEAR OF HEIGHT; A MAN CALLED DIKKO, AND MEETING SIDNEY POITIER!

Another memorable programme I did was to climb Nelson's Column in Trafalgar Square. Nelson was being given its periodic clean, and scaffoldings, with a ladder, had been erected around the column by the workmen. Of course, everyone wanted to climb the ladder to see the great man face to face. A Nigerian colleague from the Hausa Service and I were delegated to climb the ladder making a recording with commentary culminating with the moment of coming face to face with the great Lord Nelson.

Up until then, I had no idea that I suffered from *vertigo* . I began to realise this only when halfway up, I had to look down to record what I could see from that height. My Nigerian colleague was recording his impressions in Hausa, but I froze for what seemed to be ages, and could not speak wanting desperately to turn back. I was petrified as I looked down Whitehall towards Parliament and the river beyond. The workman who was accompanying us had to assist me to speak into my recording microphone. I did eventually make it to the top and came to face with the great man himself, and recorded my impression for all the world to hear. But everyone who heard the broadcast must have noticed the fear in my voice, as I looked down and spoke into the mic. It was the most terrifying experience of my life and one I would not wish to repeat. In fact I never listened to the piece again, even though colleagues in the office pulled my leg about it constantly. The things we do for money

As I have mentioned, I went up Nelson's column with a Nigerian colleague from the Hausa service; his name was Umaru Dikko. Many of you reading this would not have heard about him in those

Reflection on my life

days, but in the summer of 1984 his name made headlines in Britain when men, said to be from the Israeli secret service Mossad, and the Nigerian government of the day, conspired to kidnap him in broad daylight in Bayswater in London. After working at Bush House for a while, Umaru had returned to Nigeria, became a politician and businessman, but fell out with the government and moved back to London where he set up a business.

One day he was seized outside his house in Bayswater, bundled into a van, and taken to Stansted airport, where a Boeing 707 cargo aircraft was waiting to repatriate him to Nigeria, to face corruption charges. His captors had handcuffed and drugged him, and stuffed him into a large crate with a doctor by his side, maintaining a tube to keep him breathing. The doctor and another of his captors, a diamond dealer, were Israelis; the other two were a Nigerian ex-army major and a Tunisian-born shopkeeper. Lucky for him, his secretary had witnessed the kidnapping and called the police, and various airports around the country were alerted. When two suspicious crates arrived at Stansted airport, they were opened in the presence of Nigerian officials, to find Umaru unconscious, but breathing. He was taken to hospital where he recovered. The doctor and the shopkeeper were sentenced to ten years in prison, the Israeli organiser of the snatch, received fourteen years, and the Nigerian Military man twelve years in prison.

Umaru denied accusations made at the trial that he was a corrupt man who had caused poverty and starvation in his country. The Buhari government, he said, wanted him because he had been the Chairman of the Shagari presidential task force on rice. The government said that he had forced up the price of rice for his own gain, something Umaru denied. He was given British security protection during the trial and when it ended, he asked for political asylum. But the British government, not wanting to embarrass the Nigerian government any more, refused. But he was given temporary permission to stay, which was extended several times.

ARNOLD AWOONOR-GORDON

He went on to study law, and was called to the Bar at Middle Temple in 1991. When the government of Nigeria changed, he was invited back to his country, where he set up a new political party. Towards the end of his life he was chairman of the disciplinary committee of the People's Democratic Party of the President Goodluck Jonathan. He died in London recently after a series of strokes.

Another interview, which I must say was one of the highlights of my broadcasting career, was the one I did with Sidney Poitier. He was visiting London soon after he had won the Oscar for his part in *Lillies of the Field,* and his London agent had set up a press conference after which I was to interview him. As his arrival was delayed and the press conference cancelled until the following day, which was a Sunday, his agent, whom I knew well, said that I could do the interview in his suite at the Dorchester hotel, if I did not mind however late he arrived. I agreed to this, and he said he would call me when Poitier arrived. I sat at home that Saturday evening, with my recording machine, waiting for the call. It came at around midnight, and I jumped into a taxi and was at the hotel within twenty minutes. Sidney Poitier was most amiable and gave me a long interview. Although he had been travelling from city to city in Europe, attending press conferences and giving dozens of interviews during the day, I had imagined he would be tired and would want me out of the way as soon as my interview was over. Not a bit. He was top of the form, and after the interview asked me where was the best joint in London for dancing. This was a time when London was swinging, and I am sure he wanted a slice of the swing that was London on his very brief stopover. I knew just the place, somewhere that was my favourite joint in London. Although his agent, the public relations lady, and another person I took to be his minder and bodyguard, did protest that he should rest as he had a busy day ahead, he said nonsense, and overruled them. Soon we were all squeezed into a limousine and went to the club, the *Bag of Nails,* off Regent Street behind Hamlyn's Toy shop.

Reflection on my life

I was well known to the security men at the door of *the Bag of Nails*, who were letting people in as there was always a queue to get in. But I need not have worried because Sidney Poitier's face was easily recognisable, and we were waved in. We were put in the cordoned off VIP area, and the champagne flowed; the bill was picked up by the agent. I introduced Sidney to my gang of friends and he danced and danced what was left of the night away. It was after five in the morning when we left the club, and it was daylight when we came out into Regent Street to take them back to the Dorchester, and me to my humble flat in Notting Hill Gate. It was one of the most memorable interviews I ever had and the most memorable time of my life, when I partied with Sidney Poitier in Swinging London.

I was scheduled to do an interview with Mohammed Ali when he came to London for his fight with Henry Cooper. I attended his press conference with a lady colleague from South Africa. At the end of the press conference, his minders told us that we could have a one- to-one interview with him later in his hotel suite. Fortuitously, or by design, the lady colleague turned up earlier than me. As soon as I got to the hotel suite, it became obvious that the reason we had been invited to the hotel for the one-to-one interview, was because of my colleague, who was a beautiful young Indian girl, and not me. I understood the situation perfectly, did a short interview and made my excuses and left. She got an interview in return for what else, I don't know. I never forgave her.

Chapter 23

AN OLD TWISTER DINES WITH THE QUEEN, AND HOW I MET ENGELBERT HUMPERDINCK

EARTHA KITT

Reflection on my life

One other memorable interview I did was for the TODAY programme on Radio 4, where I was doing freelance work. This was with a Chief from somewhere in Eastern Nigeria, whose name I have forgotten. He was in London to attend a meeting of the world wide Freemasons, whose head was the Duke of Kent. This chief, who claimed to be ninety-five, was full of fun and, amongst other things, told me that he used to dance the twist with his great grandchildren, and would put them to shame. He was a jovial man and it was fun to interview him on all kinds of subjects, including his twenty wives and his many children, grand and great grandchildren. The interview was broadcast in the programme the following morning, and soon after the programme ended, the producer on duty at Broadcasting House received a call from of all places, Buckingham Palace. They wanted to know where the chief was staying as the Queen would like to invite him to lunch.

He was very pleased when he was told this, and three days later, wearing his full chieftain regalia, he went to have lunch with Her Majesty the Queen and the Duke of Edinburgh. I called on him later that day when he returned from the Palace, and he was still full of bonhomie, and told me about the lunch. Apparently during lunch, where he had the queen, the duke and the other guests in stitches telling stories about his life in his court, the queen asked him whether it was true that, at his age, he could do the twist with his grand and great grandchildren. Without being asked, he got up and gave the Queen, the Duke and her assembled guests, an impromptu demonstration of the twist with his robes and regalia flying all over the place. I was not there, but he said that the Queen, the Duke and her guests laughed so much that tears ran down their eyes. I could just imagine the scene as he twisted with his gold chain of office flying all of the place. He was full of fun with no holds barred. One thing this made us realise was that the *Today* programme is listened to at Buckingham Palace, whether by the Queen herself, or her minions, I don't know.

On other occasions, I attended press conferences for Sophia Loren and Charlie Chaplain, who were in London to announced their collaboration on the film *Countess from Hong Kong*; Elizabeth Taylor and Richard Burton promoting the film Cleopatra, Ella Fitzgerald, Satchmo, Duke Ellington, and several others. At the time I did not realise the importance of being in the same room with these celebrities. I was just doing my job. It was many years later that it dawned on me what I had done and the importance of meeting these people. Now, I can appreciate the beauty of Sophia Loren, the purple velvety eyes of Elizabeth Taylor, and the aura of Mohammed Ali, and I can only thank God that I was able to be in the same room, however fleetingly, with these great people, most of whom are now no longer with us.

Another person I did meet briefly was Frank Sinatra. It happened this way. My colleague and best friend at Bush House at the time was the famous Pete Myers, who presented Good Morning Africa Programme on the African Service. Pete was amongst one of the first broadcasters employed by Radio 2, when the pirate stations were closed down, and the BBC for the first time started to play pop music. Pete had the graveyard slot on Saturday night, which was between 9 pm and 1am. Sometimes I would go to the studios to meet him so we could go clubbing after he came off the air. He used to have some of the celebrities who were in town, on his show. That day, he had Frank Sinatra on his programme and I sat in the outer 'Green Room' to listen to the rest of the programme with Frank Sinatra. At the end of the programme Sinatra came into the Green room to collect his partner, who had also been waiting with me, and they left. It was much later that I realised that it had been Juliet Prowse, the dancer and actress he was dating at the time, who had been sitting in the Green Room with me. I kicked myself later for not realising who she was, so I could have chatted with her while she waited, and perhaps she could have introduced me to Old

Reflection on my life

Blue Eyes himself. But I can genuinely claim that I brushed against the great man himself, if only for a few minutes.

And talking about brushing against celebrities, this happened many years later when I was working for Radio Netherlands in Hilversum. I had been in London for a short holiday and was flying back to Schiphol airport. Sitting across the aisles from me was a very big black man with straightened hair. Even before the plane took off I noticed people coming up to him with pieces of paper for him to sign. What surprised me was that they never said anything or asked his permission for him to sign the papers they thrust in front of him with a pen. After this had happened a few times, I was annoyed and leaned over and said to him 'They don't even ask your permission, just thrust a paper and pen and expect you to sign.' He smiled and in a very deep voice said 'I don't mind, I am a singer and I am used to it.' I then assumed that, with such a deep voice, he must be an opera or classical singer.

You can imagine my surprise when we landed to find hundreds of girls and young women shouting 'Barry White.........Barry White...Barry White' It was then I realised that I had sat next to the biggest box office singer in the world, and I did not know it. I could have kicked myself for not pushing a piece of paper and pen across to him for his signature. I have dined on this story for many years, but most people who hear the story are surprised that, working in the media, I had never heard of Barry White. Until then I had never heard of him, but I must say I began to follow him from then on until he died.

Another celebrity I had the pleasure of interviewing was Engelbert Humperdinck. His real name was Arnold George Dorsey, but his agent changed his name to that of the German composer, who wrote the opera Hansel and Gretel. This was a very smart move, because it was a name that called for attention and one that cannot be easily forgotten. His first hit record was Please Please Me, which went to number one immediately it was released.

It was arranged that I should meet him at the studios in North London, where he was busy recording his follow-up record. I arrived and was asked to wait in an anteroom outside the recording studios. But from there I could hear him rehearsing the song over and over again, with various stops for the recording producer to give advice and so on. After a while, I realised that if I opened my recording machine I could surreptitiously record the song and perhaps broadcast it with my interview. After several hours of this, the recording was complete, and he came to meet me. He was very charming and apologetic for keeping me waiting, and gave me a long interview. He then offered me a lift as he was going to Soho to have dinner with some friends. I accepted, and he drove me in his very new open top Triumph, and I sat there enjoying the pleasure of being driven by a singer in the top ten, and in a smart car to boot.

When we got to Soho, he said that if I had nothing on, I could join them for dinner. I declined as I had arranged to go to the cinema with some friends. Looking back now, I could easily have cancelled my cinema date, and gone and have dinner with someone who, for the last fifty years or so, has been one of the most famous singers in the world. But, again, looking back at the time, I am proud that I was doing my job of interviewing people, and not to become friends with them!

Although, as I said, I had surreptitiously recorded him making his second record, we were not allowed to use it, as it had not yet been released, and the BBC could have been sued for using copyright material.

Someone did ask me whether I had ever interviewed the Beatles, and of course, I replied that I had not done so. Because when the Fab Four became famous, you could not get an interview with them for love or money. But sometime later, and before he died, I was

Reflection on my life

able to get an interview with their manager Brian Epstein, but only because his butler and cook was a friend of mine, and he persuaded him to grant me an interview. As Conan Doyle said about hind sight, it is easy to be wise after the event, because I now wish I had kept all those recordings of the interviews I did at the time. I would be a rich man today selling them.

But two of the nicest persons I had the pleasure and honour of interviewing were the now famous actress Judi Dench, now Dame Judi, and Eartha Kitt the African/ American singer and cabaret artist whom Orson Wells referred to as 'the most exciting woman in the world'. Judi Dench was then an up and coming young actress, and had gone to Freetown with a group of young actors, under a programme sponsored by the British Council. The group worked with the Freetown Players, then the most prominent group of local actors, holding workshops with them and later on putting three performances at the British Council hall at Tower Hill.

We had arranged for the interview to take place early one evening at her flat in Hampstead, but when I arrived she was not there. I waited outside for about half an hour, when she turned up with profuse apologies for keeping me waiting, and invited me in. It turned out that she had been rehearsing for a new play and the rehearsals had gone on for much longer than she had anticipated. Anyway she offered me a drink, and sat down to give me one of the most interesting interviews I had then. She talked about her time in Freetown and her interaction with members of the Freetown Players, whom she said was a most professional group, and praised them for their dedication to the old established craft of acting, mentioning them all by name, and sending them her best wishes for the future.

Then after the interview she invited me to stay and have dinner with her, and she cooked a mean spaghetti bolognaise, which we had, washed down with several glasses of red wine. She told me that she had got fond of groundnut soup when in Freetown, and had brought back the recipe, which she intended to cook one day. She was warm and bubbly and friendly, and I shall never forget the evening I spent with Judi Dench. Today she is one of Britain's most accomplished actress, winning awards after awards, including an Oscar. She was the first woman to play the part of 'M' in the James Bond franchise.

I interviewed Eartha Kitt when she was in London appearing at the London Palladium and an interview with her was arranged. Normally in these cases where celebrities are concerned, we went to them at their hotel and not them coming to us at the Bush House studies. But in this case, she came to us rather than us going to her. For she said that she was more comfortable recording or being interviewed in a studio setting rather in a hotel.

So one Saturday morning she arrived at Bush House surrounded by her manager and other hangers on. Whenever a prominent person or celebrity came to Bush House, the bosses and other high profile staff would all assemble to welcome him or her. So it was in this case that some of the great and good were there, bowing and scraping and fawning and smiling and shaking hands with this world renown singer, completely disregarding me, who had to do the interview. Anyway she was charming and full of fun laughing all the way to the studios. She arrived with lots of rings on her fingers and yards and yards of bangles on both arms, and when we sat down to do the voice level tests, the engineers found that every time she moved her arms, or touched the studio table, her rings and bangles made the most awful clatter, which was not what was needed.

The engineers suggested that she should remove her rings and bangles, but who was going to tell such a high profile person to remove her jewellery, which was a part of her personae. After some behind the scenes consultations it was decided to bring a cushion on which she could rest her hands and arms, and provided she did not move them, the recording could go through. She thought this was funny and willingly agreed to it. So we started the interview with her hand still on the cushion, but from time to time she forgot and wanting to emphasis a point, she would move her arms and the jangle of the bracelets would be heard. In this she was also very funny, as whenever it happened she would say 'oops' and burst into laughter, then rest her hands again on the cushion. Instead of this spoiling the interview, in fact it enhanced it and added to the fun.

At the end of the interview I asked her which of all the songs she had recorded she would like me to play, and laughing she said 'You choose one.' Without hesitation I said 'I want to be evil'. She burst out laughing and said 'That's the one' and then sang a few lines stressing 'I want to be evillllll, I want to be baaaad' And that was the song I played at the end of the programme. Later on she sent me an autographed photograph of herself.

ARNOLD AWOONOR-GORDON

Chapter 24
TENANTS FROM HELL, A NIGHT AT THE BALLET, AND CHAMPAGNE WITH THE QUEEN MOTHER

LEADER OF THE VOLUNTEERS AND THE VISITORS TO THE OLYMPIC GAMES IN

Reflection on my life

2012

THE PRIME MINISTER

10 DOWNING STREET
LONDON SW1A 2AA

13th September 2012

Arnold Gordon
35 Cobden Road
Chatham
Kent
ME4 5HW
United Kingdom

Dear Arnold

I wanted to write to thank you personally for the part you played in making the London 2012 Olympic and Paralympic Games such a huge success.

To see tens of thousands of people giving up their time to support London 2012 has been truly inspiring. As a Kent Ambassador you have ensured that thousands of people have enjoyed the London 2012 experience by the welcome and spirit that you have shown visitors to your local area. You and your fellow volunteers have been an essential ingredient in a remarkable summer that millions of people across the country have shared and will remember for a lifetime. You have sent an incredible message about the warmth, friendliness and can-do spirit of the United Kingdom right around the world. Quite simply, the Games couldn't have happened without you.

I have heard for myself that, for many, the Olympics and Paralympics have provided the inspiration to volunteer for the first time. But whether this has been a new experience for you, or you have volunteered before, I hope the wonderful memories you have taken away from the Games will encourage you to continue to make a difference.

Thank you again.

Yours sincerely

David Cam—

LETTER FROM THE PRIME MINISTER DAVID CAMERON THANKING ME FOR VOLUNTEERING AT THE OLYMPIC GAMES IN 2012

During the World Cup tournament in London in 1966, the one and only time England won the FIFA World Cup, there was a great demand for accommodation. So I decided to rent out my flat in Notting Hill Gate for the duration, while I took a holiday in

Holland, Germany and France. I got tenants through an agency called Universal Aunts and they found me two young men from Spain to take the flat. It was the worst thing I ever did, for when I returned at the end of the tenancy, they had trashed the flat. I had been told that the flat would be let to two young men, but in my absence, those hoodlums brought all their hangers-on to use the place. They slept on the floor, couch, corridors and the bedroom, so by the time the flat was handed back I did not recognise it. Anyway, the agents paid for the damage and I had the flat painted anew. But one thing I could not forgive them was that they threw out my jar of *ogiri*, which I had left in the fridge. They said they thought it was something that had gone bad. The *ogiri*, a specially fermented condiment, had been made lovingly and specially for me by my mother, and I had been using it sparingly. Now it was in the skip. Madding!

When I returned from holiday, I interviewed Sir Stanley Rouse, the only British President to date of FIFA, the International Football Federation. England had won the World Cup for the first and only time, and there was much talk and discussion about the total lack of African teams in the tournament. Although Egypt had taken part in the World Cup in 1934, yet in 1978 Tunisia was the first African country to win a World Cup game, when they beat Mexico 3-1. But between 1938 and 1966, Africa had not been included in the World Cup, although football was very popular on the continent. Not until 1970 did Africa take part, much of which was due to the FIFA President, Sir Stanley Rouse.

Amongst our gang of like-minded young people who enjoyed swinging London, was an Australian who worked in the press department of the Royal Opera House. From time to time he would get us free tickets to opera, ballet and concert at Covent Garden, and although they were not the best seats in the houses, and although we were so far in the Gods we had to use binoculars to see what was happening on the stage, it was thrilling to be at this world

Reflection on my life

famous venue. In general, the music was good and it enabled us to see Maria Callas, Placido Domingo, Luciano Pavarotti, Joan Sutherland and some of the great singers of the day.

One particular event which I shall never forget took place at the Royal Opera House. Our friend was able to get us four tickets for a gala fundraising performance at which Rudolf Nureyev and Dame Margot Fonteyn were to perform. Such gala performances required full evening dress, but my friend Malik decided that we would go in our national costumes. Not having a Sierra Leone national costume, I borrowed a three piece agbada from a Nigerian friend, and Malik, who was from Malaya, wore his national costume, which included a skirt like part of it. My costume was blue damask and Malik's was pink silk. Our other two friends were in full evening dress with white ties and stiff collars.

For once, we had some good seats in the stalls and we sat there looking pleased with ourselves. The gala was attended by Queen Elizabeth, the Queen Mother, and Princess Marina, the Duchess of Kent. Of course, we all had to stand up when they arrived in the Royal Box and the national anthem was played. During the interval, imagine our surprise when one of the opera house lackeys came to us and said that the Queen Mother had seen us from the royal box, and would like to meet the two gentlemen from the Commonwealth. Of course Malik and I were the two gentlemen from the Commonwealth, and got up and followed him. During the walk to the lift and in the lift he told how to behave in the presence of Royalty. Not to speak until we were spoken to, then to bow from the waist and say 'yes mam,' 'no mam,' etc, etc.. As you can imagine, we were all nerves at being invited by the Queen Mother and meeting royalty for the first time.

When we reached the royal box, the Queen Mother and the Duchess could not have been nicer in putting us at ease. The Queen Mother asked where we came from and what we were doing in London.

Taking the lead, I said we were journalism students. How could one tell Royalty that we were not students, but died in the wool London swingers? Anyway, the Queen Mother said she had never been to West Africa, but had been to South and East Africa. The Duchess, on the other hand, told us that she had been to Ghana when she had represented the Queen at the Independence ceremonies, and mentioned the Kente cloth she had been presented with by President Nkrumah. She still had it and, which, one day she hoped, will go to her grandchildren.

The Queen Mother asked whether we had been to Scotland while in the UK, and when we said we had not, but intended to do so, she said that we must go to Scotland. She was born there and has a castle there, which she escapes to now and again. All this time we were holding on to our glasses of champagne as we dared not take a sip in case we missed our mouths, so nervous were we. Soon the Queen Mother held out her hand signifying the meeting was over. We shook her hand, and she said she hoped we will enjoy our stay in England, and the rest of the show. We bowed and retreated backwards. It was then Malik and I realised that the Queen Mother was wearing pink, like Malik, and the Duchess light blue, like my blue Nigerian Agbada. We laughed all the way down in the lift. Naturally, we dined on that story for ages, and am only sorry we did not have our photos taken with the only members of the Royal Family we were lucky to meet.

Once I had to go to Christies, the Bond Street auction house, where they were auctioning some sculptures from Africa, including some by the great Nigerian artist, Ben Enwonwu. As I arrived clutching my recording machine, a Rolls Royce pulled up and out stepped a large and wealthy looking American, puffing at the inevitable large cigar. He spotted me and, without asking, clutched my hand in his own large paw and, still puffing at his cigar, said to me 'Come with me to give me luck.' Not waiting for me to say anything, he briskly dragged me into the building. He turned out to be a multi-

Reflection on my life

millionaire owner of a Gallery in California, which specialised in African art. Naturally, being one of the big spenders in the art world, he was very well known at Christies, and was greeted and given special treatment and a prominent place during the sale. Of course, having dragged me to give him luck, I too had a prominent place next to him during the auction. Every time he bid he clutched my hand for luck. I must say he was lucky and bought most of the sculptures on sale, including one of Enwonwu's famous works, the *Anyanwu* (Sun). The original of this work I later found out, had been donated to the United Nations Organisation in New York, by the Nigerian Government. After the sale, I was entertained to a slap up dinner at the Savoy Hotel where he was staying. I enjoyed it and revelled in it, as it was the first, and last, time I was at what is one of London's, and the world's top hotels.

Chapter 25
BACK ON THE HOME TURF AND MY DUTCH DAYS

WITH VERONICA WILSON GETTING OUR TICKETS FOR A TRIP TO FREETOWN, WEARING UNISEX CLOTHES.

While I was working freelance I was able to report on, and interview representatives of many companies in London dealing with Sierra Leone. One such company was the British United Airline, (now no more) an airline that had a weekly flight from Gatwick to Lungi Airport in Freetown. I interview the Managing Director, who was so impressed with the publicity his company received, that he offered myself and a BBC colleague, Veronica Wilson, a free trip to Freetown, which we readily accepted. At the same time we had done some promotions for a clothing company that had designed a unisex outfit which could be worn by both men and women. We had been photographed wearing the outfits by the departure desk of the airline, which was published all over the

Reflection on my life

place.

Anyway, Veronica and I flew to Freetown on what turned out to be the day of the 1967 General Elections in the country. This shows how out of touch I was about politics in Sierra Leone, to arrive in the middle of an elections. Although I was supposed to stay at the family house, Michael Crowder, my former travelling colleague, was then Dean of the Faculty of Economics and Social Studies at Fourah Bay College, and he invited me to stay with him. Freetown was in Election fever and in a state of upheaval later that day, as the All Peoples Party (APC) under the charismatic leader Siaka Stevens had narrowly won the election over Albert Magai's Sierra Leone Peoples Party (SLPP). The swearing in ceremony was to take place on the 21st Of March.

People had got the impression that I was there to cover the elections for the BBC, which was far from the truth. I was there on a freebee. Anyway I was asked by some of the APC supporters to witness and report on the swearing in ceremony. I had gone to Delco House to see a friend, and as came out of the building, some people I knew were celebrating on the terrace of the City Hotel, and called me over to help them celebrate and have a beer. I was happily downing my Star beer when I realised that I should be at State House at 4 o'clock for the swearing in Ceremony. I rushed out and ran up to the Cotton Tree clutching my recording equipment, intending to be in at the swearing in ceremony. But my path was blocked by gun totting soldiers who had setup a cordon around State House, and no amount of pleadings would they let me through. I finally found my way to the Paramount Hotel, where the APC supporters were celebrating, and I joined them.

It was while there that we heard Brigadier David Lansana over the radio that Siaka Stevens had been deposed and put under house arrest, that the elections had been scrapped and a curfew imposed. I hurriedly made my way to Mount Aureol, where I was staying with

Michael. Then followed the most bizarre week of coups and counter coups; for a few days later Brigadier Lansana was himself overthrown and arrested by Lt. Colonel (later Brigadier -General) Andrew (Jockstrap) Juxon-Smith, who then set up the National Reformation Council, with himself at Chairman. Continuing the merry-go-round, almost a year later, a group of non-commissioned officers over threw the Juxon-Smith regime, and invited some senior military officers, led by Brigadier Bangura to form a government. Bangura had been exiled to neighbouring Guinea, on the suspicion of being a supporter of Siaka Stevens before the elections. He was soon joined in Guinea by Siaka Stevens in exile.

Now aware the Siaka Stevens had won the elections, however narrowly, Bangura invited him to return in triumph from exile to resume office. Since, given the convolutions of politics in Sierra Leone, historians have argued about whether it was a wise move on the Brigadier's part. For in less than five years, he was arrested, tried and executed by hanging by Siaka Stevens on what many suspect was a trumped-up charge of attempted coup. So much for Sierra Leone politics.

I was asked by the BBC whether I could show someone around, who was from a sister radio station in Holland. The lady was over in London to study the workings of the BBC African Service, as the Dutch were in the process of starting a similar service. So, for one week, I took the lady round and showed her what we were up to. At the end of her visit, she asked me whether I would like to move to Holland to work for them. Without hesitation I agreed and within a month I was established in Hilversum, Holland.

The job was not too difficult as I was left on my own to make programmes, which were sent to be broadcast by the various radio stations in Africa. I could make one half hour programme that could be broadcast as it stood, or make several shorter items that could be broadcast as part of a longer programme. As I did not know the

Reflection on my life

country, I was able to travel all over the place meeting Dutch people and collecting stories and interviews to make my programmes. I also found some of the African students living and studying in the country and recorded messages from them to their families and friends at home.

I liked living in the Netherlands and although I never learned the language, living there was a great pleasure. I did not learn the language because the Dutch speak the most beautiful English, almost without an accent. From a very early age they have to learn

English, German and French for, as they themselves say, no one can speak Dutch except a Dutch person. So, as everyone spoke English, day to day interaction in shops, markets on the transport is easy. I must say that the radio authorities wanted us foreigners working for them, to learn the language, and I was sent to a language school in the south of the country run by nuns. But after six weeks in very pleasant surroundings, I came back as ignorant as I went.

It is interesting how such a small country like the Netherlands, which is mostly under water, has been able to become such an expert on shipping, trade and land management and engineering. When I first went there the emphasis was on reclaiming the land from the sea, and I was able to visit some of the great engineering projects taking place in the North Sea. I was amazed that a country which was previously known around the world for its windmills and clogs was now one of the economic powers in Europe. After I had been there a year, the station opened a training school to train broadcasters from the developing countries. This meant another source of students for interview. The first set of students included several from Sierra Leone. The electronic company Phillips also had a training school where students from various countries came to study. Then a television service was started which added another dimension to the work I did.

ARNOLD AWOONOR-GORDON

VERONICA WILSON WITH JEWELLRY MADE WITH DIAMONDS MINED IN SIERRA LEONE

Reflection on my life

ME BEING HOISTED BY GAMBIAN WRESTLER MASAM BULA BEFORE TAKING PART IN IN INTERNATIONAL WRESTLING CHAMPIONSHIP IN LONDON.

Then I went on holiday to Freetown and was offered the job of

ARNOLD AWOONOR-GORDON

Director of Television, which I accepted. I returned and packed up and went to Freetown. Having been away from Sierra Leone politics I did not know what I was letting myself in for. In the beginning all went smoothly as the person in overall charge was an Englishman and we did everything by the book. But as soon as he was manoeuvred out of the job and a local person took over, the inevitable palaver set in!

When I took on the job a house provided by the government went with it. These 'government quarters' were at a premium, but it was fortunate that I had been given an introduction to the Minister of Housing by his brother in London, and he promised me that I would be allocated the house, then occupied by an expatriate worker who would be returning to the UK in a month's time. I went and looked at the house, which was a bungalow in a compound at Cockerill South, on Wilkinson Road. I liked it immediately and arranged to store some of my belongings there with the permission of the occupier. Just as well, because two days before he was to move out, a young lady came and told him that she had been allocated the house and demanded the keys. He refused and told me about it. I informed the minister, who immediately called the person in charge of allocating government houses, and told him that the house had been allocated to Mr Gordon, and he would be taking the key from the present occupier as soon as he was ready to leave the premises. I can still see the face of the fellow, whom, I got to know later, had in fact allocated the house to one of his girlfriends, a very junior secretary in his department. So I moved in and spent some happy times there.

It is interesting to note that my neighbours at the time were some young Italian engineers, who were working on the Bunbuna hydroelectric project. They seemed to have parties every night and I am not surprised that the project took so long to complete. I inherited a Siamese cat called Mortimer, from the previous occupier of the house. It was a very independent cat, but one very loyal and

Reflection on my life

would stay by my side when I went down with malaria. One day Mortimer disappeared and search as much as I did I could not find him. By then the house where the Italians were staying, had been turned into a Chinese restaurant, and inhabited by a Chinese family. I will not say more. But I had to admonish the family when I saw them open the septic tank and started to bail out the contents to use as fertiliser. They stopped when I told them that no one would eat at their restaurant if they knew how the vegetables were fertilised.

When I took over as director of Television, the studios were in a dilapidated state and needed much upgrading. As I was friendly with the people who ran the Diamond Corporation, I persuaded them to help fund an annex to the main studios.

While on a visit to London, I discovered that as the BBC TV was then changing to colour, the black and white equipment they used in their training department was surplus to requirement. So without much arm twisting, I persuaded them to donate them to us, which they readily agreed, but on the understanding that we had to pay for the shipment from London to Freetown. Again I turned to my friends at the Diamond Corporation, and again with much arm twisting, they agreed to undertake the cost of shipping all the television studio equipment to Freetown. And so we had some of the most up to date equipment, which included portable cameras which allowed us to go outside of the studios to record programmes.

One of the first programme we recorded and showed on Sierra Leone Television, was the annual Kenema Agricultural Show which brought to people in Freetown all the activities of an agricultural show for the first time. I was able to order new programmes, including children's programme such as Sesame Street, print a regular television programme, which was distributed free of charge, and soon television, which had lagged behind radio, became the much watched medium in the Freetown area at least. I was informed that the sale of television sets increased two-fold. I was made aware of how popular television had become in the country when an episode of the popular American series 'Peyton Place' did not arrive from London. We had to apologise on air that we had to suspend the series until the episodes arrived. The howl of protest, especially from the ladies of Freetown, that greeted me everywhere I went, cannot be imagined. There was much relief when the presenter announced that the episode had at last arrived and was broadcast.

One thing I wanted to upgrade was the presentation of the programmes on air. I was able to recruit some boys and girls, and, with luck, a Dutch television presenter arrived in town to visit her husband who worked for Shell. For several weeks she trained our presenters in the art of presenting on television, and viewers remarked on the high standard we had achieved. She not only trained them in presenting but also in what and how to dress, how to speak into camera, etc, etc. She also had a go at the newsreaders and their standard of reading the news also improved.

Because of the nature of my job, I became friends with many foreigners living there. The American Ambassador Michael Samuels and his wife, the German Ambassador and his wife, the Italian Ambassador and his exuberant wife, and many others working in various areas of commerce in Sierra Leone. One particular German and his wife I became friendly with, worked for the construction company building the Freetown to Bo road. He was an avid collector of Sierra Leonean art, and had the largest collection of old bundoo devil masks I have ever seen. He had a very sneaking way of collecting them. Because his work took him to villages along the route of the road, he would have a new bundoo mask made in Freetown and offer them in return for the 'old' ones that the ladies had used for decades for their masquerade. They were pleased to have a new one to replace their 'old and decrepit' one and willingly gave him the old one. They did not realise that

Reflection on my life

they were exchanging an antique and precious one for the new and glittering one. Although I did not approve of his methods, there was nothing I could do about it.

He also had a collection of about twenty very old clay pots which he said had been excavated when the road was being built. The site had over five hundred of these pots, but he was only able to bring twenty with him, and wanted to go back to get the others. But by the time he returned two days later, the site had been levelled, on the instructions of the local chief. When asked he said that they had opened up a site where sacred pots had been buried in much earlier times, and he did not want a further desecration of a sacred site. So my friend was never able to add another loot to his collection.

I had never played golf before, but I was persuaded by Hugh Clarke, who was then the chairman of the Freetown Golf club, to try and play a round with him. He loaned me a set of golf clubs, and after a round and some drinks at the club house, he asked me how I liked it, and when I said I did enjoy the round, he immediately got me to sign up as a member. I did not have a set of golf clubs but the Dutch manager of KLM had a set, which came with the job, and as he was not a keen golfer, had never used it. So I 'borrowed' the clubs and from then on until I left the country and returned them. I was a regular player, but not the best golfer but I enjoyed the round and the comradeship of like-minded people.

The caddy master assigned a very young man to be my caddy. He must have been about eleven or twelve, and I realised that he could not read or write as he had never been to school. He told me he was keen to learn, so I arranged for him to go to night school, and in no time he was so ahead of his class made up of houseboys and taxi drivers, that he was making money on the side teaching some of his classmates who could not find the time to attend class. In order to make some extra cash, he offered to do my laundry, which I agreed to. He did not have the strength to squeeze the clothes and had to ask the houseboy next door to help him squeeze the clothes after washing.

He asked me whether I could teach him to cook European food, but as I only cooked Sierra Leonean food, I asked an English friend of mine if he could help. He did and for nearly a year Sheka, as he was called regularly turned up for lessons and eventually became a paid cook for my friend. He grew up, got married, had a son and got a job with one of the American embassy staff.

While he was a young lad he was caught having sex with a young girl of the same age, and her parents, wanting money from him, which he did not have, reported him to the police and he was arrested and charged. I had to go and stand by him when he came before the juvenile court. This was a thoroughly farcical experience. The three magistrates were very elderly men, all respected Justices of the Peace. The prosecutor was also a mature policewoman with a severe face. She read out the charge and the statement of the girl, which included the words 'And he put his tone into my virginal, and started to rock up and down.' It was all I could do not to laugh aloud, but held a handkerchief to my mouth as my shoulder shook with suppressed laughter. No one laughed as the policewoman read out all the details of the case, leaving nothing to the imagination, with her stern expression.

Things got worse when the lead magistrate in, admonishing the young man said 'You are a young man and you should not do these things, you should leave it to people like your master who is older than you.' Meaning that the young man should not indulge in sexual activities. By then I could not control myself and was doubled up with laughter. I feared I would be asked to leave the court, or be charged with contempt. But no one took any notice of me, and the case went on as if I was not there. The long and short of it was that he was sentenced to six strokes of the cane. When I went to the police station to find out how this was to be done, I was told

Reflection on my life

that until they had a doctor to certify that he was fit to be caned, he would be locked up. I was told that if I could find a doctor this could be done immediately.

I went to the City Hotel, where I was sure I would find a doctor, found one, explained the situation to him, and for another star beer, he willingly came with me and signed the form. It was then I realised that the police had been holding another fifteen young boys in custody as they could not, or did not have the inclination of finding a doctor to certify they were fit to be caned. So my doctor had not only to sign a certificate saying my young man was fit to be caned, but had to do it for all the others, some of whom had been there for months. They were then all lined up and all the policemen in the building, with canes, started to beat them as they ran out of the station. I must say I felt sorry for them, as they thanked me for bringing the doctor to deliver them from their incarceration.

I also became a member of the Freetown Aqua Sports Club, and although I did not possess a boat the whole time I was there, yet I had many friends who did. So I was not short of invitations to go fishing or to visit Banana Island, or make a trip to Bunce Island. During the time I was a member, the club had several scares with people going out in their boats and failing to return by the end of the day. Search parties had to be hastily organised to go in search of the lost seaman, and of course most members had to stay at the club until they were found.

I remember one such incident when a prominent Lebanese businessman, failed to return in his very expensive boat, even though it had all the navigational equipment on board. As it got dark the club was crowded with most of the Lebanese community in Freetown, who were deciding whether the President, who was a friend of the person missing at sea, should be informed. Like who should bell the cat, none of them had the guts to get on the phone to inform the President that his friend was missing at sea. But they need not have bothered, because much later in the night he was found by the search party and towed back to the club. It seems that the engine of his very expensive boat had broken down.

In those days, to become a Commodore of club you had to be a boat owner, but this is not so today, where any member can be voted Commodore. I don't think many of the new members of the club today, know the background of the forming of the Freetown Aqua Sports Club. The club was formed in 1967 by a group of prominent Sierra Leoneans and Expatriates, and the first Commodore was Peter Bartlett the General Manager of the Aureol Tobacco Company. Nearly all the members, whether local or expatriates, had their own boats, and the companies such as The Aureol Tobacco Company, Sierra Leone Brewery and the British High Commission, had their own large boats on which they entertained lavishly. The club really was a hub for all the movers and shakers in the town and the hive of all the gossip, both political and otherwise. It is interesting to note that during the Commission of Enquiry that followed the 1967 army coup, every Sierra Leonean who appeared before the commission, was asked the question 'Were you ever a member of the Freetown Aqua Sports Club?' the impression was given that the members of the club must have been in the know about the coup, and in fact, the coup may have been hatched there. Nothing was far from the truth. I am still in contact with the wife of one of the founder members, and she tells me she spent many days, sitting in the Kingsway Stores drumming up new membership.

Through membership of the club, and the kindness of other members with boats, I was able to make frequent fishing trips to Banana Island, Plantain Island and Bunce Island, catching some of the biggest barracudas ever seen. Another good thing about belonging to the club, was that people were very generous with their catches, and would hand out their surplus fish to all who wanted them. So my freezer was always full of fish that I had either helped to catch or been given by someone who had caught too many. There was one Lebanese member however, who always brought back a boat full of fish of every description. The general gossip was that the fish was not caught by him, but he bought them off the illegal foreign trawlers fishing in our waters, and passed them off as having caught them himself.

I was a Rotarian for a very short while, but the ambiance felt uncomfortable, so I left. I was also a member of the Hill Station Club which at one time had a nightclub in the basement called THE TALK OF THE TOWN. It was a popular club where all the young and beautiful people could be found on a Saturday night. It was run by Fennel Greene, who was able to play some of the latest records from the UK, and the young people flocked to hear and dance to the latest from the UK. At one time I was the Catering member of the club, and held a Tuesday buffet lunch, where one could come for lunch and be back at work in no time. I soon gave up as it was not as popular as Provilac, the restaurant run by Mrs Vicky Bishop of Paramount fame. Her Wednesday African buffet lunch was so popular that one had to book well in advance to get a table. On any Wednesday one would find Politicians, lawyers, CEOs of all the big companies, entertaining their guests to Vicky's African buffet lunch.

At the Hill Station Club, we put on an annual Christmas pantomime, which was attended by the members and their children. On New Year's Eve we had a fancy dress dance, where members tried to outdo each other with the ingenuity of their costumes. At midnight we would let off fireworks, but this was stopped, when one year, the noise of the fireworks alarmed S.I.Koroma, the Vice President, who at that time was residing in the Presidential Lodge, close to the club on Hill Station. It appears that he thought that the noise was the sound of guns going off, which in those days could signal the start of a Military coup.

During our merry making that New Year's Eve, the club was

surrounded by a squad of soldiers wanting to find out what we were up to. Members of the management committee of the club, dressed in their fancy dress costumes, had to go with the soldiers to see the Vice President to explain themselves. I must say he saw the funny side of it, but cautioned that it should never happen again as the sound of fireworks could frighten the populace. I think it was from that time that the letting off of fireworks was stopped in the country.

I was in Freetown in 1977 when the students of Fourah Bay College demonstrated against President Siaka Stevens. I was at home that Saturday, listening on the radio to the Convocation ceremony that was taking place at Mount Aureol. Suddenly I heard shouting and protest as the President got up to speak. The radio went dead and they started to play music, and I knew something was wrong. Later I learned that as he got up to speak, the students started to protest, holding up placards accusing the President and his government of corruption. The ceremony was abandoned and the President made a hasty retreat back to town. The students did not get away so easily, for the next day, some of the All Peoples Party (APC) young men stormed the campus, beat up the students, and some said, raped the female students, and did a great deal of damage to the College premises.

My nephew Richard Olu Gordon was one of the ring leaders of the protest, and was among those arrested for organising the protest. The college was closed down. The protest soon spread to town and on the Monday, school children joined in demonstrating with placards that read 'no college, no school'. It was reported that the disturbance soon spread to the provinces, and those around the President said that he was visibly shaken, and called on the Internal Security Unit (ISU) to put down the protest. They, it was reported, refused to shoot the children, and Cabinet ministers were also reported to be fleeing Freetown to return to their homes in the provinces, fearing for their lives, so hated they were.

Reflection on my life

After some religious leaders prevailed on the student leaders to call off the protest, they did so and the children went back to school. A meeting was arranged between the student leaders and the government to have a dialogue. Looking back now, it appears that the students did not come prepared, because their demands were so far-fetched, and not something the President could meet easily. Such as sacking his ministers, some of whom they said were not too well educated, and bringing in better educated people to run the ministries and so on and so forth. I think if they had sat down and thought it through and put forward more sensible demands, their demands would have been met. But soon everything died down and the students went back to college.

President Siaka Stevens had his network of spies all over the place, and knew everything that was happening in the city. I remember when his wife, Mrs Rebecca Stevens, who was friendly with my mother, came and asked my mother to accompany her to inform the President that one of their sons wanted to get married. When they got to his sitting room, one of his Vice-Presidents, Kamara-Taylor was with him. After they had informed him of the coming nuptial of one of his sons, he said, addressing his wife 'I was waiting to see when you would come to see me about the wedding, for I understand the girl is five months pregnant. How can she go down the aisle with a large stomach?' In Krio he said 'are bin dae wait for see ustem you cam for tell me. Are yeri say de pikin get big big belle. How e go go down the aisle wit big big belle, are nor know?' This was a shock to Mrs Stevens and my mother, as they did not know about the pregnancy. He said a lot more, but Kamara-Taylor, being the diplomat that he was said 'These days it does not matter, as they will design the bridal dress in such a way, that no one would notice the bump' In the end he agreed and asked for details of how much they would need from him to organise the wedding. How he knew about the pregnancy when even his wife did not know, remains a mystery to me. But he knew everything that was happening in the city, and the country.

ARNOLD AWOONOR-GORDON

I used to be surprised at the number of overseas businessmen who visited Freetown, meet the respective minister and want to be taken to see the President. I am sure the President had lots on his plate, but somehow time would be made to see them. If these people saw the Minister of Information and Broadcasting, and wanted to see the President, the Permanent Secretary would call me to accompany him to the meeting. And there were some strange people we did take to meet the President.

One visit I remember was from a film company who were scouting for location for the film 'Mosquito Coast.' They had come to see whether they could find a suitable location to film. I accompanied the Minister to the meeting and the President graciously received us. The film people gave the President a summary of what the film was about and told him that the peninsula area would be ideal for them to do the filming. They told him about the director, Peter Weir and the films he had directed, and the people who were to star in the film. These were Harrison Ford, River Phoenix, Helen Mirren and Butterfly McQueen, the black film star who had made her name as the maid in 'Gone with the wind'. The film was adapted from the book of the same name, written by Paul Theroux, a distinguished American author. They also told him about the budget which would include money spent on hotels, transportation and the hiring of many local people as extras.

The President listened intently, but did not ask any questions, but said that he would think about their proposal and would communicate his decision through the Minister. I was very excited as I imagined myself as the local fixer who would be rubbing shoulders with such international Hollywood stars. But as we left the room, the President called the Minister back as he wanted to discuss something with him. We waited in the secretary's room adjacent to the President's office until he came back. As soon as I saw his face, I knew something was amiss, but I did not relate it to the meeting we had just had. The film people departed to their hotel to wait the decision of the President and we went back to the office.

As soon as we got back, the Minister called the Permanent Secretary and myself into his office, and told us the news that the President had scuppered the project. He felt that the name of the film 'Mosquito Coast' would forever be associated to Sierra Leone, for he pointed out that Sierra Leone had been known in the old days as 'The Whiteman's Grave' owing to the prevalence of mosquitoes. So because of that he did not give his approval, and we lost some much needed foreign currency. And I did not get to rub shoulders with the great and good of Hollywood. The film was eventually filmed on the coast between Nicaragua and Honduras, and was a financial success.

But the President did give his approval for the BBC to film a television programme about the meeting between Stanley and Dr Livingstone, which originally took place somewhere in East Africa. But Sierra Leone stood in for East Africa, and gave employment to several people who were hired as extras. I was the 'fixer' on the film, and it opened my eyes, which were shut at the time, as to how to go about bribing people, some in high position, in order to get things done.

After the producer, actors and film crew had been in the country for a week, they needed written permission from the Ministry of Information and Broadcasting in order to travel around the country and begin filming. I knew that permission had been granted by the President, but their seemed to be a stumbling block within the Ministry to obtain the necessary permission. I mentioned this to a friend of mine who was an old hand at this game, and he asked me whether I had 'sweetened' the hands of the people who were holding up the filming. When I looked unsure at what he meant, he then gave me the scenario as to how to get things moving.

I was to buy a brown envelope, stuff it with Leone notes, and hand this to the people who were in the way, and hey presto, all barriers would be removed. I told the BBC people about this, and they being old hands at filming in various African countries, knew the drill and agreed to this. So I bought two brown envelopes, stuffed them with small denomination Leone notes, so the envelopes looked bulky and passed them on. As one of the people who received his envelope said to me 'Arnold, now you are talking'. Doors where open, the necessary permits were received and we were away. This was my first experience with 'brown envelopes' and it was not my last.

Another group of people I had to accompany the Minister to see the President were a group of Swedish entrepreneurs who wanted to open an FM station in Sierra Leone. They had opened one in the Gambia, which was very successful and received wide coverage all over the area, including Senegal. The President listened carefully to their plans, and after they left, he said to us that he did not want a private radio station operating in the country, as the Sierra Leone Broadcasting Service did a good job, and was under government control. And then added that if he allowed a private station to operate in the country, it could be used as propaganda tool by the Opposition Party, and even to announce a military coup. I laugh when I think of it now, when I see the proliferation of radio stations that now cover the whole country. Shaki would turn in his grave.

I think the most unusual people who arrived in the country and wanted an audience with the President, were two smart alecs and conmen from the United States of America. I think they thought we were all fools, for what they wanted to see him about was for Sierra Leone to invest in a 'unicorn' which they had found in the jungles of an African country, and were seeking funds to organise performances around the world to show this mythical beast to the public. The Minister was very sceptical and called me into his office told me so. I suggested that he tell them to go to the American Embassy and they would in turn call the Foreign Minister

Reflection on my life

to arrange the meeting. We never heard anything from them again. But much later I heard that they had conned money from several gullible people in town, and scuppered never to be seen again.

One of the most interesting persons I got to know very well was Miss Erica Powell, special assistant to President Stevens, helping with the writing of his book 'What life has taught me.' For those who don't know or remember Erica, she was the Englishwoman who was first Secretary to, and later Personal Assistant to Dr. Kwame Nkrumah, the first President of Ghana. She first went to the Gold Coast as secretary in the Secretariat in Accra then under Colonial rule. She was deployed to the staff of Dr Nkrumah before independence, and rose to become his special assistant after independence. She became one of the most powerful women in Ghana, and it was said that she was Nkrumah's gate keeper, and no one got to see him without her approval.

She was on leave in England when the Military Coup, which overthrew Nkrumah, took place, and when I got to know her in Freetown she was working for President Stevens. She told me that she was lucky to be out of the country when the coup took place, for, she said, the least that could have happened to her was being raped by the soldiers. The worse, she said, would have been she would have been tortured, quartered and hung, and then shot. She was a great raconteur, and told stories about her time in Ghana with much relish. She constantly denied the rumours that she was Nkrumah's lover and said that he was not a womaniser. In fact he was weary of Ghanaian women, as they had too much family baggage with them. That was the reason he did not marry one of them, but asked his great friend, President Nassar of Egypt, to find him a wife. Fathia had several children with him, and lived in Ghana until the coup when she returned to Cairo.

Nkrumah, she told us was very superstitious and believed in African juju. Something which seemed to have rubbed off on Erica, for she also believed in African juju. She also vehemently denied that she had been planted by the Colonial government as a spy in the office of the President, a denial many people took with a pinch of salt.

Erica and Fathia, Nkrumah's wife, never got on, and she told stories of them keeping a distance from each other, and communicating through emissaries when they had to. It is interesting to note that both women died on the same day in 2013. Fathia in Cairo and Erica in a small English village, and what it also coincidental, is that they were both buried the same day. Fathia with a lavish state funeral in Accra, and Erica in a small English village church and cemetery with only a few close friends, as she had no family. I was glad that she had not been forgotten, as the Ghana High Commission in London sent someone to represent them at the funeral. He gave a very moving tribute to the work she did in Ghana.

She was working in Freetown when Nkrumah died in Conakry, and President Stevens had her included in the Sierra Leone delegation that went to the funeral. I can still see her now holding court at the Sunday curry lunch at the Atlantic restaurant, a place she visited regularly. Not many people can boast that they had worked closely with two of the most charismatic African leaders, before, during and after independence. She did write a book entitled PRIVATE SECRETARY (female) GOLD COAST, which unfortunately is now out of print. May her soul rest in peace.

One day in Freetown I was introduced by the German embassy to a young German who had arrived to set up the SOS Children's Village at Lumley. I set up a small committee to help with the initial setting up of what today is a very successful charity in the country. The charity brought funds to construct several houses, each with a house mother to look after several children, in a family atmosphere. The village was officially opened by President

Reflection on my life

Stevens, and I remember him being taken on a tour of the village, accompanied by a young girl of about six or seven, who without any prompting, took hold of his hands and accompanied him around the place, to the delight of the President. I was chuffed when visiting the village on one of my recent visits to find that one of the original boys the village took in, was now the director of the village. He was quite a handful in his young days and gave his house-mother a lot of headache. But the village did manage to turn round his life, to the extent that he now looks after young people who were orphans like he was at the time.

I got involved with two very important charities while I Freetown. The first, which I helped to set up, dealt with trying to stop young people taking drugs, mainly smoking marijuana (diamba). This was at the instigation of the World Health Organisation (WHO) in Geneva Switzerland. The charity aimed to bring to the attention of families the dangers of drug taking, especially amongst young boys. We decided to aim our campaign at mothers, for it was found, that it was they who came more in contact with their sons on a daily basis than even teachers. My job was to go round to talk to women's groups and show them what the marijuana plant looks like, and how it smelt when smoked. I did not smoke it myself, but burned it for the smell. So, I would turn up with my pot of pot, a marijuana plant in a pot, with some already made up. I could then show them what the plant looked like when growing, when dried and what it smelt like. This way we hoped mothers would be more alert if their sons should grow, smoke or have the drug in their pockets. I am not sure to what extent we were able to prevent the spread of drugs amongst the youth of Sierra Leone, but I am proud that we made a noble effort.

The other charity I was involved with was the Planned Parenthood Association, which was set up to help prevent the birth of unwanted children. There again the emphasis was on women, to teach them contraceptive methods to prevent them having too many mouths to feed. But we soon found out that however we tried with the women, it was the men we had to target, for as one woman told us, the men wanted sex, and would refuse to help with the precautions we had taught them. Surprisingly, some of the women did not want to indulge in any form of birth control for various reasons. One excuse we heard repeatedly was that God gave every woman so many babies in their bodies, and they had to bring them out, or they would die inside them. So, if God gave you ten babies, you had to bring them all out. A rather cock-eyed reason, I think.

So we set up men's groups to teach them, first that they should not have too many children as it affects the health of their wives and partners, and secondly the health benefits of using the condom. This was the most difficult part as the men had all kinds of reasons why they did not want to use the condom to prevent their women having too many babies. Their reason was that putting on a condom was like having sex with a raincoat on, the same reason that men all over the world give for not using the condom. We did our best to convince them, and show them how to put on a condom using the convenient banana, but to no avail. They also felt that condoms were too expensive, so we decided to distribute them free through the Fullah shops. We suggested to them that whenever a man purchased something, he should be given a condom. But this brought about violence against a woman, whose husband caught her with a condom and accused her of having a lover. But she told him that she had got one for him, as she was going to persuade him to use it. You cannot win, whichever way you try.

Chapter 26
IN THE BELLY OF THE BEAST

ATTENDING THE UN GENERAL ASSEMBLY IN NEW YORK WITH SIERRA LEONE DELEGATION

During my time as Director of Television I had to learn a great deal about politics and the part it played in the life of people in the country. The Sierra Leone Broadcasting Service was under the Ministry of Information, and when I joined we had an illiterate minister who was always interfering with the work we were doing. As television became popular every young girl wanted to work for us, and the Minister was always sending his favourites to me with a note, asking me to employ them. If I rejected them, he would call me and berate me for not employing this or that girl he had sent to me.

I was fortunate that he did not last long in the job, and was eventually hanged for ritual murder, after having been found guilty of making juju with the unborn child of a woman. The story that came out at his trial was long, gruesome and complicated, and is too sickening to repeat here. But people in the country at the time will remember the case. I heard that at the time of the case President Stevens was heard to remark that in the old days it was the Mendes who were accused of cannibalism, but things must have now come to a head when now the Temnes have turned to eating people.

The new Minister was more enlightened and he and I came to an arrangement about the pestering power of his girlfriends and relations who wanted to work on television. When he sent them to me, I would go through the recruitment process with them, put them in front of a camera to read the news, then write a summary of their deficiency, which would be sent to him. It was then up to him to break the sad news to the young lady that she did not pass the required test to become a TV presenter.

When I was at television I always had to tread carefully not to offend the political authorities, and had to watch what we put out each day. I got into big trouble when we designed our programme to celebrate the anniversary of the country's independence from Britain. We searched for films in our archival library, and put together a programme with films that were taken in 1961, during the independence celebrations. The commentary on the historical Ceremony of the lowering of the British flag and the hoisting of the new Sierra Leone flag was by the veteran broadcaster, John Akar, the Head of the SLBS at the time. Our programme went out on the anniversary day, and I think it was well received by a nostalgic audience.

However, the following day, the Minister of Information called me

Reflection on my life

in agitation to his office. When I got there he was in a state, because the President, Siaka Stevens, had called him to say that he had heard that we were praising John Akar on television, and he wanted to know what it was all about. I must point out here that the President and John Akar, who at one time was our Ambassador in Washington, had fallen out for some reasons too long to restate, and he had been sacked. So he was not in the best books of the President. I explained about the programme and said that it would have been difficult to exclude the voice, although not his face, from the programme. He calmed down then and asked me to accompany him to see the President to explain what had taken place.

When we reached the office of the President, we had to wait for an hour until we could see him. After I explained what had happened with the programme, the President said that he had not seen the programme, but had been informed (dem congosa wan dem) that we had been praising John Akar on television. Then he said something that we, the Minister and myself, may have misinterpreted. The President said that he was surprised that we still had tapes in our archives with the voice of John Akar. And if he was in our place he would not keep such tapes in the archives. The Minister and I took this to mean that we should destroy any tapes in the archives that had the voice of John Akar, both film and audio. He, therefore, ordered me to find a way of destroying the tapes. I felt gutted having to destroy archive materials that were so pivotal to the history of Sierra Leone. I shall regret doing so for the rest of my life.

The question then was how to get rid of so many cans containing several reels of television programmes that had nestled in the archival library since Independence? I appealed to the minister for some direction, but he was no help. We could not just bury them as they would take too long to degrade. We could not just burn them as that would not be good for the environment. It was one of our junior engineers who came up with the answer. Why not, he said, go and dump the lot out at sea where the tapes would be destroyed by the sea?. It was a most sensible solution, but the logistics proved more difficult to carry this out than at first thought. But after a great many telephone calls and letter writing, we managed to secure the services of a launch from the Ports Authority to help us carry out this dismal task

So one morning we loaded up all the television tapes from our archival library onto a van and took them down to the Queen Elizabeth 11 Quay. I am afraid I chickened out at the last moment and did not go out to sea with the library and engineering staff. But I instructed them that they should go as far from the shore as possible, and they should open every can and remove all the tapes and cut them up before dumping them into the deep. It was the last time we saw those tapes that had caused so much raucous. I regret doing this to this day.

As I mentioned, one had to be very careful what we said in our broadcast so as not to tread on the toes of the people in power. There was one incident I remember very well which I think was more to do with interpretation rather than deliberate. The President had made one of his regular 'meet the people' tours of the country. This time it was to the shores of Lake Sonfon, in the North East region of the country. The Ministry of Information reporter who covered the tour filed a copy, for broadcast stating that the President had a picnic by the shores of the lake. All hell broke loose the following day from State House. The President had objected to the fact that the listening audience had been told that he had 'gone on a picnic', when in fact he had gone on a working tour to meet the people of the area. The objection was to the word 'picnic,' which was interpreted to mean 'an outing', something that people did at the beach on public holidays. It took some convincing to explain that what was meant was that the President had had an alfresco picnic lunch provided by the people on the shores of the

Reflection on my life

lake.

Another incident happened when I worked in Freetown, which in the event had nothing to do with my work. My family owned some land at Goderich on the main road by the Milton Margai Teachers College. One day I passed by and noticed that the land was being cleared, and when I enquired who had given permission for the workers to clear the area they told me that it was a government Minister and gave me the name. The following day I wrote to the Minister to inform him that the land belonged to my family and perhaps someone had sold it to him by mistake. I received a letter from the Minister on his official letterhead, informing me that he owned the land, and that he had instructed his workers, that if I was to set foot on the land they were to beat me up and, if possible, kill me and he would take responsibility for it. The letter duly appeared in a newspaper.

That evening I was at home when I received a call from his residence saying that the President wanted to see me. As I drove to the house, my heart was beating wondering what I had done to offend the President that he wanted to see me at his home. But I need not have worried.

He had read the letter from one of his top ministers to me in the newspaper that day, and wanted to know what it was all about. I told him that it was a dispute over our family land, and he sent me home to collect the letter. When I returned with the letter, he read it and then sent for the Minister. When he came he was berated by the president for using his ministerial letterhead to write such an insulting and criminal letter, and wondered how a man from Koranko country would have the cheek to claim lands that had belonged to a Creole family in Freetown for generations. He warned him that if he did not write a letter of apology to me, with a copy to him, and remove his workers from the land by midday the following day, he would be sacked. I was sorry to see someone who went strutting around town in his official car, reduced to a gibbering wreck as he grovelled in front of me, and the Vice-President, who was also present. I received the letter of apology the following day, and although the press wanted a copy to publish it, I refused. The poor man had been humiliated enough.

As I mentioned earlier I was very naive about the intricacies of Sierra Leone politics, and gaily sailed on doing my job, without realising the intricacies of the politics at work. Then, suddenly one day, all the staff at both the radio, television and the information division of the ministry, were called to a meeting with the Secretary to the President, who was also the Head of the Civil Service. The meeting was held to inform all of us about the changes that had been decided. The SLBS radio and television were to be merged under a new post, that of Director-General of Broadcasting. This meant that my post had been abolished, and I was to be transferred to the division of information in charge of writing the daily radio and television news bulletins. The confusion was what was to happen to the post of Chief Information Officer. Was he subordinate to the Director-General? And in what hierarchy was the Director-General in the scale of the Civil Service? Somehow, these questions were fudged and were never answered to anyone's satisfaction. The other heads of government departments wanted to know their positions in the hierarchy of the civil service.

I moved from my office in New England to a shared office in the ministry in the middle of town, and carried on with my work. It was while at the Information division that something happened that made me realise that if I wanted to get on in the country, I had to try and beat them at their game. When I ran television I became very friendly with some of the ambassadors and high commissioners assigned to the country. One such was the Lebanese ambassador, who with his wife became very good friends of mine. He arranged for me to visit Lebanon for a three weeks visit. In those days, I am not sure whether this still exists, before a senior civil servant left the

Reflection on my life

country for a visit abroad, permission had to be obtained from State House. The ambassador wrote to the Permanent Secretary at the Ministry of Information and Broadcasting extending to me the invitation to visit his country. The Permanent Secretary then wrote to State House requesting permission for me to make the visit. I saw a copy of the letter. Imagine my surprise when the reply came from State House granting the permission to make the visit, but instead of my name, the name of one of my colleagues in the ministry had been substituted. Until today, I do not know how that happened, as the colleague denied all knowledge of why my name went forwarded to State House but his name came back. The Permanent Secretary was also aghast. But I can say, with some satisfaction, that he never made the trip, as the ambassador cancelled it.

This and other things made me realise that I had to learn the mechanism of politics and backstabbing, and started to make friends in high places. I began to pull some strong strings, and soon the post of Public Relations Officer in the Ministry of Foreign Affairs was created for me. This was thanks to the then Minister, who had become, and is still a good friend of mine. Although I called the job 'Senior Bag Carrier' yet it gave me the opportunity to travel with the minister abroad. I visited Ethiopia, Kenya, and the US, where we attended the meeting of the General Assembly. As I was in a position to see all the invitations that arrived from various countries for visits abroad, I was able to take advantage of some very interesting sponsored trips abroad.

But it was not to last and out of the blue I was sacked by the President of Sierra Leone. It came about this way. The BBC had been broadcasting stories about the country that could only have been sent by an insider in the government. The President was furious, and brought down his wrath on the Minister of Information and Broadcasting to find out who the source was. It happened that at one cabinet meeting the President had promised to sack the minister if he did not find the mole in the government who was leaking inside information to the BBC.

After that meeting, the minister went to have lunch with his mistress, who was a close friend of mine. He was in high dungeon going on and on about this person who would make him lose his job. Now, according to the mistress, she jokingly suggested that perhaps I was the mole, because of my connection with the BBC. She later swore to me that she meant it as a joke. But the minister did not see it that way and, clutching at any straw to save his job, he went straight to the President and reported that he had found the mole, and he was Arnold Awoonor- Gordon. Promptly the President wrote a memo to his Secretary, who was also Head of the Civil Service, that my appointment should be terminated with immediate effect.

I knew someone who worked in State House and he rang me to find out what I had done to make the President so angry that he had ordered the termination of my appointment in the civil service. Of course, I did not know what I had done, until the next day. For early that morning, even before I had got out of bed, the mistress came to see me at the bungalow I was living at in Cockerill south. She was also in a state, and after I had calmed here down with Earl Gray tea, she then told me that she had done something very wrong by telling the minister, jokingly, that the mole in the government was me. She was sobbing as she spilled the beans about what had led to my downfall. But I calmed her down and she left. By the way, I did forgive her and we are still good friends.

Even before I received the letter of termination, I went to see the Head of the Civil Service, and his view was the word of the President was the law of the land and he could do nothing to change it. Before I left his office I made the remark that, according to the civil service General Orders, there are procedures laid down for sacking a civil servant. First a letter of query would be sent to the person, which the person had to reply to, before a final decision to terminate the appointment was made. I shall never forget what he told me in his small squeaky voice 'Mr Gordon, you are talking about the old time civil service. This is the new civil service. If the President says sack you, sacked you are.' And so I was sacked.

My mother, who was a staunch member of the women's wing of the ruling All Peoples Party, and a close friend of the wife of the President, went to see him one evening in his house at Kingharman Road, to plead my case. He was most gracious to her and said he wasn't there, but it was what he had been told that I had done. He also informed her I would be given all my gratuities and allowance. He assured her not to worry, and that being an international man I would not find it difficult to get an international job. And so I left the Sierra Leone Government.

A few years later when I was working for the American Embassy, I accompanied the first female American ambassador to State House to present her credential to the President. After the presentation ceremony, as they were having refreshment, I heard the President saying to her that she had got a very good man in Mr Gordon working for her. He praised me to the sky, gave her a summary about my family background, and the international work I had done, and so on. I could not believe my ears listening to the praises coming from the man who had given me the boot from my job. The ambassador was also very surprised, and I had to give her the background to the high praise from my head of state later on.

Soon after I was sacked, I made arrangement to return to Holland where I knew there would be a job waiting for me. But as I was nearing the completion of the house I was building, I decided to get a job until the house was completed so I could rent it out. But first I had to move out of the government quarters, and so started something like farce from people wanting to take over the bungalow. First a very senior officer from State House came and told me that he had been allocated the house, and I was to hand over the keys within a month, the time I was given to quit the premises. I promised to call him to come to collect the keys the day I moved out

Then one day I returned to find a truck outside the house full of furniture and a lady saying that her husband had been allocated the house, and would I mind if she stored her furniture until I moved out. I informed her that the house had been allocated to someone at State House, but she said the house had been allocated to her and her husband as they had just returned home after a stint at an Embassy abroad. I called State House and the guy was at the house within fifteen minutes. Then a fight broke out as to whom the house had been allocated. While they were fighting and arguing, as I had moved out all my stuff, I drove to the Ministry of Housing and handed over the keys. I never found out who ever got the house eventually.

It was while I was a civil servant that I decided to build my own house. I already had some family land at Gbendembu, Goderich, so I approached the assistant manager of Standard bank for a loan. He was an English man and he gave me some good advice. He suggested that I should build the house in stages. First make an estimate of how much it would cost to do the foundation, then borrow money to do that. After paying off that loan, then make another estimate of the cost of putting on the wall to a certain height, borrow to do that and so on. This way, he advised, although it would take a long time to complete, the house will eventually be completed. What a good advice he gave me, and this was how I struggled until the house was completed.

He was very good to me, because sometimes before I had finished paying of the loan, I would go back for a top-up, because I would need to purchase some materials that arrived and would be snapped up before I had finished the loan. He would grumble but would

Reflection on my life

oblige me. Even when he left the company to return to the UK, he informed the Sierra Leonean who took over from him about our arrangement, and that man continued with the arrangement. I thank both of them for their help in getting on the property ladder.

As a practising Christian I did not believe in juju or anything associated with the occult. I found out that one could alter the building of the house here and there, buy some cement and do some plastering, buy some blocks and raise the height, etc, etc,. But when it came to floating a floor, everything had to be in place as the work had to be done in one go. So enough cement, sand, iron rod, boards, sticks and electrical cables all had to be ready for the big float. I met a friend who had completed his house, and I mentioned that I was finding it difficult to get all the materials in place for the float. He then asked me whether when laying the foundation, I had done the ceremony to appease the ancestors. I said that I did not know anything about it, and he then enlightened me. I should have cut the throat of a white cockerel (UGH) put some coins in a jar, dig a hole in the foundation, and called someone to come and invoke the ancestors 'to open the way', as we say in Sierra Leone, for me to complete the house. He said he also did not believe in the ceremony, but he had done it and was able to obtain the funds to complete his house.

I decided to try it, but drew the line at the white cockerel. Incredibly, one month after the ceremony to appease the ancestors, I received a windfall from some shares I had in a company in the UK that I had forgotten about. So one Sunday morning we started on the floating of the floor, which was completed in five hours. It appeared that, sometimes, invoking the spirits of the ancestor works. So, although my house was incomplete when I was sacked, I had installed the windows and doors, water and light had been connected, and it was only the floor tiles for the downstairs and the bedroom upstairs that I still had to get. I could move in while I completed the house.

ARNOLD AWOONOR-GORDON

While I was still employed by the Sierra Leone Government, I once got caught up in a situation between a cabinet minister and his girlfriend, which made me nearly lose the government quarters I had been given as part of my job. She was a girl I had known for many years, first in London and later on in Freetown. She was the girlfriend of a married Cabinet minister who had rented and furnished a house for her. I don't know what happened between them, but they fell out, and he ordered her to leave the house where she was staying with her teenage daughter. Rumour had it that he had caught her with another man and threw her out. Anyway, one night she turned up at my house with all her belongings, and asked whether she and her daughter could stay, until she could find somewhere else to move to. Lucky for her, an expatriate friend of mine had gone on leave and left the keys to his house for me to look after while he was away.

So, I gave up my house to her and moved to the house of my friend. Two weeks later, I received an official letter from the Ministry of Housing, which was in charge of allocating government quarters, that it had come to the notice of the Minister that I had moved out of the quarters allocated to me, and rented out the house to another party. And I was given three days to give up the house, if this was true. The letter was not signed by the Permanent Secretary, as would have been the usual practice, but by the minister himself, who was a good friend of the friend of the lady in question. I went to her and I said in Krio. Titi, you wan make are loss me ose?. Do ya muf wan tem en go fen oder place for tap'. I must say she understood where it was coming from, and moved out to stay with a girl friend of hers.

She was not a good person, because I later learned that she seduced the boyfriend of the lady she went to stay with, had a child for him, and moved on. The last I heard was that she met a German working for a road building company, who married her, adopted her son and daughter and they went to live in Germany, where I hope she is still

Reflection on my life

living the good life. The coda to all this was that my houseboy, who had quarters attached to the house, informed me when I returned, that one night he heard noises outside, and when he looked out of the window, he noticed her burying something in the garden. The next day when she went out, he dug up what she had buried, which turned out to be a paper with Arabic writing on it. He peed on it and burned it and told me that he thought she was burying something to make me leave the house so she could take possession of it. I didn't believe it then, and don't believe it now. But it taught me a lesson to be careful whom to trust in the country.

I was at the SLBS when it was decided that women were to be recruited into the army as other ranks. There were already women officers but they were in the medical section as matron and senior nurses. Recruitment notices went out on radio and in the newspapers, giving the qualifications needed which if I remember, that candidates had to have achieved certain educational standards with the right qualifications.

All the applicants were invited for an interview at the Army Headquarters at Wilberforce. I was not there so cannot vouch for the truth of what happened, but I was told this by someone who was there. There were over five hundred young ladies who turned up hoping to get into the armed forces and put on the smart uniform. Realising that many of them did not have the required academic qualifications, after welcoming them, the senior officer who was in charge of recruitment, told them about the academic qualifications required to enter the armed forces. He and the other officers present, were leaving the room, he told them, and by the time they returned, all those without the necessary qualifications had better leave the room, otherwise if they were caught out, they would be sent straight to the guardroom as they were all on military property. By the time he returned only about a quarter of the applicants were left. The others, fearing being locked up in a military guardroom, had thought it wise to leave.

I later heard that one of the young ladies who had left, complained to her boyfriend, who was a senior politician, and who had recommended her for one of the posts, about not even being seen. His reply was that you told me you had the right qualification, obviously you didn't, and that is why you were never seen. As I say, I was not there, but this could be one of those urban myths that circulated around Freetown at the time.

I grew up in the center of Freetown and used to hear stories about the Maroons who were some of the first people to be settled in Freetown. But I did not know the background until my very first visit to Jamaica, and was taken to an area where the Maroons still live. Their history is a fascinating one. When the British captured Jamaica in 1655, the Spanish fled leaving a large number of African slaves. Some of these slaves fled into the hills and fought the British, who were hampered by the terrain, which they did not know. Tired of fighting an enemy they could not defeat, the Governor signed a treaty with the Maroons, promising them 2500 acres of land in two locations, on condition that they were to remain in the five main towns.

Later a new Governor tore up the treaty with the Maroons, and a war broke out, and all but one of the five towns were destroyed. Only one, the Achampong remained. Many of the Maroons were deported to Nova Scotia in Canada, and some to Freetown, accompanied by some that had been sent to Canada. Thus Freetown originally was separated into three sections occupied by the Maroons, the Nova Scotians and the Recaptives. The church built by the Maroons, St John Maroon Town Church is still on Siaka Stevens street, and descendants of the original Maroons still worship there.

But not all the Maroons were happy in their new homeland, and in 1840 two hundred of them petitioned the governor to be allowed to return to their old hometown of Jamaica. They were refused free

Reflection on my life

passage, so an old Maroon widow, Mrs Mary Brown, bought a schooner and on January 1, she, her daughter and son-in-law and other like-minded Maroons, set sail back to the scene of their long-remembered memories.

Because of the Maroon connection with Freetown, I was very keen to visit Jamaica to find out more about this connection. I did so much later in my life, when I visited Jamaica for the first time. I found that the Maroons in Jamaica today, are to a small extent autonomous and separate from Jamaican culture, and today live amongst the most inaccessible place on the land. But they still maintain their traditional African celebrations and practices. On the 6th of January each year they have a large festival to commemorate the signing of the peace treaty with the British. I was fortunate to attend the festival the year I visited, where there was singing and dancing, drum playing and preparation of traditional foods. There was also a masquerade of African devils such as can be seen in any West African ceremonial festival, and brings tourists from all over the country to take part in something that harks back to the days of slavery. And they still have African names like Kodjo, Kwame and Quashie.

When visiting Jamaica there were three places I wanted to visit. The first was the birthplace of their most famous son, Bob Marley. He was born in a small village in the hills called Nine Miles, in the parish of St Ann, of a Scottish father and a Jamaican mother. He was christened Robert Nesta Marley, he never used his middle name, moved with his mother to Trench Town, in Kingston where he started his musical career. Of course the village where he was born has become a mecca for not only people who liked his music, but also for those who supported his philosophy of using marijuana as 'a healing sacrament'. Although the possession of, and dealing in marijuana is illegal in Jamaica, yet Nine Miles is a law unto itself, and the weed is sold and smoked openly everywhere.

Naturally it attracts hundreds of young people who come to the area from cruise ships, to get high on the real stuff. But they are warned by the villagers that they could smoke and get as high as they like within the village confines, but taking the stuff down into the town or back to their ships, they could be arrested.

Bob Marley used the weed, which he said was prevalent in the bible, reading passages such as Psalms 104:14, as showing approval of its usage. He said of its usage 'When you smoke weed, it reveal yourself to you. All the wickedness you do, the weed reveal your consciousness to yourself', and this is the philosophy that still exists in the village today, and which attracts the tourists from the cruise ships.

The two other places I wanted to visit while in Jamaica, was the home of the late playwright and actor Noel Coward and that of Ian Fleming, the creator of James Bond. Called Firefly the home of Noel Coward was his vacation home. Situated on a mountain top it was originally owned by the infamous pirate and Governor of Jamaica, Sir Henry Morgan. Coward is buried in a marble tomb in his garden, in a spot where he used to sit, commanding a view of St Mary's harbour, from where the Pirate Morgan used as a lookout. A statue of him sits there looking out to the sea.

Named after the luminous insects seen at night, it is at Firefly that Coward entertained the great and good including the Queen Mother, Queen Elizabeth 11, Sir Winston Churchill, Sir Lawrence Olivier, Sophia Loren, Elizabeth Taylor and many more, all of whose photos line the walls of the sitting and dining rooms. The house has been kept as he left it when he died in 1973 aged 73, and is open to tourists by the Jamaica Nation Heritage Trust, which owns it.

Another house in Jamaica with a former famous owner, which is worth a visit, is Goldeneye, the name given by Ian Fleming to his estate on the northern coastline of Jamaica. Situated on the edge of

Reflection on my life

a cliff, overlooking a private beach and the Caribbean Sea. Fleming said that he got the name 'Goldeneye' from the novel by Carson McCullers's Reflection in a Goldeneye and Operation Goldeneye, a contingency plan he developed during the Second World War, when he worked in MI5.

It was there that he wrote all his James Bond novels, and a number of the James Bond movies, including 'Dr. No' and 'Live and Let Die', were filmed near the estate. The name of the estate became the title of the seventeenth James Bond movie, and the first to star Pierce Brosnan as James Bond. After his death the estate was sold to Bob Marley, who later sold it to the owner of Island Records Chris Blackwell. It now operates as the Goldeneye Hotel and Resort, an upscale hotel consisting of Fleming's main house and several cottages. Nearby is the appropriately named James Bond beach.

Chapter 27
GETTING TO KNOW UNCLE SAM'S PEOPLE IN FREETOWN

After I was sacked, I took a temporary job with British Caledonia Airways, which allowed me to travel to London frequently. The Airline at the time had a contract to run the Hotel Bintumani at Aberdeen. At the opening of the hotel, we had a posse of journalists from abroad and the local press. The opening ceremony was performed by President Stevens, during which an incident took place which I shall never forget. The Vice-President S.I.Koroma arrived late, after President Stevens had already arrived. Luckily the manager had been informed that he was running late and kept delaying the ceremony by showing the President around the hotel, while I was stationed at the car park. As soon as a sweating VP arrived, I whisked him through the kitchens to his place at the dais before the President arrived there. No one noticed anything amiss. But he was one long sweaty VP.

I was with British Caledonian Airways for only ten months when, at a cocktail party, I met the Public Relations Officer of the then United States Information Service (USIS) whom I had got to know when I was Director of Sierra Leone Television. He asked me what I had been doing since I left the government, and when I told him I was with British Caledonian Airway prior to going back to Holland, he told me to come and see him at the embassy the following day. Without hesitation, he offered me the position of Senior Foreign National Officer in USIS, which I held for the next eight years.

The Organisation of African Unity (OAU) conference took place in Freetown in 1980. A great deal of money was spent in constructing a conference centre, villas to house the Heads of State, new street lights, the widening of roads from the villas in Hill station to the conference centre at Aberdeen, and the purchasing of a fleet of Mercedes cars to convey the delegates to and from the conference.

Reflection on my life

Each delegation had a Cabinet Minister attached to it, and after the conference ended, there was a scramble by the Ministers to acquire the cars for themselves. By then I was not in the government and so was not involved directly with the conference, but watched the shenanigans as a spectator.

I must say that contrary to what the populace thought before the conference started, the conference was well organised and went off without a hitch, and it showed that when we put our minds to it, we can come up trumps. But I shall never forget what I was told by David Williams, editor of the weekly magazine, West Africa. We were having a drink at the bar in the conference centre on the last day, and I was congratulating ourselves for a job well done, when he said, 'Now you will begin to pay for it'. And how true his prophecy was. For within a few months the exchange rate for the Leone to the Sterling, went from two to one, to eighty to one. As I write today it is Le7500, or more, to one pound sterling.

So for the next eight years I worked as a Foreign National officer for USIS within the American Embassy. My duties included organising the visits of musicians, lecturers and artists from the US to visit and perform in Sierra Leone. I organised a photographer who came and photographed all the Paramount Chiefs in the country, the photographs were not only exhibited in Sierra Leone but across the US as well.

I had five different American bosses during the eight years I spent in the job. Initially, each of them felt they had arrived to invent the wheel. As a senior person in the department, I had to help them as much as possible so that they would not fall flat on their faces. Some listened to my advice that we have been doing things in a certain way and to have it changed would not be in the best interest of the service. I must say I had my work cut out, but all in all I got on well with most of them, except for one Edward Sullivan. Although we did not exactly quarrel, he was nevertheless the antithesis of what a boss in his position should be, or how he should behave in public and private!

Ed was a bluff, hard drinking, womanising but very likeable person, and he soon made it clear that he did not like to do any work. As he put it to me, 'you have been here long enough, and I am sure you can carry the department'. And carry the department I did. His day went like this. He would arrive in the office at around eleven in the morning, when by then I would have collected the unclassified cables from Washington for him to see. He would glance at them and pass them back to me to answer. I would then remind him that the classified cables needed to be collected by him, and that he should reply to them personally, as no other eyes should see them. He would reluctantly go to the classified section of the Embassy, a part no Sierra Leonean employee should enter, collect the cables, glance at them and pass them over to me to reply to. I would point out to him that only Americans are allowed to see classified cables, and his reply would be that there is nothing secret about any of the cables, and any way I had been in the Embassy long enough to know all its secrets. So I would do what my boss told me to do: read the classified cables, draft a reply to each and hand it over to him to read. Again, he would just glance at them, sign and I would send them off for transmission to Washington.

Luckily, as he was always mentioning, I had been there long enough to know how to frame my replies. By lunchtime, Ed would be off to some local dive, and drink and get drunk. He would then return to the office just before closing time, say hello to the staff, find out whether there was anything important that needed his attention, and off he would go to meet his local drinking buddies. Every night one would see the official car parked in some corner of the city, places at which he would pick up a girl for the night. Time and again, before Ed showed up for work, one of the security guards would come to inform me that some girl or other was outside asking for Ed, and would not leave until she had seen him. I

Reflection on my life

would go out to find out what she wanted. The reply was simple: Ed had not paid her for her services the night before. I would then pay the girl, so as not to embarrass him to the other Americans in the embassy.

But when Ed did appear at the office and I told him that I had paid his debt, he would say that I should not have paid her that much as she was not too good in bed anyway. He would then jovially refund what I had paid. I don't know how he did it, but I received word from Washington authorising me to collect, read and reply to classified cables from head office. I was later to find out that this was most unprecedented in the annals of USIS.

At that time I was not to sure whether his other Embassy colleagues knew about his exploits, but I found out later that they did. Ed slowly built up enough problems for himself to have him recalled to Washington. One blatant example was Ed going to the airport at Lungi to collect his own boss from Washington, who was on one of his periodic visits to the USIS in West Africa. Ed went with the office driver using the official car. According to the driver, Ed drank all the way on the ferry to the airport full of bonhomie, buying drinks for all and sundry. They arrived at the airport an hour before the flight was due, and, of course, Ed spent the time in the airport bar. He must have been completely blotto, because instead of waiting for all the passengers to come through customs and immigration, Ed ordered the driver to take him back to the ferry as he had not seen the person he had come to meet. The driver, being an old hand at this, suggested that they wait until all the passengers had come through before leaving the airport. But Ed overruled him and they left for the ferry terminal, where Ed went straight for the bar drinking until the ferry left.

I was at home when the Ambassador, who was a friend of the visitor, and with whom he was to stay, rang me to find out why no one had gone to the airport to meet his guest. I told him that Ed and the driver had gone to the airport and I did not know what had happened that they did not meet the visitor. It transpired that the visitor had indeed arrived and waited to be collected, but no one showed up. So he had got someone from the airport to call the Ambassador to find out what was happening. Luckily a Lebanese friend of the Ambassador had travelled on the same plane and was able to bring the visitor to the residency.

I had to drive down to the ferry terminal to meet Ed to inform him of what he had done, but he shrugged his shoulders and said he had made a mistake. I would have loved to be a fly on the wall when he met the Ambassador and his big boss from Washington the following day.

Ed's downfall took place at a dinner the Ambassador and his wife gave for some of the Sierra Leoneans who had been on visits to the US under the auspices of the USIS. Amongst the guests was the Minister of Education and his Russian born wife. Ed must have arrived worse for wear and, sitting next to the wife of the minister, started to insult the Russian nation. I tried to deflect his criticisms at one end of the table so that the Ambassador, sitting at the other end of the very long table, would not hear him. Unfortunately, the Ambassador's wife heard what he was saying and quietly asked Ed to come with her. I later heard that she quietly told him to leave her house and to start packing to leave the country immediately.

After all the other guests had departed, and there was only myself and the Political officer left, it was then it all came out about the exploits of Ed which were known by everyone in the Embassy, except the Ambassador and his wife. The ambassador did berate me for not bringing all this to his attention, as I had been friends with him and his wife, even before he became ambassador. But I defended myself by saying that Ed was my boss, and there was no way I was going to shop him.

Early the next morning there was a heavy knock on my door, and

Reflection on my life

when I opened it there was a contrite Ed apologising for his behaviour the night before, and asking whether I could put in a good word for him with the ambassador. I promised to do so and he left. That was the last time I saw of Ed Sullivan. He was packed off to stay at the airport hotel at Lungi until the next plane out of the country the following day. I heard later that he died of drink. We the staff, received letters of thanks from Washington, for the way we had run the department during the reign of Ed, and we were promised some compensation. Of course we all hoped that it would be some extra dollars in our pay packets, but we were disappointed. The compensation turned out to be a desk computer for each member of staff so that we did not have to use the only one we had until then. Ed was a great story teller and he claimed that he was in Rio drinking with the writer of the song THE GIRL FROM IPANIMA and knew the girl about whom the song was written. But I have since learned that most drunks in America, will tell the same story when they are really in their cups.

Ed was not the only American member of staff of the embassy to be packed out of the country in a hurry. One day I was in my office on the ground floor of the embassy on the Siaka Stevens side of the building, looking towards the Cotton tree. Suddenly I heard the screech of car brakes the blowing of car horns, and noise of people screaming. I looked through the security bars on the window and noticed some Leone bank notes floating from above and people scrambling to collect them, as they whirled to the middle of the road. I assumed that perhaps someone from the Nigerian embassy next door had dropped a wad of bank notes and that people were scrambling to collect some free money. This went on for a while, as the crowd became larger and the traffic became snarled up. I left my office and went outside to find out what was happening.

I had not gone out of the building when I was informed by the security guards that it was the US Marines, who had been sent to guard the embassy, who were throwing money from the roof of the embassy for fun, just to see the locals scrambling for free money and taking pictures. I cannot vouch for this, but I heard later that as the crowd grew larger and the noise grew louder, President Momoh heard this in his office at State House and began to make preparation to flee as he thought the crowd was coming for him. The long and short of the story was that the Marines were called in for a grave dressing down by the Lady Ambassador, and told to pack and go to stay at the airport until they could leave on next plane out of the country. The ambassador was called to State House to explain the antics of the marines and had to give an unqualified apology to the President.

The lady ambassador under whom I served was a formidable woman who had been appointed to her first ambassadorial post by the President of the United States. She had been a formidable fundraiser for him, and arrived in Sierra Leone with an older husband and two boys in their late teens. Now, I ask you, what can two American teenage boys do with themselves in Freetown? Nothing, but get up to mischief, which they often did and I had to rescue them from time to time. By then, both the American and some local staff had walkie talkie communications equipment, and we all had a call sign. My call sign was Headman. The downside of this was that everyone listened to every communication as we had to keep our equipment open in case we were needed. So I could not sleep well as every now and again the equipment would crackle into life as someone from the embassy would require a driver or other assistance.

So it was that, one night, I was awaken by the ambassador seeking my assistance to go and locate her boys who were somewhere on the town. I did not have a car at the time so she ordered a car to collect me to go on the search. I knew where to find them, as I had heard rumours that they frequented a bar on Lumley beach. They were reluctant to return with me and begged me to tell their mother that they could not be found. But I refused and brought them home to mama, who gave them a good dressing down. I don't remember if she thanked me for getting me out of my warm bed to find her loving sons. Her husband got a job heading the American school.

Down from the American embassy, on Walpole Street, was the Russian embassy, and as the cold war was then at its height the Russians suspected that those of us working for the Americans were all spies, and treated us as such. Of course they had their pet journalists amongst the local hacks, who from time to time would publish stories linking us to some spy plot or other. But we never took any notice of what they wrote, and were glad that they supplemented their meagre salaries with what they could get from the Bolsheviks!

As I mentioned earlier, Madam Ambassador was a large and formidable lady, and brooked no nonsense from anyone. At one time the embassy was looking to employ a local staff with economic experience, and as luck would have it, an experienced economic graduate, who had worked his way up to become a Permanent Secretary in government, had just retired. He fitted the criteria perfectly and, after an interview, was appointed. Two days after he took up office, a journalist, who was obviously in the pay of the Russians, wrote a headline grabbing story which intimated that the poor man had been in the pay of the Americans while serving the Sierra Leone government all along, and had been passing government secrets to his paymasters. And to compensate him, they had given him a well-paid dollar job in the embassy on his retirement.

On the morning the story appeared, the CID people came to the Embassy, and took him in for questioning. As soon as the ambassador arrived for work and heard about the arrest, especially as it took place at the embassy, thus American grounds, she left her office, came out of the building to get her car, and asked me to accompany her to State House up the road from the embassy. Unfortunately the car was not there, and instead calling for another embassy car, she took to walking up the road, furious and puffing until she reached State House. She demanded to see President Momoh at once, and of course she was ushered in to see him without any ceremony.

I stood there as she berated our Head of State about the protocol around a foreign embassy, the sanctity of which was inviolate. And how dare they imply that a nation as important as the U.S. would plant a spy inside the Sierra Leone government etc, etc. I never saw Momoh so apologetic in my life. After listening to her outburst, he was able to pacify the ambassador and assure her that there was no truth in the newspaper allegation; I suspect he had not even seen the article. He immediately ordered his secretary to see that the person was released at once, and to find out who had ordered his arrest in the first place!

After she had been pacified by the President, she was offered a cold drink, which she accepted. By the time we returned to the embassy, the man had been released and back at work. I never found out what happened to the person who ordered the arrest in the first place. As I said, she was a formidable lady. I left the embassy before her time came to an end, and always wondered what happened to her. But a colleague who also worked in the embassy with me at the same time told me sometime later that she had met one of the sons in Kigali, where she was working for USAID, and he was working for one of the UN agencies. So he did make good after all.

Not all the Americans who worked at the embassy were that bad. The wife of one Ambassador, who was an academic and was a highly paid Professor at a prestigious university in Washington, gave her time freely to Fourah Bay College. She was given the six students who were doing their master's degree, and she drove regularly up to the college to supervise them. When there was one of those palavers that students have from time to time, and the college had to close for some weeks, she told her students that if they could come to the Residency at 10 o'clock in the morning, she could continue her lectures, and, what was more enticing, provide them with lunch. She did this for six weeks until the college reopened. Many years later, I met one of her students who was working for one of the UN agencies in of all places Indonesia. She could not praise the Ambassador's wife too highly, for seeing her through her studies, to the point where she was able to secure an international job. She was very sad when I informed her that her benefactor had died earlier that year.

ARNOLD AWOONOR-GORDON

Chapter 28
IN THE LAND OF BARBEQUE AND THE GRAND OLE OPERY

Visiting the United States of America for the first time can be daunting for anyone, as I found out when I first went there. Of course I had seen photos and films of the place and had been amazed at the tall skyscraper buildings especially of New York. So, when I flew in one morning, after an overnight flight from Dakar, I had the impression, as we flew over New York that the plane would be dodging between the tall buildings. But we flew over them and landed safely at the airport. It was then I experienced what is known as jet lag.

I had to change planes at the airport as my final destination was Washington. Whilst waiting in the departure lounge I remembered that I had been given several stamped addressed envelopes to post for friends, and seeing a post box by the checking in counter I posted the letters. And horror of horrors, I saw myself posting my passport as well. It was like a bad dream, watching myself posting my passport with the letters. I told the nearest check-in clerk what I had done, and she told me that if I was lucky the post box would be opened before my plane left, but if not, she advised that I write my Washington address on an envelope she gave me, and she would see that the passport was sent on to me when the post box was cleared.

When I told my hosts in Washington what had happened, they, and everyone who heard the story said the same thing. I would be very lucky to get back my passport as all New Yorkers were thieves and robbers, and a passport so easily found would be sold on the black market in no time. They were all wrong. For three days afterwards my passport arrived safely. This was my first taste of the friendly rivalry that exists between not only Washington and New York but also between cities and states in that great country.

I must here recount something I saw in New York on a later visit. It was at the end of summer, when the air was turning cold and I was waiting at a bus stop in the centre of town. I noticed a young man sitting by the pavement, begging. No one took any notice of him as people rushed to and fro on their way to their business. What I noticed was that the young man had no shirt, tee shirt, top coat or jacket, and was half naked. Then a student type young man stopped, knelt down by the beggar and spoke to him. He then took off the top coat he was wearing, removed all the things in the pocket and helped the young beggar to put it on. Then he was on his way. I must have been the only person standing at the bus stop to notice this act of kindness, as all the others were intent on looking out for the next bus. Who says New Yorkers are not kind?

Whilst working for the Americans I had the opportunity of visiting the United States on several occasions, mostly to attend courses in order to enhance the work I was doing. I remember one course in particular. It took place at the University of Chicago, and it was to do with the media and public relations. One of the tasks we had to perform was to take a video camera and go out in the streets to make a ten minute film about any subject of our choice. I decided to make a film about the fat people. I had noticed in the streets that the people, especially the black women, were indeed very fat, and I had to film surreptitiously so that I would not be caught filming. But I was caught by a very large black woman, bulging out of her top and wearing shorts which exposed her very large thighs. She angrily approached me and said 'What you doing boy?' In a very small voice I said I was making a film for my school work. I think she realised that, by my accent, I was not an American. She said 'Where you from, boy?' 'West Africa,' I replied. 'You from Africa?' she asked with a broad smile, and when I said yes I was, she shocked me by saying 'let me embrace my roots,' and she clasped me to her very ample bosom and nearly squeezed the life out of me. She then posed for me to film her. I stopped the filming then and ran back to college to relate my experience.

Once I happened to visit the United States in the summer, and during the July 4 Independence celebrations I received several invitations to spend the day with American hosts families, and from some Sierra Leone families too. I chose the Sierra Leone families for no other reason than that I was tired of eating the same American food over and over again, and wanted to eat some good home Salone food. I was mistaken, because every Sierra Leone family I visited wanted to show me how they had assimilated into the American way of life, and to do so, they organised the same old backyard barbecue. I got fed up with eating burned hamburger and sausages, I don't like them anyway, and hinted to one of my hostesses that I would prefer some home cooking. She took the hint, by going to her vast freezer and pulled out a bowl of dry fish palm oil stew, which she thawed, cooked some white rice, and this did the trick. Palm oil stew had never tasted so good, and I have liked palm oil stew since then! Two fingers to your backyard barbecue.

One thing I found amongst Americans was how ignorant they were, not only about Africa, but also the world in general. All their news was about what happened in the area they lived in, and to hell with the outside world. How insular they were is illustrated by this example. One place I wanted to visit, while in the States for the first time, was Nashville, Tennessee, the home of country and Western music. The African-Americans I met could not understand why I liked what they termed 'White folks music' and were surprised when I told them that Jim Reeves was very popular in Africa, even after he was dead. But I did not listen to them and was very pleased when my African- American hosts arranged for me to attend one of the weekly country music stage concerts at the Grand Ole Opery. I

Reflection on my life

could not persuade them to accompany me, and looked wide eyed when I sang some of the songs I knew from listening to Jim Reeves when I was young.

Dedicated to honouring country music, Grand Ole Opery, which I understand it is a corruption of GRAND OLD OPERA, showcases a mix of legends and contemporary chart-stoppers performing country, bluegrass and folk music. They attract hundreds of thousands of visitors from around the world, in addition to millions of radio and internet listeners. Rightly called 'the home of American music' its' famous stage has seen the likes of Jim Reeves, Johnny Cash, Dolly Parton, Hank Williams, Patsy Cline, Garth Brooks and the Carter Family, nearly all the most famous and well known country singers. Although when I visited none of these singers performed during my visit, just being in the home of country music was enough to last me a lifetime.

I must here recount something that happened to me, which I am sure has happened to some of you. That of eavesdropping on the start of a conversation by someone, and not finding out the end. I was in a department store in Chicago and stopped to look at the jewellery counter. Standing there were two very well dressed Jewish ladies in fur coats, examining some jewellery with the assistant. Another lady, who was not so well dressed, joined them, and she was introduced to one of the ladies. This is how the introduction went. 'This is Sarah. She was a friend of Anna Frank.' Of course my ears pricked up, as I wanted to hear about Anna Frank from someone who had been a friend of hers. I moved closer so I could hear what was being said, but I was disappointed. For the lady she was introduced to said 'Nice to meet you, Sarah. But what have you done to your hair? It is a mess. I must take you to my hairdresser and she would do wonders with your hair,' and so on and so on, but nothing about Anna Frank. So after a few minutes of this stuff about hair, I drifted off as there was no point in lingering because it was obvious that nothing would be said about what I wanted to hear.

Another incident like that happened to me at another time. I was waiting for the lights to change at Piccadilly Circus in London, opposite the Haymarket. Standing next to me were two old ladies, one leaning a walking stick. Suddenly I heard the one with the walking stick, pointing towards the Haymarket, say 'I lost Ethel down there one day.' My ears pricked up to hear more about Ethel and how she got lost. But before she could say another word, the lights changed and we all moved as one body to cross the road. Till today, I wonder who Ethel was, and how she got lost down the Haymarket in the West end of London.

And while on the subject of Embassies I was around in London when Sierra Leone gained its independence, and took part in the tableau to celebrate it. The High Commissioner was Dr Richard Kelfa-Caulker and his wife Olivette. The celebrations took place in the Guildhall in the city of London, and I shall never forget the emotions we felt as the union jack was lowered, and the new Sierra Leone flag was raised in its place. We then sang our new national anthem, which we had learned, for the first time. It was a most memorable event.

I was also in at the beginning of the purchase and occupation of our new High Commission building at 33 Portland Place, a building which we have now lost. The interior was used for the film, The Kings Speech. It was a splendid building at the time and much suited to showcasing our country. It was centrally located and even had a mews flat at the back. It is sad that we no longer have use of such a splendid building.

And while we are on the subject of the High Commission building, it was there that I witnessed a most bizarre incident, something that was heart stopping when it happened. It involved the Star of Sierra Leone. This gem weighed 968.9 carat and had been found on 14 February 1972 in the Diminco alluvial mines in the Koidu area of

Reflection on my life

Sierra Leone. It ranks as the 3rd largest gem-quality diamond and the largest alluvial diamond ever found. The diamond had been brought to London for sale, and of course there was much publicity given to the diamond, and a press conference was arranged at 33 Portland Place to which hundreds of people from the media were invited. In fact the place was so full that people were standing in the corridors and by the lift shaft. The High Commissioner at the time was Dr Davidson Nicol, former Principal of Fourah Bay College. There was much expectation as the great stone was taken out of its case, unwrapped and handed to the High Commissioner. As he took it, for some reason he dropped the diamond. There was an audible gasp from the assembled audience, as it rolled under the table. But we need not have gasped, as the man from the company laughingly reached under the table and rescued the Star of Sierra Leone. He then explained that a diamond is one of the hardest stones on earth and dropping it on the floor made no difference to the quality or hardness of the stone. We all breathed a collective sigh of relief. In October that year the President announced that Harry Winston, the New York Jeweller, had purchased our most valuable asset for under $2.5 million. Oh Salone!

I was also around when Sierra Leone became the one hundredth member of the United Nations, and enjoyed the party that took place to celebrate the momentous occasion.

Chapter 29
IN THE SEASON OF LIFE AND DEATH

During the time I was with USIS in Freetown, I kept hearing about HIV/AIDS, and in fact one of the members of our gang in London, had the dreaded disease and was dying. In his last letter he wrote me, he said that I should do something to help especially black people, who had no support. He then said, why not return to London to help start something? After he died I kept thinking about what he had said in his letter, and made up my mind to pack in the job in Freetown and return to London to see what I could do. As soon as I got back to London, I got myself attached to the Terrence Higgins Trust, the only charity then doing something to help people with HIV/AIDS.

The name Terrence Higgins, now so well known, was at the time a name to bring fear into the minds of people. Terrence Higgins, aged 37, was a gay man who was one of the first persons in the UK to die of the disease on the 4th of July 1982. Because much was not known about the disease at the time, he was treated very badly in hospital, was isolated with everyone afraid to go near him. He died a miserable death. And even when he died, the undertakers shunned the body and it took a great deal of persuasion before he could be buried.

His partner and his friends were so shocked and angry at the way he was treated in life and in death that they set up the charity in his name. It was to raise funds for research as a way of preventing suffering due to HIV/ AIDS. The trust was named after Terrence Higgins in order to personalise and humanise the sensitive if delicate issue. Today the trust is considered to be the UK's leading HIV and AIDS charity and also the largest in Europe.

But, when I joined the Trust as a volunteer, it was still struggling to raise funds to help and support people with the disease, and also to educate the public that HIV/AIDS was not a gay man's disease, as the newspapers were fond of calling it, but was something that can affect anyone who engages in unprotected sex. The trust organised training course to train people on how to handle people with HIV/AIDS, and I went on one of the courses. The training covered HIV/AIDS counselling, sexuality and homosexuality, how to deal with death and loss, client centred counselling skills and special issues on HIV/AIDS. We were also trained in budding skills.

After the training ended, I was put with a trained counsellor to conduct counselling of young people who had the disease, and as I progressed, I was able to conduct counselling on my own. Some - times this took place at the centre or in the hospital where the person had been admitted. It was the trust which started the budding scheme, which has become a part of the help and support for people with HIV/AIDS. Early on it was found that people with the disease were shunned and became estranged from their families and friends, and no one wanted to be with, or visit them. So in order to provide help and support, each person we dealt with was provided with a buddy, someone who was not ill him/herself, who would visit them, take them out to hospital appointments and generally be a buddy to them. In no time at all we had a network of over two hundred people willing to become buddies. They received training, especially on how to handle death and loss, as at that time, before HIV/AIDS drugs were developed, people who caught the disease, died like flies. So one had to be trained to be able not to grieve over the loss of the person one was buddy to. I also did some training to upgrade my skills in face to face counselling with the National AIDS Trust.

It was while I was working with the Terrence Higgins Trust that I realised that although there were black people who had caught the disease, yet there were no support mechanism especially for them. The trust had been set up in response to the threat of the AID/HIV virus which it was felt affected everyone and open to all, whether gay or straight, men and women, white and black people. But unfortunately at the time, because the trust was set up by gay men and many of the people they supported were gay men, black people, straight men and women did not feel comfortable mixing with gay men at the centre, or to be with them in group counselling or at meetings.

I questioned this mixing of the people, especially as I realised that there were many black people needing help and support, equally as the gay men, who were predominant and were forceful in claiming their rights within the charity, as it was felt that the trust was set up and run for them, and for them only. The people who were in charge also felt the same, but when I questioned them they said they were open to everyone and they did not discriminate against anyone. I was not happy with this, and so, with some friends, I decided to setup another charity that would help and support black people who needed help.

From the front room of my house in Balham, South London, the Charity Blackliners was born. The mission statement of the charity stated that it was to provide for the welfare of people of the African, Asian and Caribbean communities in Britain, who are living with, or affected by HIV/AIDS; to enable better sexual health amongst the target communities, and to provide for the general health of the communities. I chose a logo of a telephone at one end and a man beating a drum at the other; it was like a means of communication from one instrument to the other, one African, the other European. We started with a telephone helpline, and I was surprised at how ignorant black people were not only about the disease, but health issues in general. I remember one of the very first calls we received was from a Caribbean man who wanted to know whether he could catch the disease from using one condom over and over again. We had to tell him that condoms should be used once and then disposed of. He then said that he could not afford condoms as they were too expensive. But by then, as condoms were being provided free by

Reflection on my life

the government, I was able to point him in the right direction to obtain free condoms.

At the time we started the helpline, there were stories in the media that AIDS came from Africa and from monkeys. We used to receive calls asking whether this was true and how many black people we dealt with and so on. People from the press would pretend they were black people and call hoping to catch us up to give them the information from our data base. But we needed the press to get the word out that we were there for the black community, and turned to the black press for this. I must say at first they were not too enthusiastic about getting involved with HIV/AIDS, but with perseverance we did break down the barrier of suspicion.

The churches and the black population were not too keen on getting involved as, at the time; the disease was associated with sex, and gay sex at that, something that should not be spoken about too loudly. But this has now changed. The year we started was the year that World Aids Day, on December 1st, was inaugurated by the WHO.

I printed and published a Blackliners Helpline World Aids Day Declaration on AIDS and the Black/Ethnic Minority Communities poster. I was happy when over forty prominent black celebrities such as Earth Kitt, Nene Cherry the singer, Clarke Peters, the actor, Steve Pope, editor of the VOICE newspaper, Keith Vaz, MP, Dame Jocelyn Barrow, Hugh Masekela, South African musician, Paul Boateng, MP, and the footballer John Fashanu signed the declaration, which called on the British government to become more sensitive to the needs of black people where the issue of HIV/AIDS was concerned.

The Vicar in charge of the Church where I worshipped regularly was the Rev. John Sentamu, now the Archbishop of York. I approached him to find out whether he would be willing to say something about HIV/ AIDS in his sermon to the congregation on World AIDS DAY, which happened to fall on a Sunday. He was very supportive and based his sermon about compassion for sick people in general, and people with HIV/AIDS in particular. I was not at church that day as I had to attend a service in London to mark the day. But when I next saw him he said that a few of his parishioner, did mention after the service, that HIV/AIDS was not something to preach about. This was not surprising as ninety percent of the congregation were from the black community in the area.

But with perseverance we succeeded in obtaining funds from the local council, for by then the government, through the Ministry of Health, had woken up to the spread of the disease, which was decimating large numbers of people, and costing the National Health Service a great deal of money. As the only charity helping the black community in London, we were able to obtain funding to move into offices in Brixton, buy furniture and pay salaries for two people to run the charity. We were also able to get some volunteers to man the helpline so it could be opened for a longer period.

As soon as we got charity status from the Charity Commission we were able to attract a number of high profile patrons, such as Lady Colin Campbell as chair, the Members of Parliament Paul Boateng and the late Bernie Grant, Benjamin Zaphaniah the Rap poet, Carmen Monroe, actress; Dame Jocelyn Barrow, Nene Cherry, singer, Hugh Masakela, the South African musician, John Roberts QC and the High Commissioner for Sierra Leone, HE Caleb Aubee. We had a ten strong board of directors to set policy and oversee the charity. They appointed me Director/Counsellor to run the day affairs of the Charity.

During the first eight months of the helpline opening longer, we handled 358 calls directly concerned with advice, counselling and support from black people needing our services. By the end of the first twelve months, six hundred and fifty-seven calls had been received by the helpline, with seventy-five percent coming from men, and the rest from women. Some of the main queries and types of problems of concern to the callers, ranged from where to obtain condoms, to infection from oral sex, to whether it was safe for pregnant women to take the HIV/AIDS antibody test; was AIDS a gay Whiteman's disease, the problem of false positive tests and the pros and cons of the AZT drug.

The AZT drug was in its trial stage at the time and we got the impression that black women in particular were being pressurised into going on the trial. The majority of the calls we received came from London, but as our name spread, we were getting calls from Scotland, Manchester, Birmingham, Bristol, Cardiff, Leeds and Liverpool. We even received a call from Rome and Paris, where there were no facilities for the black community.

One of the problems faced then by people with the disease was housing. It was bad enough for people from the white community, but it was much worse for a black person. People with HIV/AIDS were regularly thrown out of their accommodation when the landlord found out. This was brought home clearly to me when just as we were closing the office at midday on Christmas Eve, a young black youth of about nineteen came to see us to report that he had been thrown out of his room by his mother, when she found out first that he was gay, and second that he had caught the disease. On Christmas Eve, where in London were we to find accommodation for a young black man with AIDS? Luckily one of our volunteers, who had the disease himself, had a spare room in his house and he offered to put him up.

It was then I realised the extent of the housing situation for people with AIDS and decided to do something about it. I approached several Housing Associations in the area to find out what their attitudes were to black people in particular, who were HIV positive.

Most of them had not realised that there was a problem, but were not too keen to get involved, except for one: The Threshold Single Persons Housing Association, whose director I came to know very well. The idea I put to her was that perhaps we could raise funds to purchase a house and convert it into rooms that we could let out to black people with HIV/AIDS. She put this to her board of Trustees, as I did to mine, and they agreed.

Now, we had to raise the funds. Of all the companies and organisations we approached with our plan, only one invited us to go and see them. It was the charity arm of one of the large and well known housing construction companies. I remember well going to see them at their offices in Notting Hill Gate and being made very welcome by a rather young man, whom we later learned, was the head of the charity division of the company. He was very gracious as he listened to the plan we had brought for him to see. Our plan was to raise the funds to purchase a house and do it up into rooms, to be let out to single young black people who were HIV positive. He listened to our spill rather impassively. When we had finished, what he said made our hearts sink. He said the plan we had would be too expensive to carry out, as, from experience, renovating a house had lots of dangers. Then he said 'Why not build something from scratch? Then you can have something that would suit your needs, and it will not be as expensive as renovating an old house.'

We looked nonplussed. Where were we going to raise that much money to construct something from scratch? Seeing our down cast look, he said 'Go find the land and we will build it for you.' He saw that our eyes were wide open, with a mixture of joy and apprehension: joy at the prospect of his building the house for us, but apprehension about where to get the land. Then, as though we were hearing a fairy godfather come to our complete rescue, he added: 'I know our company has some land in Lambeth. I will see whether it is still free. Leave it to me and I will get back to you.' We could have fallen down and kissed his feet as he ushered us out of his office. As soon as we were out of site in the street, we hugged and kissed each other like school children.

So it was that both charities were able to design and build six one-bedroom bungalows, with all the conveniences that a person suffering from the disease would need. Soon we had a long list of young men needing our accommodation. We did have some palaver with the local council who wanted to be the sole organisation to select tenants for the accommodation. They wanted to cash in on the very hard work we had done.

While I was working for the charity, I realised that I was lacking in administration skills, and so took a part time course in Public Administration and Policy at Birkbeck College, University of London. After I completed the course, I had the opportunity of doing a full-time degree course in the same subjects, but it would be at Bristol University, miles away from London. It would mean having to give up my job with the charity, as I could not do both at the same time. I was in a dilemma. Go to Bristol and get some more academic experience or stay in London and continue working for the charity. Rather reluctantly I gave up the job and moved to Bristol.

But I left the Charity, which was my baby, in very good and capable hands, and I must say the hands were very capable. For they took the charity to a point where within a year they had raised enough funds to expand it to include more housing projects, providing home care and support, providing a more ethnocentric counselling for men and women, having a drop-in centre, expanding the volunteering to provide more support in budding and home support, organising educational and outreach programmes in schools and colleges in all London boroughs, domiciliary home-care for people housebound. During that period the full-time paid staff reached ten in order to provide these services, and soon the charity became not only a service to help people in the black community who are HIV positive, but a fully- fledged health service providing for the needs of the black communities. They had partnerships with the Primary Health Care Trusts, with all the London National Health Service Trusts, and with the Family Planning Association. I must say that I was very proud with the development of the baby I had given birth to from the front room of my house in Balham!

Working in the HIV/AID field with African and Caribbean people, had its traumatic sides. I was contacted by the Governor of one of the prisons in London and invited me to come and see him. It appears that he had the first confirmed HIV/AID prisoner in his care, who was an African, and he wanted advice as to how to treat him. The young man's case was a sad on. He came from Uganda with his wife and two children, and soon after they arrived in the UK, they were both diagnosed as HIV positive. Like most people I came across at the time when not so much was known about the disease, he was in denial and accused his wife of passing on the disease to him. They had a flaming row, as she accused him of sleeping with prostitutes, catching the disease and passing it on to her. He hit her, she fell and hit her head and passed out. She was taken to hospital and died two weeks later leaving the two children under five. Of course he was charged with manslaughter and sentenced to five years in prison. Unfortunately, the newspapers had a field day, with the headlines that claimed the disease did indeed come from Africa and people should be afraid to be with people from the African Continent.

So the prison Governor wanted to know how to support the young man, as he had to be isolated from the other prisoners, who would harm him if he mixed with them. One of the problem he had was the diet of the prisoner, as he had to be able to provide the type of food he wanted. I assigned one of our volunteers, who were from Uganda to become a buddy to him, and who would visit him twice a week, to support him. On the food side, this was difficult as we

Reflection on my life

were not allowed to bring him any food from outside. But with the help of his buddy, a menu was drawn up for the cook, and twice a week he was able to eat food from his country. I don't know how he fared as by then I had left the charity to go to Bristol.

The other case I remember was referred to us from one of the largest hospital in London that had a ward set aside for people with the disease. This guy was born in the Caribbean, came to the UK and worked for several years, before moving to New York. He was there at the outset of the HIV/AID epidemic, when New York was a place for free love and where the disease spread like wildfire. He was thrown out of his apartment, and at that time, the blacks in America had their heads in the sands, and thought the disease was a whiteman's disease, and blacks did not get it. So, of course all his friends would have nothing to do with him, and he ended up sleeping in his car. It was then he decided that he would return to the UK where medical treatment was free and non-judgemental.

As soon as he arrived he was admitted into the hospital. The welfare officer contacted us so that he could support him as he had no family or friends here. We arranged for weekly supply of Caribbean food to be frozen and sent to the hospital for him, and I or someone used to visit him once a week. When I told him that I was going to New York for a visit, he asked me to bring back some 'coke' for him as the 'coke' in New York was better than everywhere else. You would not believe it, for when he asked for 'coke' I honestly thought he meant 'coke' as in Coca Cola. It was when I mentioned it to the friends I was staying with in New York, that they enlightened me that he meant 'coke' as in cocaine. Of course I did not bring back any, but it would not have made any difference as he died while I was away.

Chapter 30
A BEND IN THE RIVER: MY LIFE GOES ON A NEW PATH

While I was in Bristol, I stayed in touch with 'my baby' by working part time for the Alex Richard Trust, an HIV/AID charity that, like the Terrence Higgins Trust, had been founded in the name of one of the first persons in Bristol to die of HIV/AIDS. I only worked between lectures so it did not disturb my studies in any way. I would also volunteer for Blackliners whenever I was in London. It was during one such visit that I was introduced to the director of the London Marriage Guidance service, an organisation that provided counselling and mediation for couples who were separating or divorcing, and did not want to do so in an adversarial manner. She asked me what I was doing and what I had done, then mentioned that her organisation were not getting any black couples coming to them for mediation and counselling. She wondered whether it was because not as many black people separated and divorced as couples from the white community. I said that I did not think this was the case, and she offered me a short contract to do some research into this.

I started my research in Bristol before the end of my course, as Bristol had a large black population, something I did not know until I went there. I started with the solicitors dealing with divorce in the city, and expanded my research to London when I returned. My researches showed that many black people as white people, did divorce and separate, but they did not know about marriage counselling. It seemed that it was not in the interest of their lawyers to tell them about the alternative to the adversarial system of separation and divorce. It was all about money. While doing the research I got the idea that a marriage counselling and mediation service, set up especially for the black community, would work

Reflection on my life

well, just as I had established Blackliners. So, after submitting the report of my research, and as I completed my course and had my degree, I decided to create the African Caribbean Family Mediation Service in Brixton, with the support of the London Marriage Guidance Service. The logo I chose for this charity was of a black family, father, mother and two children, a boy and a girl standing together in silhouette.

As usual, with my contacts in the black community, it was not difficult to find like-minded people to come on the board of Trustees. I applied for, and received charity status from the Charity Commission. I also applied for, and was fortunate to obtain funding from the National Lottery Charities Board. Our patrons were the late Sir Banja Tejan-Sie, Ambassador Arthur Lewis, Paul Boateng MP and John Roberts QC. The statement of intent of the charity was to develop a family mediation service that was child-centred, for people from Africa and the Caribbean, who are divorcing or separating, that will respond promptly to take advantage of new developments in the divorce laws of the United Kingdom. To make mediation accessible to as many black people as possible, to train and support more black family mediators to provide an ethnocentric family mediation service.

After advertising and recruiting ten men and women to become our first mediators, they were given intensive training by the National Mediation who also provided a practice supervisor to help us during our initial stage of operation. As soon as our funding came through I was appointed full time director by the board of trustees, and set about seeking fund to expand the service. As the service became well known in the black community, we began to receive more and more referrals so that by the end of the first year we had received 22% of clients from Lewisham, 30% from Lambeth, 18% from Southwark and 27% from Wandsworth. We also received funds from eleven funding sources, which enabled us to expand our helpline service and recruit and train more mediators.

One of the biggest problems, when mediating between divorcing or separating couples, was how to deal with the children. They became our paramount problem as families started to disintegrate. What to do with them when the father lives apart from the mother and how is he to have contact with them? Research has shown it is better for the young ones to have contact with both parents during what is a stressful period for all concerned. We found that the only place the children were taken to meet the father, usually, was at MacDonald's or at KFC. They needed a safe and secure place for them to meet. So we raised funds to set up a child contact centre, which was opened and staffed by a trained supervisor and her volunteer helpers drawn from local colleges and institutions. The centre became an integral part of the African Caribbean Mediation Service, and is still up and running until today under a new management.

While we were concentrating on mediating between separating and divorcing couples, I received a visit from a black lady who had a problem. Her son had been expelled from school and needed someone to help her mediate between her and the authorities so her son could go back to school. I informed her that we only mediated between couples and not between parents and schools. She looked downcast and said that she thought mediation was mediation, and it was between people whether couples or schools. Just to please her, I agreed to help.

The Head of the school was very accommodating when I went to see her, and welcomed my intervention. She explained that the boy in question, who was only fourteen, was very bright and could do well, but he was always playing truant and although she had given him several warnings, he had not changed. I asked whether she had told his mother about his truancy, but she said she had never met the mother, even though she had sent several letters to her. I asked whether she would like to meet the mother with me there, and she agreed. It transpired, later, that the mother was not too literate and

Reflection on my life

the son had never given, nor read the letter to her. The outcome of the matter was that, at that meeting with the mother and her son, it was the first time the mother knew about the truancy of her son. We discussed what to do if he was reinstated, and she promised to walk to school with him every morning, which I am sure the young man would not like. She would also call the school each day to see whether he was there. The mediation went well as it was the first time all three had got together to sort out the problem. It was something the head said that set me thinking. She said that, if only there was someone to mediate between her and the parents, her life would be made easier. She longed for the old days when each school had its own truancy officer, a post that had been abolished in schools during her lifetime as a teacher.

This seemed a valid concern, so I decided to discuss the matter with the trustees. It was agreed that I should look into the possibility of setting up a home/school mediation service, where we could have trained mediators who would mediate to defuse situations that could lead to the expulsion of pupils from schools. I investigated this and found a charity in north London that had such a scheme. I worked with them and put together a plan in order to obtain funds to set up the scheme. With such an innovative project it was very easy to obtain the funds to set it up, and we were very fortunate to recruit a wonderful and brilliant young lady by the name of Gillian Bowen as Project Co- ordinator, who within a very short time had the project up and running. After training the mediators, they were attached to eight schools in South London, six secondary and two primaries, and soon more and more schools were requesting our services. The service was able to provide mediation between teacher and pupils, which was very rewarding, when both parties were given a chance to appreciate the sensitivities and purpose of the different roles.

One of the situations that the mediator was able to defuse, and which I remember to this day, went like this. The boy was from a single mother family, who came from Somalia. He was always late for school, and was in danger of being excluded. Fortuitously, a teacher called in one of our mediators to find out why this pupil was always late. It turned out that his mother had two other young children and was trying to keep a job as well. So, in the morning, she had one child in the buggy, and she needed the school boy to help her take them to the child minder. By the time he had done this, he was invariably late for school. The problem was solved when we twisted the arm of Social Services to provide a double buggy for the mother, so she could take both children to the child minder, thus releasing her son to go to school on time.

At the end of the first year of operation the service was evaluated by the National Children's Bureau, which found that the Home/School Mediators had established contact with, and solved 153 situations that would have led to expulsion. I am afraid the Project Co-ordinator did such a good job that, in her second year, after I had left, she was headhunted by the Department of Education to set up a division to run Home/School Mediation nationwide. I am sure she succeeded in her new position.

By then I was getting tired as age was creeping up on me. So I retired as the Director/Counsellor of the charity and relocated from London to Chatham in Kent, the garden of England. By this time the charity had grown beyond all expectation, with a thriving family mediation service, a child contact centre and the Home/School Mediation Service. Later a men's counselling service was added. The full time paid staff had grown to six with the addition of a full time administrator/finance officer, and a business manager. With funding from the Lord Chancellor's Department, the service had also set up partnership with London Marriage Guidance Service as an outreach service in South London. The year I left we had provided mediation and counselling for over 145 couples, some on a short term and some on long term basis, and the number of children who used the contact centre regularly numbered 45. So,

Reflection on my life

when I retired, the service was fully established and being well managed.

One of the most unusual mediation cases we handled was the one I referred to as 'The man with two wives.' The background of the case was this. The man from Nigeria, had been in an arranged marriage for five years and sadly he and his wife were still childless. As a result the family back home persuaded him that they would find a younger wife for him, who would produce the children he so much craved. With the consent of his wife, he agreed. This I think was his, and hers first mistake.

He went back to Nigeria and 'married' the young lady according to native law and customs of the tribe, and brought her back to London as his 'sister', to live with the other wife in the marital home. Things went well and the young 'sister' gave birth to twins, one boy and one girl. The older wife, was glad and took to looking after the children gladly. Things went on peacefully, and the 'sister' had another child, a boy this time. And again the older wife cared for the new child as her own.

Everything would have gone on as it was, if the new wife had not met some friends from her home town, whom, we later learned, informed her that her marriage was not legal in the United Kingdom, and if and when the man was tired of her, he would send her back home and take the children away from her. She, therefore, started to put pressure on the man to divorce his wife and marry her. He refused, of course, and the atmosphere in the house became unbearable, so much so that the first wife could not stand it any longer. She asked the husband to get rid of his 'sister' or she would report him for bringing her to the UK illegally.

There were rows and arguments almost every day, which came to a head, when the 'sister' stabbed the older woman and was arrested and charged with attempted murder. It was then we were brought in by the solicitors to mediate between the husband and the wife. In order to save the 'sister' from going to jail for a long spell, it was decided that the wife would plead that in fact she had started the row that lead to the stabbing, claiming it was entirely her fault that the row had got out of hand. But, at her lawyer's instigation, she would agree to do so if she was given full custody of the children, and also agree to divorce her husband so he can marry his paramour, as the lawyer called her. The mediation went on for several days, with each side wanting more and refusing to give in. In the end we came to an agreement whereby the wife would have custody of the twins, she would then divorce the husband who would then marry his paramour and keep the son. The husband also had to agree to let the wife have the marital home, and a monthly allowance to bring up the children. While we were taking part in the mediation process, it was discovered that the 'sister' was again pregnant. The outcome of all this was that the 'sister' wife was found guilty of the lesser charge of grievous bodily harm, and given two years suspended sentence. I left the charity soon after and did not know how it all ended. I hope that the man married the young 'sister', she gave birth to a girl, and they all lived happily after. The surprising thing was that the fact of her illegal entry into the country was never revealed during her trial.

During my journey in this life I have visited many countries, met many people and observed many cultures and customs. One of the most memorable trip I made in my life was to China. I had in my mind's eye the old China of houses with umbrella shaped roofs, and people walking around in pyjama type clothes, and the traditional bamboo hats. I was disappointed, as cities like Beijing looked like cities in other countries of the world, with sky scraper buildings, wide boulevards with lots of new and shiny cars causing the usual traffic jams, and polluting the air. Not a house in sight that was the symbol of what I had come to imagine China was like. This was the old China, but the new China was a modern and vibrant country, with the people dressed like people all over the world, and no pyjama style clothes in sight. I understand the people from outside

Reflection on my life

the large cities were not allowed to dress in that way to come into town, nor were they to wear those bamboo hats.

So what we came looking for had disappeared. But right in the middle of Beijing, a small corner of old China had been preserved, and this became a tourist hot spot. The houses were as we had imagined, some of the people wore the pyjama style clothes, and above all, the old type bamboo hats. There were also rickshaws to take us round. Of course like rubber neck tourists everywhere, we dashed around snapping people and houses and going into the latter to see how the people lived. I must say they were used to tourists and did not mind us in the least.

Of course the place we all wanted to visit was Tienanmen Square. It was a place we have all heard of, because it was the focal point of the students protest in 1989, a pro-democracy movement that was so brutally put down by the authorities and broadcast on the world's television. And the most ironic and famous image that appeared on our television screens, was that of the lone man standing in front of the moving tanks who refuses to move, even when the tanks tried to move around him. For many years the international media have been trying to find this man, with no success.

The name Tienanmen means 'the Gate to the Forbidden City', and was designed and built in 1651, and enlarged to its present size in the 1950s. It has been at the centre of some of the most turbulent events to take place in China. Apart from the students protest in 1989, perhaps the most notable was the protest during the May Fourth Movement in 1919, the proclamation of the People's Republic of China by Moa Zedong in 1949, and the Tienanmen Square protest after the death of Premier Chu En-lai. Today the square is dominated by the large portrait of Mao Zedong on one side of the square, on the other side is his mausoleum, and the Great Hall of the Peoples and the National Museum.

The Forbidden City to which the square leads, and which we

visited, was the Chinese Imperial Palace, built in 1420. For almost 500 years it served as the home of the emperors and their household, as well as political centre of the Chinese government. No Chinese person was allowed to set foot in this city, who did not belong to the Royal Household. Thus its name. It now houses the Palace museum and is a UNESCO World Heritage Site.

One place I was anxious to visit was Xian in Shaanxi province, to see the Terracotta Warriors and Horses. This is a collection of terracotta sculptures depicting the armies of the first emperor of China. It is a form of funerary art which was buried with the emperor in the 210-209 BC, the purpose of which was to protect him in the afterlife. For thousands of years the figures had been buried, until discovered in 1974 by local farmers digging a well. The area was approximately 1.6 kilometres from the real tomb of the Emperor.

When I eventually had the chance to visit the terracotta warriors and horses, I was dumb founded at what I saw. The whole area stretches for about two football fields, and only part have so far been excavated. The terracotta figures are life-size, and vary in height, the tallest being the generals, in uniform and hairstyles in according to their rank. It is said that they originally held real weapons, swords or crossbows which it is said were looted or rotted away. They were painted in bright pigments, including pink, red, green, blue, black, brown, white and lilac, which have faded or flaked away. The figures included warriors, chariots and horses, and it is estimated that there are three pits containing 8,000 soldiers, 130 chariots with 520 horses and 250 cavalry horses, the majority of which still remained buried in the pits nearby. Other terracotta non-military figures found in other pits included officials, acrobats, strongmen and musicians.

One of the farmers who discovered the find, was at the museum as part of the exhibition, and for a small fee, would recount how he

Reflection on my life

came to unearth what today is the largest archaeological find in history. According to the guide book, work on the mausoleum began in 246 BCE after the Emperor Qin ascended the throne at 13. The project eventually involved 700.000 workers, and the figures were manufactured in workshops by the government labourers and local craftsmen using local materials. Heads, arms, legs and torsos were created separately and then assembled. It is believed that the warriors' legs were made in much the same way that terracotta drain pipes were manufactured at the time. On completion the terracotta figures were placed in pits in precise military formation according to rank and duty. It was an inspiring feeling to stand and be photographed amongst the items that look so lifelike, even though they were made over one thousand years ago.

ME AMONGST THE TERRACOTTA WARRIORS

AND

ON THE GREAT WALL IN CHINA

ON THE GREAT WALL IN CHINA

Another thousand years old site we visited was the Great Wall of China. This is a wall which stretches from east to west of the country, winding over mountains, across grasslands and through

Reflection on my life

deserts in numerous twists and turns. Spanning a total of 5,600 kilometres, it starts from the banks of the Yellow river in the east and meanders towards the west. Its gigantic proportions of construction, long history and great magnificence, has made the wall known throughout the world, and brought it the status as one of the Seven Wonders of the World.

In fact the Chinese Great Wall is one of the only man made construction project that can be seen clearly from space. This was verified by Neil Armstrong, the first man to walk on the moon. The wall is one of UNESCOs World Cultural Heritage site, and has long been a symbol and the soul of China.

The construction of the wall was started between the 8th and 5th centuries in order to keep the nomadic barbarians out of the country. The wall successfully defended the country and kept out the Manchu invasion, until 1644 when they were able to breach the wall and reached Beijing, where they reigned until the 18th century.

In all my visits to various countries of the world, I was fascinated by the various cultures of the people. But two that stick out in my mind was the culture of a village in visited in East Africa. It was made taboo to have sexual intercourse with a woman on the ground or up against a tree. The reason for this was to protect women from being raped while they were away from the village tending to their farms. A sensible taboo to my mind, and one that could be taken up by villagers in many countries, especially to protect women from being raped by soldiers.

I noticed in several African countries that certain cultural differences exist between tribes, even those who have been living side by side for generations. These include the problem of intermarriage between peoples of different tribes, or having sex with someone from another tribe. In Kenya when I visited some years ago, there was a court case that I am sure would need the patience of Job to sort out. Two very well educated professional lawyers from different tribes, married, had children and were successful and wealthy. When the husband died, his people wanted to take his body home from Nairobi, where he and his family had

1IN TIANANMEN SQUARE IN BEIJING

lived for many years, for burial. The burial ceremony for this tribe included a purification ceremony at which the wife was to become involved.

Naturally, the wife refused to give up the body to his family and so a court case ensued, which when I was there had gone on for nearly a year. I don't know how it was settled but I hope to the satisfaction of the wife. When I mentioned this to an old lady in Accra, she told me that in her younger days, intermarriage between tribes was frowned upon by her family, and her mother drilled into the ears of she and her sisters, not to befriend a man of a different tribe.

Another case of cultural differences between tribes I read about took place also in Kenya. The men of one tribe were circumcised and the men from a neighbouring tribe were not. The

Reflection on my life

uncircumcised men were not allowed to become friends, date or marry women from the other tribe unless they agreed to be circumcised. But as people were mixing more and more, especially in the towns, the men from the circumcised tribe were kidnapping the other men and forcibly having them circumcised. Naturally this has caused much tension leading to violence between the tribes.

ARNOLD AWOONOR-GORDON

Chapter 31
HOW I BECAME AN INTERPRETER

After a year doing nothing but writing, I looked around for something to do. I wanted something that was not too taxing but interesting, so I became a Mystery Shopper, and an Interpreter in the Krio language for the Home Office Immigration Appellant Authority, which I think was one of the most interesting and rewarding jobs I have ever done in my long working life. First the mystery shopping. This is something anyone with any intelligence can do, and it is great fun. One worked at one's pace and when one was available and although the pay is not something to write home about, the perks are great. As soon as I signed on I was given a code number, which I had to use every time I logged into the company's computer. There I would find all the jobs that were available, where they were, the number of days they would be available and the deadline for completing them. The jobs ranged from visiting a posh restaurant as a customer and reporting on how you are treated, the manners of the waiters, the cleanliness of the place, including the toilets, to visiting a betting shops and pretending one is new to betting, and report on how the staff treated you as they showed you how to place a bet. Other jobs included visiting an airport, or a clothing shop to make a purchase, a fast food restaurant, a shoe shop or a car dealer, pretending you wanted to purchase a car, or going to a football match or race course. In all these places one had to keep an eye on the service and make a report back, naming and shaming any of the staff who did not come up to standard.

Apart from being paid for the work, we were also paid our fares and other expenses on production of receipts. As I mentioned earlier, we were not bound to accept any assignment and I only accepted ones that were within a short radius of where I lived. As a mystery shopper I have had some very good meals and drinks and bought some expensive clothes that I could not otherwise afford. I do not relish going to a betting shop though, as I am afraid that I would get the betting bug. But I must say I have some winnings when I do. Every now and again, when I have some spare time, I log in to find out what interesting assignments are there, not too far from me. I understand that some companies that organise mystery shopping do have some assignments that include travelling abroad to exotic places, but, sadly, mine only has assignments that do not require travelling out of the area. What a pity.

Training for the job.

Training to become an Interpreter was also one of the best things I have done. The idea came about when I was asked by someone I knew, who worked at Gatwick airport, whether I spoke Krio as they were getting a large number of people from Sierra Leone arriving who did not speak or, as I later found, pretended they did not understand or speak English. Most were claiming asylum as they were fleeing from the rebel war that was raging in the country at that time. I agreed and went to the airport, and as they did not have anyone who could interpret in Krio, I was welcomed with open arms. So, for several months, I spent every day interpreting as the arrivals, many of whom were young men, told hair-raising stories of running away from the rebels who wanted to force them to join up. The girls also told stories of being raped and, in some cases, about their children being taken from them and killed. It was difficult to know whether all these stories were true or not, but the authorities had to take their stories at face value, and put them on track for asylum status.

I realised that I did not have the relevant skills to do in-depth interpreting so I went on a paid course that gave me the skills that I needed. Unfortunately I did not know any other language than Krio and so the only work I could get was with the Immigration

ARNOLD AWOONOR-GORDON

Appellant Authority, was to interpret for Sierra Leoneans who claimed not to be able to speak or understand English, and who were appealing the refusal of their applications for asylum status being turned down. One of the first cases I had to deal with was a young man, who when asked by the Home Office Solicitor why he should not be sent back to his country, said 'If am I sent back to my country I fear that I will be dragged into the bundoo bush and female genital mutilation will be performed on me.' 'But,' said the Home Office Solicitor: 'Female genital mutilation is carried out only on females and not on males." "How do you know that?" the young man asked angrily "It is a secret society and unless you belong to that society you never know what they do there. Whether they do it on women only or on men, I don't want to know. I am not going back to find out.'

Welcome to the Immigration Appeals Authority Court, where I have spent several years interpreting the lies and evasion from people who have had their application for Asylum turned down by the Home Secretary, and are appealing against the decision. And, in the case of the young man above, I had to interpret word for word, even though I knew, and the Adjudicator and the Home Office Representative knew, and the Appellant's Solicitor knew and the young man in question also knew, that he was not telling the truth. But we all had to go through the motion according to the law, and hear his case through to the end, and the reason why he should not be sent back to his country.

The Immigration Appellate Authority or IAA as it is commonly known, is a tribunal set up by act of Parliament under the Immigration Appeals Act, 1969, although since that date it has been subjected to numerous changes. A full right of appeal to an Adjudicator was first created by the Asylum Immigration Appeals Act 1993 and is governed by the Immigration Act 1971, with changes made by the Immigration Acts in 1993, 1996, 1999 and, most recently, by the Nationality, Immigration and Asylum Act

Reflection on my life

2002, also known as the 2002 Act. This last Act has made significant changes to Asylum and Immigration appeals, and new rules governing the procedure to be followed in Asylum and Immigration appeals were also formulated, under the Immigration and Asylum Appeals (Procedure) Rules 2003 (2003 Rules). With all these changes, (and the new Coalition Government has made some more changes) I wonder how the Home Office Representatives, the Immigration Judges and Immigration Solicitors, can make any sense of Immigration and Asylum in the United Kingdom.

Like all other Interpreters my role is to help the Appellant understand what is being said and to also help the Adjudicator and the Home Office Representative understand what the Appellant is saying. Interpreters provide simultaneous translation, which means interpreting while a discussion is taking place, as well as consecutive interpreting, which means interpreting after a statement has been made or question asked. As Interpreters, we can make notes to help us, but no written work is required of us.

One of the things stressed over and over again is that an Interpreter has to be fair and unbiased and should not take sides. An Interpreter should not talk to the Appellant or his/her Representative before or after the case, and should not be seen to fraternize with the parties to the case outside the court. These are no-go areas and can lead to instant dismissal if these rules are broken. The Interpreting service is provided and paid for by the IAA, and only the Interpreter provided by them can take part in the proceedings of the hearing.

In order to become an Interpreter for the IAA one must be a British National or entitled to work in the United Kingdom, be able to speak English fluently and the other language well, have no links with any Government, Political Party or Organisation that could affect the fairness of the Court service, and should be over twenty-one. Apart from completing an application form, which after approval, the prospective Interpreter is expected to attend an interview, a briefing and an Assessment Test. At the Assessment the prospective Interpreter will take part in a ten-minute consecutive interpreting role play and a ten- minute simultaneous interpreting test, talk in English and the chosen language in order to verify interpreting, linguistic and professional skill in English and the other language. If the Candidate is accepted he/she will be given further training before being let loose in front of an Adjudicator and an unsuspecting Appellant.

These are the following qualities of an Interpreter: 'The Interpreter needs a good short-term memory to retain what he/she has just heard and a good long-term memory to put the information into context. Ability to concentrate is a factor as is the ability to analyse and process what is heard.

The complexity of Translating

I have been asked by friends whether I have, to my knowledge, misinterpreted at any time during a hearing. I can remember doing so on two occasions. The first was when the Appellant said that he had met his wife at a *pull nar do*. This in the Krio language strictly means the outing of a child. This is a ceremony at which a new born child is presented to the elders and other family members and friends in the community. This usually takes place seven days after the birth of the child. The name of the child is usually made known at this ceremony. In my haste I translated this that he met his wife at a 'Christening Ceremony' which technically was not correct. I should have said they met at a 'Naming Ceremony' which is different from a Christening Ceremony. It did not make any difference to the case, as Christening was accepted, although not strictly correct.

Then there was the time when the lady was asked why the Bank had loaned her the money without Collateral, she said that it was due to her 'sababu'. Because I did not have time to think, I said that it was

Reflection on my life

due to her Good Grace. This was accepted, but was not technically true. Several people have given me their interpretation of what she meant, including 'Lappa power'.

An issue of Gender

Another time was during a case involving Female Genital Mutilation. The Appellant stated that the Operation was performed on women when they reached Puberty. In my haste I translated it as when they reached their Menopause. I did realize my mistake immediately and was able to correct it. In this case my mistake would have made a difference to the case, as the Home Office Representative questioned her at length on her knowledge about the Secret Society and what took place there.

One of the most interesting cases in which I had to use my interpreting skills was the one mentioned at the beginning of this Chapter. The young man arrived in this country during the height of the Rebel War in Sierra Leone. He was given leave to stay for four years and at the end of that period, the Home Office wrote to him asking him to return home. The reason they gave was that the War had ended, the country was now stable and in fact the rebels had formed a political party, had run for election and some of their leaders were now part of the Government. At the time this was true.

He appealed against the Home Office decision and one of the reasons given for the Appeal was that he was afraid of being captured by the members of the Bundoo Secret Society who will perform Female Genital Mutilation on him. Now I realise that most of the people who appeal against being sent back to their country of origin tell a lot of lies. But what I could not understand is why their Legal Representatives do not school them in getting their lies to match up. Because even the most stupid of student lawyer should know that, as its name implies, Female genital Mutilation is performed only on females and not on males.

When the Home Office Solicitor pointed this out to the young man, his brusque reply, which I had to interpret, was "how do you know what takes place there? It is a Secret Society and no one knows what happens in the Bush where they perform the Ceremony. How do you a white woman who has never visited the country know what they do? I have lived there, and do not want to find out whether the Ceremony is performed on a woman or man. I do not want to know so I don't want to go back to find out." It took a lot of effort for me not to burst out laughing. By the way the Adjudicator is the Judge, the Appellant is the person making the Appeal, the Home Office Representative is the Solicitor representing the Home Office as its name implies, and the Representative is the Solicitor representing the Person making the Appeal. I always have to explain to the Appellant the Adjudicator is the Judge, the Home Office Representative is the Lawyer for the Home Office and his Representative is his Lawyer, so that they understand who was who when they are called upon to speak to put or defend the case.

Reflection on my life

Chapter 32
A MAN WANTED BY HIS OLD PALS

One of my very first cases was interpreting for a young man who was appealing against the Home Office rejection of his application for Asylum status and against being sent back to Sierra Leone. The Case was heard by a very sympathetic Adjudicator, an Asian who was blind. The young man had stated that he was living in a Town in Sierra Leone when the rebels attacked, and he and other young men were forced to join the rebels and become Carriers, taking their loot from place to place. He stated that he had been forced to stay with the Rebels, moving from one town to another, until he was able to escape. He did this after one attack on a Village, by straggling behind with a particularly heavy load, and when the rebels and the others had gone ahead, he dropped the load and fled into the bush.

He said that with three other young men and a woman he knew, they fled to a village near a large Town. Although at first the villagers were suspicious, taking them for rebels, they were able to persuade the chief that they were not, and so they were allowed to stay. How were you able to persuade the Chief that you were not rebels? He was asked by the Home Office Representative. The woman with them, he said had been an itinerant Trader and she had visited in that village before, and the Chief recognized her. She was able to persuade the Chief that they were not rebels. He eventually found his way to another Town where he met a man called John who worked for the United Nations. John was able to get him on a helicopter to the neighbouring Country, and it was from there that he made his way to Europe and eventually to the United Kingdom.

The Home Office Representative, of course, was intent on finding holes in his story in order to show why he should not be allowed to stay in the Country. She questioned him at length and the more he was questioned, the more his story changed and got more and more complicated. Unfortunately his Solicitors had sent a very junior Trainee to represent him. She was a young lady of mixed race origin, and had originally come to the Court to ask for an adjournment of the Case. The reason was that they had only that morning received his files from his former Representative and they had not had time to study it. The Adjudicator did not agree to an Adjournment as he saw, according to his copies of the Case, that the files had been sent a month earlier. There was ample time for them, he said to have done something about it.

He sympathized with the young lady, but said that he would give her an hour and a half to consult with her Client and study the Case file, before resuming with the Case. In the meantime, another Case in which I was not involved went ahead. When the Case resumed later, the young lady produced two new pieces of Evidence in support of her Client's Appeal. The first was an email from his Uncle in his country, in which he mentioned that although Elections had taken place, and to all appearances, the War was over, and the rebels had now become a part of the Political system, there was still an undercurrent of anger and resentment amongst the people. There was, the email went on, a lynch-mob mentality against the former rebels and against those who helped them, such as the young man who was in front of the Adjudicator. The reformed rebels, on the other hand, were still resentful that their leader was still being held by the Authorities, creating much tension within the various factions of the Government in power. The email also mentioned that the young man was being searched for by the rebels who had a grudge against people who had been with them, either willingly or unwilling, and who had escaped and turned against them. They were secretly meting out their own form of Vigilante Justice especially in places outside the large Cities, where Law and Order had still not been restored.

Reflection on my life

The Uncle advised the young man to stay where he was and not return home, as his life would be in danger from the former rebels. The second piece of Evidence was a copy of a local newspaper, which carried an Article with the heading YOUTH HUNTED BY REBELS, and with a photo of the young man. The Article stated that the rebels were on the lookout for the young man as they felt he had betrayed them, and had stolen some diamonds from them. The young Trainee Solicitor told the Adjudicator that these two pieces of Evidence were proof that the young man's life would be in grave danger, and faced constant threat of being killed, if he was sent back. This, she pointed out would be gross violation of his human rights under Article 8 of the Human Rights Act.

The Home Office Representative, who incidentally was also black, said that she had only now seen both pieces of Evidence and was very suspicious about the authenticity of both. She asked the Adjudicator to accept both the Article and the email with caution and suspicion. First she wanted to know how the Uncle who sent the email was related to the young man. Was he his Mother's Brother or Father's Brother? The young man said that they were not related by blood, but they came from the same Village and he always called him Uncle. The Solicitor tried to dismiss this, but the Adjudicator said that this was not important as in such Communities Cousins, Uncles and Aunts do not necessarily mean blood relatives as it does in countries in the West. Everyone older is an Uncle or Aunt, and everyone your age group who is not a Blood Brother or Sister is a ousin. The Home Office Solicitor had to accept this. I suspect she knew this already, but she was doing her job and needed as much ammunition as possible.

Next, she questioned the language used in the email, which she said sounded as if it came from a very educated person, and was self-serving. The inference she put on this was that someone who was of superior intellect and education had dictated the email. She asked the young man what the occupation of his 'Uncle' was and the young man said that he had been a Teacher. What subject did he teach?, she asked. Literature, the young man said. What Literature? he is asked. English Literature, he replied.

The Adjudicator then said that this must be the reason why the email was so well written. Turning to the Article in the Newspaper, the Home Office Representative, in trying to infer that the Article had been made up and printed specially to help his case, asked the young man how he had found out that the Article had appeared in a Paper in Sierra Leone when he was living in Hackney, London. The young man said that the man in whose house he was staying, had told him that someone had seen the Article and his photo, and he got hold of a copy of the Paper for him.

She desperately tried to pick holes in his Story: about how he had got hold of the Paper; who sent it; when did it arrive, was it sent by Post or hand delivered etc, etc? The young man did hesitate before answering some of the questions, and those he did not know, he said he did not know. She wanted to know why the Article appeared on the Sports page on the back of the Paper, and not in the inside or front page; whether the Paper was a National or Local Paper and whether it was a tabloid like the Sun or a broadsheet like the Independent in the UK to all of which he gave a negative response. Some of the questions seemed silly to ask, but she was doing her job and needed to ask them in order to find reasons to persuade the Adjudicator to uphold the decision of the Home Office to send the young man back to his country.

Eventually she ended her interrogation saying that she would have to obtain a copy of the Newspaper independently in order to access its validity and authenticity. In trying to pick holes in the original Statement that the young man gave when he arrived in the UK, she asked him to recount how he got to the UK. The young man said that the man called John got him on a helicopter to a neighbouring

Reflection on my life

country on the first stage of the journey. *'How did you come to meet this John'*, he was asked. *'I met him soon after I escaped from the rebels, and when I told him my story he took pity on me and said he would help me to get out of the country.'*

'When you got to Guinea, the neighbouring country, why did you not seek asylum there?'

'The Guinean people made it very clear from the outset that they did not want us there. It appears that some of their soldiers on the border had only recently been attacked and some killed by the rebels from Sierra Leone. So we were not the most welcome at the time. That is why I did not bother to seek asylum in Guinea, as I was not welcome.' He recounted how the man in whose house he was staying in Guinea, had purchased a ticket for him and he had boarded a plane for Brussels.

'But you said when you arrived in the UK that you did not know you were going to Brussels, now you say you boarded a plane for Brussels. What is the truth?' she asked.

'I only found out later on when I arrived here that Brussels was my destination' he answered.

'Did you not stay long enough in Brussels to know where you were?'

'No I spent only about an hour before I was given papers and told to board a plane for the UK'.

'What kind of papers were you given? Was it a ticket?'

'I don't know, but when I presented the papers at the gate of the plane I was allowed on board. So it could have been a ticket.'

The young man's Representative did an excellent job of defending him, given she had such short notice. This impressed the Home Office Representative, who after it was all over, congratulated her

Opponent on doing such an excellent job under such trying circumstances. She had been sent to ask for an Adjournment but ended up defending the client. She really had been thrown in at the deep end, and did a very capable job of it.

In her Summary to the Adjudicator, the Trainee Solicitor started by saying the young man had been credible in his answers, and where he did not know the answers he had said so, rather than try to fob the answers. He had been very cooperative. Addressing the Articles and the email, she said that it showed, beyond reasonable doubt, that the young man had a genuine fear of persecution. He would not be arrested and charged by the Sierra Leone Authorities, but his life was in danger from former rebels who accuse him of turning against them, and for stealing diamonds from them. I don't know the outcome of the Case, but I am convinced that the young man was successful in his Appeal because of the R e p r e s e n t a t i v e he had to argue his case.

Reflection on my life

Chapter 33
WE WERE ALWAYS IN THE DARK

Whilst on the subject of the outcome of cases, we Interpreters never know how the Cases do turn out, whether the Appeals are granted or not. The reason is that the Adjudicators never make their decisions on the spot. They would inform the Appellant that they have heard the reasons for and against from their Representatives and also the Home Office, and they have their notes and all the documents associated with the Case. They will go home and study everything and write up their decisions which will be sent to all Parties in between ten to fifteen days. Sometimes, when we leave the Court the Appellant will approach us and ask what we think will be the outcome. We would tell them that, as we are employed by the IAA, we are not allowed to discuss the Case with them. They will sometimes become hostile and we would have to make a quick getaway.

This one was a strange case: In the first place the Representative of the Appellant arrived late. The Adjudicator and the Home Office Representative were in the middle of discussing what to do with the Case, when he arrived quietly and sat in the back of the Court. He did not take his place in the seat reserved for the Representative of the Appellant. He had his files and papers in a plastic carrier bag and although he was dressed in a dark suit, none of us took him to be a Solicitor. He soon realised that the Case being discussed was the one he had come to defend, and got up to address the Adjudicator. I am sure he lost the case.

In another case the Appellant was not in court as will be seen. The case being dealt with revolved around a young man who had arrived in the UK in 2000 and had applied for Asylum. His Application had been turned down in July 2001, but by then he had suffered a mental breakdown and had been sectioned under the Mental Health Act. When his Appeal was first heard in January, it was on the grounds that he was not well enough to appear himself, and a medical report had been presented stating that he was in hospital. The Case was adjourned to April. By the time the Case was next heard a letter had been received, dated the 30th of March, stating that he was now out of hospital and would be well enough to appear in court the next time.

Today was the day of his appearance to give Evidence in support of his Appeal to be allowed to stay. And again he did not appear. His Solicitor said that his non-appearance was because he had gone back into hospital that very day. The Home Office Representative wanted to know more, but the Appellant's Representative was unable to answer whether he had gone back into hospital as a voluntary patient, or had again been sectioned.

The Adjudicator suggested an Adjournment in the circumstances, but the Home Office Representative insisted on going ahead with the Case. But after a lengthy discussion between the Adjudicator and the two Representatives, the Case was indeed adjourned for the Appellant's Solicitor to produce a medical report about the mental state of the Appellant as at the date of the Hearing. Again I never knew the outcome of that Case.

But I was at the beginning of this particular Case and, for once, knew the outcome at the end. This case also involved a man with

Reflection on my life

Mental Health problems, and I knew something of the background of the case which I remember from some years back. Several years previously, the man in question had murdered his wife and put her body in the freezer. It was a Case that made headlines in all the papers, especially the fact that he ran away from the UK, and when he was found in a European country, it took a long time before he was extradited back to the UK. At his trial he was found Guilty but Insane and sentenced to several years at a secure place where he was to receive help and treatment. But the downside of the Case was that the Judge made an Order that he was to be deported after serving his Sentence. The Sentence had ended and he was appealing against the Deportation Order.

When the Hearing came up he had been released from Prison but was being detained by the Immigration Authorities pending deportation. It was obvious that the man was insane and was being heavily medicated. He arrived in Court under heavy guard, but was in no fit state to decamp or attack anyone. He was lucid enough though and answered all the questions put to him. His Case was that if he was deported to his country this would infringe on his Human Rights, under Article 8 of the Human Rights Act. He would not be able to receive the same medical treatment he was receiving in this country, in his own country. During his questioning it came out that he had days when he was lucid and docile, and this happened when he was taking his medication. But whenever he stopped taking the medication he became violent and was not only in danger of harming people around him, but also in danger of harming himself. Reports from the Prison Psychiatrist and that of the Detention Centre where he was at present held confirmed this.

This posed a dilemma for both his Representative and the Adjudicator. It was obvious that the best thing to do was to detain him in this country and place him under constant supervision. This would ensure that he took his medication regularly to keep him calm. His Representative suggested that this could be done under the Mental Health Act. But it was pointed out to him by the Home Office Representative that this would be impossible to do. The reason was that, as he was not a British Citizen, he could not be detained under the Mental Health Act. To get around this he had to become a British Citizen and that was impossible to do, for no one can force him to apply for British Citizenship, which would not be granted anyway.

So there was the dilemma; deporting him back to his country would infringe on his Human Rights, as he would not be able to receive the same level of medical treatment there. In fact, as the Adjudicator himself pointed out, he may even kill someone else, or even kill himself. But releasing him into the UK community was also dangerous, as he cannot be provided with the care and support he will need. He would need constant monitoring and support to make sure that he took his medication regularly.

Fortunately I do know what the outcome of the Case was and what was decided. The Adjudicator requested the Home Office to do some homework and find out more about the Case from the Psychiatrist at the detention centre, and the case was adjourned for another six weeks. Fortunately again, I was the Duty Interpreter when the case came up again. He was granted leave to remain so long as he was under supervision to see that he took his medication regularly.

Reflection on my life

Chapter 34
SOLICITORS AND ADJUDICATORS

Solicitors dealing with Immigration cases, whether working for the Home Office or for a Client, are a breed apart. Some are excellent, some good, others so, so, and some damn right awful. You would think that, with all the years they spent training, they would, like boy scouts, be prepared when they come to Court, with all the papers they need and with spare copies in case the Adjudicator or their Opponent did not have copies. No! They come unprepared and because of this lack of preparedness, Cases sometimes have to be adjourned. Copies of the papers relating to the case from the Appellants' Solicitors have to reach the Adjudicator and the Home Office Solicitor at least two days before the Hearing. Quite often, an exasperated Home Office Solicitor would ask for the papers relating to a Case, only for the Appellant's Solicitor to say that they were faxed to the Court or the Home Office, but they never reached their destination. If the papers consist of two or three pages then the Adjudicator would summon the Court Clerk and ask for photocopies to be made. This tended to hold up the Proceedings for a while. Sometimes, if the papers were too many, the Home Office Solicitor would ask for a break of half an hour or so, for a proper study of the papers.

Luckily, there is usually another Case ready to go. But I didn't mind; for the longer the Case took, the more money in my pocket, as Interpreters are paid by the hour. Once I had to go to a Detention Centre near Oxford on a Sunday. After signing in I waited in the Interpreters' Room for seven hours before someone found me and said that the Case had been adjourned earlier. As they had failed to inform me I got paid for doing nothing for seven hours, during which I read the Sunday Times from cover to cover.

Adjudicators are also a mixed bunch of men and women. They are all Judges. I found the women more sympathetic and helpful to the Client's Solicitors, and would lead them back on the right path when, in their eagerness to put their clients cases, they would stray down the wrong path. My most favourite was the blind Indian Adjudicator, who, apart from anything else, had a sense of humour, made jokes and in so doing put all at ease. For example, he always asked the Client to speak up; for although he said that no one in the room, except the Interpreter, could understand what he was saying, yet they would like to hear his voice. And, he would add that he too would like to hear his voice *'because you see, I cannot see whether you are handsome, tall, short and what colour your eyes are!'* Even the Client had to laugh when I interpreted the remarks to him.

It was he who cleared up the misunderstanding when the Home Office Solicitor tried to find out how the rebel- scared Client was related to the man he called his Uncle. He said that in most developing countries, people called anyone who is older than themselves Aunty or Uncle. He warned the Home Office Representative: 'Let's not go down that route or you will only get yourself in twist trying to untie Family relationships.'

The first time I did two Interpreting sessions back to back was a great strain. It was my own fault, as the Adjudicator did ask whether I would like a break, because she could schedule the next Case before my second one. I said I would carry on, which was a great mistake. First it took a lot out of me as the second Case involved a woman who said she had been raped, and, secondly, I could have added another hour or so to my time which would have brought in some more money. But as it was the first time I had to do it back to back I knew no better.

As an Interpreter, I came to realise that it was always difficult dealing with Cases involving women, because they always almost

Reflection on my life

involved them having been raped. The Home Office Solicitors and the Adjudicators are most times sympathetic towards these women, and would spare them the ordeal of bringing up the incident as much as they could, referring to written Statements they had already made. But, sometimes, if they suspect that the incidents of rape had been made up in order to strengthen their case, then the Appellant would be questioned closely with no detail spared. For example, in one case, the Appellant stated in her statement that she had been selected by the Rebel Commander as his Wife, and lived with him for one year until she escaped. During that time she had borne him a Son, who died soon after he was born. But in Court she had stated that she had been repeatedly raped by several men. There was a surprise that the Rebel Commander, having got a Wife who was carrying his child, would let her be raped by his men.

There was a hole in her Story somewhere that made the Home Office Representative not believe that she was telling the truth, and he told her so. She said that she was indeed telling the truth, and that it was after she had escaped that she was raped. She added that she was raped not by the rebel soldiers but by the Government soldiers who attacked the Rebel Camp that made it possible for her to escape. It was during her escape that she fell into the hands of the Government soldiers who took advantage of her.

The Home Office Solicitor, still not believing her, wondered why the Government soldiers, after taking advantage of her, did not take her along with them, but the Appellant said that they did not usually take women prisoners, but left them behind either to die, or if they were too brutalized, to make their way behind enemy lines. She was able to do the latter. Still the Home Office Solicitor was not happy in the discrepancy between what she said in her Statement about being repeatedly abused by the rebels, and what she was saying now in Court that the abused was by the Government soldiers. Who were the Abusers, the Rebels or the Government soldiers? The Adjudicator, a woman, intervened at this stage and told the Home

Office Solicitor, that rape was rape and it did not matter whether it was carried out by rebels or Government soldiers, she was convinced that it did take place. The Home Office Solicitor agreed with her, but said that he was trying to find out why the Story in her statement was different from what she was saying in Court. But in deference to what the Adjudicator had said, he did not wish to pursue that line of cross examination further.

Having not gone down that route, the Home Office Solicitor then turned his attention to another piece of evidence. The Solicitor for the Appellant had brought to Court a Newspaper printed in Sierra Leone, containing an Article complete with a picture of the Appellant. The Article said that the Appellant was being sought by members of the defunct RUF for stealing diamonds from them and taking them abroad. The Article also stated that if she was caught Rebel Justice will be carried out against her. Her Solicitor contended that the Article showed, without any doubt, her client would be killed by members of the RUF if her Appeal to stay was rejected and she was returned to her country. The Home Office Solicitor had contended that there had been an Election in the country in which the rebels, who were now a Political Party, had taken part. The country was now stable, Law and Order had been restored and the Appellant had no fear of Persecution or Summary Execution as her Solicitor stated. To prove his case he read from various UN, British Government and Internet Reports which stated that the country had peacefully returned to Civilian Rule and the Courts were now operating, and that the rebels were no more.

The Home Office Solicitor and the Adjudicator were both suspicious of the authenticity of the Newspaper itself, and of the Report. The Appellant was questioned at length about how she came about the Newspaper, how and when the photograph was taken (she did not know) and who was the Relative mentioned in the Article who had given the Writer the Story. The Appellant was

Reflection on my life

not able to give satisfactory answers to the Questions, and one could see that both the Home Office Solicitor and the Adjudicator did not believe her.

Perhaps the most unusual Case that I witnessed was one of the first I remember, which dealt with someone who was brought directly from Prison. He was in Court to appeal against Deportation and his Case to me was, as I say, an unusual one. He was accompanied by two Prison Officers to the Hearing. He had been arrested at Heathrow Airport trying to leave the country with a forged UK passport and was charged and sentenced to six month in prison. During the Case he gave this most improbable Defence. He said that he had arrived in the UK on the 30th April, 2000, having left his country in West Africa on the 29th.

He had travelled on a Diplomatic passport from his country and was let through. He was on his way to Canada and the Agent who organised his trip told him to go and collect the forged British passport and his Canadian ticket from someone at the airport. He did so and was caught as he tried to leave the country. The Authorities maintained that he was stopped on the lst of May and not on the 30th April as he said, and in his luggage they had found clothes and shoes that could only have been bought in the UK. They also found in his pocket a one-day Travel Card dated the 27th of April. He denied that the clothes and shoes had been bought in the UK but in his country. He said that he picked up the one-day Travel Card dated 27th April by a public telephone in order to write the address of a Priest from his country, whom he telephoned from the public telephone. No such address was found on the ticket.

He could not explain how he came to be at Heathrow airport when all flights from his country came into Gatwick, and could not explain how he went from one airport to another. Anyway, he got six month, but was now appealing against deportation. His Solicitor complained that as he had served his Prison Sentence he should not be detained in Prison but at an Immigration Detention Centre.

The Adjudicator said that was not his area of work and suggested that the Solicitor addressed the relevant Authority for his transfer. After a great deal of debate between the Home Office Solicitor and the Solicitor for the man, the Adjudicator dismissed the Appeal against deportation. The Appellant's Solicitor asked for Bail whilst another Appeal was mounted, and although there were two Sureties present to stand the Bail for him, this was also not allowed. As soon as this was turned down the two Prison Officers got up and with one on each side, he was escorted out of the room back to Jail.

Reflection on my life

Chapter 35
THE GAINS (AND HEADACHE) OF BEING AN INTERPRETER

Many of my fellow Interpreters do work for other Agencies as well, such as interpreting for the Police, Solicitors, Detention Centres and the Courts, making lots of money annually. It is said that, in a good year, some make as much as seventy thousand pounds! One African lady, who had been in the business for over ten years and was fluent in five African languages and French, told me that she put her three children through private Education, and paid the Mortgage for a house in the Kensington area of London, through interpreting. Maybe, more people are turning to this lucrative form of earning a living, but, at one stage, bookings began to dry up and people who depended on this outlet to make an Income found themselves in a very difficult situation.

Because of the need to cut back, the Authorities began to take a closer look at the cost of booking an Interpreter for a particular job. They began to look at how cost effective it was, taking into account the travel cost and travel time, which are paid for by the Authorities, for each person. For example, if the Travel Time to a particular Centre for a particular Interpreter is three hours return and the cost is ten pounds, they will book someone whose Travel Time is only two hours with travel cost of only five pounds. This caused a great deal of manoeuvring as people cut their travel costs and times in order to get more Bookings. Many deplored this and made their views rather vocal in the Interpreters' Waiting Room and said that they were not going to compromise and make any cuts. But I was told by the African lady not to listen to them, as they all said one thing publicly and did something else privately.

Many Interpreters, she told me, were there to get as many jobs as possible and would do anything to get Bookings. As there seems to be too many Interpreters in some languages, some of them have been known to perpetuate some dirty tricks on one another. For example, if one is going away on holidays or will not be available for accepting any Bookings for a while, one can telephone the Interpreters' Booking Office and inform them, so that a stop will be put against their names until they returned. I heard of two cases where someone rang the Booking Office and using someone else's name had a stop put on the person, saying that she was going to be away for three months. So, all the jobs that she would have had went to the person who made the call.

Now, it is not the proper thing to call the Interpreters Booking Team to find out why one had not been receiving any jobs for a while. The Booking Team will not be pleased if you did. So the trick is to call and say that you are checking to confirm your upcoming bookings. This is what this particular lady did and she was then told that a stop had been put against her name because she had called to inform them that she would be away for three months. She was reinstated and continued to receive her Bookings. Someone had tried to spike her Bookings and if she had not realised it would have lost a lot of money. So one had to be on one's guard, especially with languages where they are too many Interpreters. Unlike the Krio language where there are only six of us Interpreters.

And this is another aspect to the Job. As Interpreters are paid by the hour, the longer the case takes the more money we receive. I have been booked for several Interpreting jobs where, either the Solicitor or the Appellant did not turn up or arrived late, and I would spend five or six hours waiting only to have the Case adjourned. But I was paid for those hours all the same. And this is the up side of the Job. There are very few jobs in the world where you can spend five or six hours sitting on your bum and reading the newspapers, and get

Reflection on my life

paid over twenty pounds an hour, your Travel Cost and Travel Time, with Lunch thrown in, without doing anything. Money for Jam, I call it. At one time I also decided to try and get on the Police, Court and Solicitor's bandwagon. It was not easy to do so and I did not succeed. The process was too long and complicated.

As I have mentioned before, we the Interpreters never know the outcome of the Cases that we work on as Interpreters, but in this Case, I did. Because rather at the last moment I was asked to go to Manchester to do some interpreting, and the Case turned out to be that of the lady with the baby I had met in London. Of course, as the Adjudicated in London had predicted, her Solicitor did not turn up. Two days before the case he wrote to her to say that he needed five hundred pound before he could represent her. The Adjudicator was furious because, as the lady was on Benefits, she was entitled to Legal Aid, and he had no right to demand payment from her. The Adjudicator took a copy of the letter and promised to report the Solicitor to the Bar Council. He was furious and did let rip at a section of his Profession that was letting the side down and ripping off vulnerable people. Anyway, he did decide to go ahead with the Case.

Now the Case the lady put forward was one I had heard about but had never encountered before. She said that she was a Virgin and started a Lesbian relationship with a lady in her twenties when she was in her country. Her Parents suspected what was happening and before they could confront her, she came out to them and revealed that she was a Lesbian. Her parents were naturally furious, and said that she was to marry her male Cousin who would soon put a stop to her sexual orientation. She was forced to marry him and on the night of the Wedding he raped her. Soon afterwards she escaped from him, and met the ubiquitous man who arranged for her to come to the UK. All this took place in December and her baby was born in July the following year. This is where she got her knickers in a twist.

The Home Office Solicitor asked her whether the baby had been born early or late, and she said the baby was two days late. How then could she have been raped in December and given birth to a baby in July that was only two days late. This was not possible. She got flustered and said that she was confused and could not remember dates and started to cry profusely. She could not remember the name of the lady with whom she had had the Lesbian relationship; moreover, she had not started a Lesbian or any other Relationship with anyone since she arrived in the country, and so on and so on. She said that she was afraid that if she was sent back to her country, apart from the disgrace to her Parents for running away, she would be taken away to have Genital Mutilation performed on her. The Home Office Solicitor told her that Genital Mutilation was never performed on women who have already had children, and she said that she did not know anything about that. Unusually, her Appeal was turned down there and then as she was obviously lying.

Reflection on my life

Chapter 36
WHOSE STORY IS IT, ANYWAY?

I have always asked myself whether it is the Solicitors or the Appellants themselves who make up these Stories. If it is the Solicitors, then they are not doing the Clients any favours because they know that Stories such as these would never stand up in Court. But I suppose they are doing their job and raking in the Legal Aid money, so any Story is better than none. I wonder how they can face their Clients to tell them their Appeals had been turned down. It is a dog eat dog world out there in the Immigration, asylum and Refugee business.

At one time, Newspaper Reports, with the WANTED notice printed above a picture of the Appellant, were used as a means of persuading the Adjudicator that it would not be safe to send him back. They were never able to persuade the Authorities that they should not be sent back, because the Authorities know that in some countries, one could pay for a page to be printed with a picture, and a story that the person is a wanted man or woman. We got so many of these printed Newspapers that I wonder why the Solicitors of the Appellants, use this ploy over and over again, when they know it would not help the case of their clients.

I had to interpret for a young man who was obviously a street smart boy by his body movement, his clothes and the way he talked and answered the questions. He was asked how he got to the country and he said that he came by plane. Did the plane stop anywhere else before arriving in the UK? 'I think the plane passed by Belgium' he answered. 'Did the plane stop in Belgium?' This is a tricky question because if the plane had stopped in Belgium, he should have asked for Asylum in that country as the first Port of arrival. He had obviously been schooled. 'No' he answered, 'the plane hovered over the country before arriving in the UK.' 'What did you do all that time?' he was asked. 'I slept until we touched down at Gatwick.'

When asked by the Home Office Solicitor why he had not left the country after his six months Visa expired, he said to her: 'Your people did not leave my country for over two hundred years, why should I leave your country only after six months?' 'Good on you,' I said quietly to myself.

This cCase was a mess, as the Adjudicator herself admitted. The young man had been in the country for five years and had made three applications to the Home Office to stay, and each time he gave a different name. When he got caught, his Lawyer then advised him to come clean and as he had fathered a baby born in the country, he was to apply to stay on compassionate grounds. The Home Office turned down his Application, and the case I had been asked to help interpret was his appeal.

He was a very lucky man that day. The Home Office Representative did not turn up, his Solicitor was an Asian and the adjudicator was an elderly black lady who, I think, was originally from the West Indies. He was a young and personable man and I suspect she had a child just like him, and so looked on him like her Son. If there had been a Home Office Rep present I think he would have lost his Appeal, but as one was not present she decided to lecture him like a Headmistress lecturing a truant young man. She told him that he was a Liar and a Cheat and a disgrace to the black Community. This is a good country, she told him, a country that has opened its doors to people like herself, his Solicitor and the Interpreter; that was me. It was people like him who think they could lie and cheat their way into the country that gave all of us a bad name. You have to change your ways, she admonished him, and be truthful and not lie and try to beat the system. She told him to try and emulate the Interpreter who was from his country, an upstanding and respected person in the community, who she was sure was disgusted with his behaviour and letting his country down.

Reflection on my life

The young man hung his head in shame and apologized profusely and said that he would speak the truth and not lie any more. The Adjudicator then said that she was willing to adjourn the Case, and directed the Solicitor how to go about making a new Application. The young man had to write a letter withdrawing the present Appeal and another instructing his Solicitor on which grounds he was to appeal against the Home Office decision. During the conversation that followed it came out that the young man had a child born two months earlier. Where was the Mother? He was asked. It appeared that she had gone home to her country, but he did not know the status of her stay in the country. It also turned out that although the young man said that he was the Father of the little girl, yet his name was not on the Birth Certificate. He said that he had applied to have his name put on the Certificate as the Father. In the absence of the Birth Certificate, it was suggested that a DNA test be carried out before the next Hearing in six weeks. She then made an Order that the Case be allocated to her for the next Hearing. In all this, my services were not needed because the young man spoke and understood perfect English, but as I was being paid by the hour I didn't mind sitting in until the end of the Case.

Interpreting in an Appeals case and interpreting in a Crown and Police Courts are different. In the latter, one has to be on the ball and be able to interpret not only what is said but also be able to explain cultural differences for the benefit of the Court. In one of my first interpreting Booking in a Crown Court, the erstwhile Appellant now the Defendant was charged with trafficking drugs, and I had to help his Barrister understand some of the cultural differences before the Hearing. For example, in his statement to the Police, he said that he had been given the bag containing the drugs by a friend called Lotto to give to his girlfriend. He thought that the bag contained clothes and knew nothing about the drugs. When asked for the name of the person called Lotto, he said that he did not know. He only knew his street name which was

Lotto. In the Charge Sheet the Police said that he was using an alias to hide the real name of his friend. Even his Barrister did not believe that one could know someone only by his street name.

I was able to explain that, in the part of the West Indies, and indeed in many parts of West Africa, one can have two names by which one was known by different people. For example, some could have a House Name by which one is known at home and by ones friends, and a School Name by which you are known by at school. This is a simple explanation of what can be a very complex social structure, and although when I was growing up we talked about a House Name and a School Name, young people today talk about Street Name and Given Name.

So, although it may look as if the Accused was trying to shield someone by not knowing his real name, it is possible that he indeed did not know him by any other name than Lotto. What was interesting about this street and given names complexity was that the prosecutor, a black woman from a small island in the West Indies, did not know about this, as her culture was completely different from the young man's in question. It did transpire that the young man had already been tried, found Guilty by a Jury and sentenced to three years for sexually assaulting a young girl of just over sixteen. The original Charge had been Rape, but as there had been no penetration, the charge was reduced to Sexual Assault. The young man said in his defence that what happened was consensual, and he only touched her breast and took off her knickers.

After the assault, without knowing that the girl had made a complaint against him, he went to London, he said, to arrange for a transfer from a college he had been attending, to one in Coventry. It was on the train that he met Lotto, who gave him the bag, which he said contained clothes, for his girlfriend. He was on his way back from London, and, not knowing that the Police was looking for him about the complaint, he was arrested at the train Station, and the drugs and two hundred and fifty pounds were found in the bag.

When the Police searched his house for Evidence of the rape, they found another one thousand pounds, which he said belonged to his girlfriend, money he said she had saved up from her Allowances from Social Services for the child she was expecting. Of course both sets of money were confiscated as profit from selling drugs. The young man was out of luck as the Judge, who had sentenced him for the Sexual assault was the same Judge trying him for peddling drugs, and he did not take too kindly to this new Charge at all. The young man's Barrister asked for a short Recess to confer with his Client, and this was allowed. During the Recess it was pointed out to the young man that if he changed his Plea of Not Guilty to Guilty for acting as a Courier for his friend, knowing that the bag contained the drugs, the Judge may accept this as mitigating circumstances, and reduce the Sentence and make it run concurrently with the time he was already serving. He agreed to this but wanted the five hundred pounds returned. After a discussion with the Prosecuting Officer, it was agreed that this would be put to the Judge.

One of the things I found out during all this toeing and fro-ing was that if a Sentence is under four years, then the Prisoner can serve only half of it. If on the other hand the Sentence is over four years then he will have to serve three quarters of the time. The Barrister was hopeful that this is what would happen in this Case, but although the Judge was sympathetic and accepted the new Plea, when he came to passing Sentence, the young man received five years in Prison, the Sentence to run concurrently. So the poor lad would be in Jail for some three and a half years. He took it in his stride and I only hope an Order was made later for the return of the five hundred pounds.

What was interesting was the way the Court was conducted. The Judge could have come out of central casting, as were the Court officials, both men and women in their black uniform gowns, as was the Barrister and the Criminal Prosecution Service Prosecuting Officer. The whole atmosphere was like watching a Court Case on television, and for a while I wondered whether television was imitating reality, or whether it was the other way round.

People who write and produce Court Room dramas for television must do their homework thoroughly in order to get it right. Even the dingy benches, Jury seats and the Dock with the Prisoner and his Guard, all looked so realistic and I felt I had been there before, even though it was my very first visit to a Court in Britain. And do the women Guards have to look so large with big broad hips, bulging out of their uniform trousers? It all looked so familiar.

Reflection on my life

Chapter 37
A GLOBAL TEAM SOMETIMES MISINTERPRETS

The few women from the African continent who are Interpreters are also a mixed bunch. Some are also doing the Job for pin money, but I got to know one who was out to make as much as possible each year. She was a very kind and helpful person and was always passing on information about how to get jobs in other areas such as the Police, the Courts and private Interpreting services, to all and sundry.

She had been doing the job for about ten years when I met her. She told me that she started interpreting when her husband, who was her country's Ambassador to the Court of St James, died suddenly leaving her with three teenage children at Boarding School and the Mortgage on a swanky five bedroom flat in Kensington. She could have packed up and returned to her country taking the children with her, but like all Africans, she was determined that the Education of her children was paramount and so she stayed on. She sold the Kensington flat and bought a smaller one with the proceeds, paid the school fees for her children for one year with what was left over, and then started to look for work. For a while she worked at the Embassy but that soon became untenable.

She then got work in Social Services and it was then she realised that she could put her language skills to better use. Several times she had to be called to interpret for people from her country who were accessing Social Services, and this then led to her being called by the Police to help and it snowballed from there. She was able to complete the Education of her children right through University and she has been at it since then. In one good year she raked in over seventy thousand pounds. In a bad year she can make forty thousand pounds. Not bad for a widow with three children. She was always immaculately turned out in expensive clothes and she deserved it. Some of the Muslim women wear their traditional dresses, with covered heads and demure colours. One of them told me that she dressed like that deliberately in order to put Muslim men and women she interpreted for, at ease. They felt more comfortable if she does look like a Muslim woman rather than a Westernised woman.

The question that arises is whether one should interpret what is said word for word or use paraphrase to get across the meaning. For example, I often hear Appellants say that they were close to the Rebel Commander and did his biddings passing on his wishes to the other rebels. Do I interpret this as his Second in Command, or as his ADC? Either is correct, but in effect he is not one of these either. From my experience of what takes place in the country I come from, he is merely a glorified Bag Carrier, carrying the Commander's briefcase and, if the person is a woman, she is also his Comfort Woman. But because the appeal is not a Court Trial, and for ease of understanding, I always translate bag carrier as ADC or second in Command. I think I am correct.

But again, is it right for the Interpreter to change things or should he/she just mouth it word for word? I got myself into some trouble when a young girl, who in this case did not know any English, said that she fled the country because she was from the wrong tribe and that there was also Racism in the country. I was taken aback by the word 'Racism' as there was no Racism where I come from. There was Tribalism but not 'Racism'. I thought that I may not have heard her properly and asked her to repeat the word again, which she did. She saw the look of surprise on my face as I did not feel that an uneducated girl like her would know the meaning of Racism. She then went on to say 'don't you know what racism is?' It was then I collected myself and translated what she had said. I am sure the Adjudicator, the Home Office Solicitor, and the Appellant's Solicitor wondered what had got into me, as I traded words back and forth with the Appellant. I am still in the dark as to what she

Reflection on my life

meant about racism being in our country.

In many of the escape stories given by both male and female Appellants, as to how they left their countries, there was always a man involved, who helped them. Sometimes he was white and sometime black. Sometimes this man worked for the Red Cross, the UN or one of the NGOs, and sometimes he was a Businessman. But one thing they all agreed on was that they never got to know his name, or he was simply known as John. In many cases, even though they were with this man for up to ten months, they never asked his name nor did he volunteer to tell them his name. One female Appellant even said that she lived with her Benefactor and several other girls for over a year and did not know the names of even her companions. She said the man told them not to speak to each other. I would be a Millionaire by now if I charged a pound for every time I heard this kind of story.

In another case, the lady had arrived in the UK to visit her sixteen year old daughter and had become very ill with a severe attack of sickle Cell disease. The Story she told was that she had suffered from the disease since she was a child and it was controllable. She got married and had a good Husband who looked after her and her Daughter in comfort. Her whole world changed, when during the rebel attack on Freetown, her Husband was killed in front of her ten year old Daughter, and her house burned down. Her Daughter needed counselling constantly, and as this was not available in the country, her Sister, who was living in the UK with her Husband and four daughters, invited her Daughter to come and live with her, which she did.

She the mother, being homeless, had to stay with various friends and went in and out of hospital as the disease got worse. To compound her problem, she received a telephone call from Social Services in the UK to say her Daughter had been taken into care as her Sister's Husband was suspected of sexually abusing her. Her friends got together and paid for her ticket to come to the UK and see her Daughter. The Case against the man was dropped at the insistence of her daughter, who said that the man had also abused his daughters, but did not relish having to go to Court to testify against their father. Her Daughter was then taken into care and is very happy with her Foster Parents.

She returned home, and again went in and out of hospital. Six months earlier when she felt better, she again came to the UK to visit her Daughter who, although happy with her new Parents, said that she missed her Mother. It was while on the visit that she had a very severe attack of the recurring Sickle Cell disease, and has been in and out of hospital since then. She has been told by the hospital that she should stay in the UK as she had been recommended to participate in a Medical trial for a new kind of treatment for the disease. It appears that people with Sickle Cell disease, which only attack people of African, Caribbean and African-American origins, very rarely live to an old age, and as she was over fifty they would like to have her help the Medical Profession with their Medical experiment. She brought to the Court, letters from the hospital and the various Professors who are conducting the Trials in support of her application for Leave to remain in the UK. This is one Case in which I tried hard to find out the outcome. She got her Leave to remain in the UK, which I was glad about.

Chapter 38
THE ENIGMATIC HOME OFFICE, INTERPRETERS AND CASES

I sometimes cannot understand the workings of the Home Office when it comes to its Immigration policies. This case is a case in point. The young man had come to the UK ten years earlier and had been given leave to stay for four years. At the end of the period he applied for Leave to stay permanently. The Home Office took another four years to reply to his Application which was turned down. He appealed against this dismissal and it took another two years before he received a reply from the HO, saying he had to return to his country. By then the young man had been in full Employment, had married a lady from his home country who was a British citizen and had produced three children.

The Case, which I had to interpret was his Appeal against being sent back to his country. Fortunately for the young man he had a very sympathetic Adjudicator trying the Case. The young man did not have a Solicitor to represent him as his funding had run out. He had asked for a Loan of one thousand pounds from his Bank, which had been granted the day before, and there was no time for the Funds to reach his account for him to transfer them to the Solicitor. He brought all the documents to the Court and asked for an Adjournment, by which time the funds would have reached his Solicitor for him to be represented. The Adjudicator said he was very impressed with the effort the young man had made about trying to raise funds to obtain representation, and granted the Adjournment. He did castigate the Home Office for the length of time it had taken to sort out the predicament in which the young man found himself, and that he would be willing to allow his appeal. I was not there for the conclusion, but I hoped the young man was allowed to stay, for he had established a stable Family relationship in the country, had been in the same Employment since he came to the country, and it would be wicked to send him back to a country he had lost touch with. Why the Home Office took so long to sort out his Immigration status I cannot imagine. Time and time again I came across such cases and the Home Office would refuse to give an answer to this question when it was asked by various Adjudicators.

There was one day when a female Interpreter stormed into the Interpreters room in a rage. She had been booked to interpret in a case involving a man from Egypt. She had not even exchanged words with the Appellant to find out whether they understood each other, when his Representative informed the Adjudicator that his Client did not want her as an Interpreter, as the Arabic she spoke was not the same as that spoken by his Client. The Adjudicator had no option but to dismiss the Interpreter, and asked for another one who spoke the same kind of Arabic as the Appellant. The Court Clerk came into the Interpreter's Room asking for someone to do the interpreting, but even though all the Arabic speakers in the room said that there was no difference between the Arabic spoken in Egypt and the rest of the Arabic world, none of them volunteered to help out.

The thinking in the Interpreter's Room was that it was a ploy by the Solicitor to get the Case to be adjourned because of the lack of an Interpreter to help his Client. And that is exactly what happened. But the Interpreter was left feeling hurt and used and left with very low esteem, as her interpreting skills were being judged and found wanting. Later on I found that several other Interpreters had had the same thing happened to them, but felt it was part of the Job. It was obvious to all in the Court what the Solicitor was up to, but not even the Adjudicator could do anything about it other than adjourn the Case

I sometimes got so mad as I sit there and listen to the Home Office

Reflection on my life

Solicitor asking questions of the Appellant that are not relevant. Some Adjudicators will pull them up and tell them not to ask irrelevant questions, but as likely as not they will not. I suppose some of the Home Office Solicitors, being human, and knowing that the Appellants were lying through their teeth, would try to catch them out by picking holes in their interview and their Statement. Do I think that some of the Adjudicators were prejudice? I can safely say yes, some of them were. One Adjudicator was so prejudice against a young woman that he did not allow her Representative to put the Case for his client, but kept on interrupting from time to time, and I could see the Rep getting madder and madder.

The Case was a simple one. The young lady had come to this country at the height of the Civil War that was raging in her country. She had been given four years Leave to remain, and during that period she had qualified as a Nurse and had a very good job. She was employed by the National Health Service, who were very pleased with her work and performance. The four years were up and she had been asked to leave the country. She was appealing against the Order to leave. The Adjudicator was not sympathetic and suggested that, as a qualified Nurse, she would be snapped up by her home Government as they were short of Nurses.

The young lady said that this would not be the case as most of the hospitals had been destroyed and many locally trained Nurses were unemployed. So although she had received her Training abroad, she would still have to be at the end of the queue for jobs. Her Representative said that her services were needed in this country as there was a shortage of Nurses, and in fact the Government actively recruited Nurses from overseas countries such as hers. The answer to this from the Adjudicator was that when she was returned home she could apply to return here, if, as her Representative said, the UK was actively recruiting people like her from overseas. It would not take more than three months for her to go through the recruitment process and she would be back here in no time.

It just shows how ignorant some of the Adjudicators were. Her chances of being recruited in her country are very slim indeed, as the stigma of having been sent back after five years in the UK would tell against her. Some Appellants get so annoyed at the Adjudicator that in one Case I was at, he threw the water jug at the Adjudicator, narrowly missing him. From then on only plastic jugs were used in the Courts. I have even heard one Appellant being asked what flowers were grown in the front garden of his house in the village where he lived.

Now and again, Articles would appear in the Papers bemoaning the huge cost of Legal Aid to the Taxpayer especially for Refugee and Immigration Appeal cases. It was usually stated that legal eagles appearing in these Cases try to string them out making one Appeal after another when they know that there are no Legal bases for the appeals. They get paid anyway, so why not go the whole hog and get as much money as possible. I am not surprised that Legal Aid has been abolished for such Appeal Cases.

I sometimes have problems with Representatives in particular, regarding the nuances of the Krio language. This was exemplified in the case of the young man, when going through the written Interview that had taken place when he arrived at the airport, During the Hearing, he was reminded that he had said then that he had fled from his country because he was fleeing from the 'poor Society', which was interpreted to mean that he was an Economic Refugee fleeing from Poverty. The Home Office Solicitor laboured this point to prove that he was lying, because, when questioned at the Hearing, he had changed his Story to read that he was fleeing from the Poro Society, a Secret Society in his country.

The Adjudicator, being a more astute man, realized that there had been a wrong interpretation put by the person who had interviewed the young man at the airport. It should have been the Poro Society

Reflection on my life

and not the 'poor Society' as he had written down. The Home Office Solicitor had realised this all the time but was using this slip in the language to demolish the Case. I was able to explain that some of the people who speak the Krio language sometimes cannot pronounce their Rs properly so that poro could sound like 'poorer'. The young man was lucky that he came before an Adjudicator who was experienced enough to know the difference.

Some Mothers would bring their Children, including very young babies, to Court in the hope of gaining some sympathy for their Case. It happened in one such Case when a Mother brought a month old baby with her saying that she did not have anyone to leave her with. The baby did sleep quietly in her carry cot besides the mother for about fifteen minutes, after which the baby became restless and started to cry. This I must say did put the Home Office Solicitor off his stride and he asked whether he could have a short Adjournment for the baby to quieten down. The Adjudicator agreed but said that we should all stay in our places until this was done. What he did not realized was that it was time for the baby's feed. And as happens all over Africa, the mother picked up the baby with one hand and with the other brought out her breast and started to feed the child.

The look of horror on the faces of the Adjudicator, the Home Office Solicitor, the Court Clerk and her Representative, all men, could be imagined. Hastily the Adjudicator gathered up his papers, call for a break of fifteen minutes and fled the room, followed closely by the Home Office Solicitor, the Court Clerk and her Representative. I was the only one who stayed, but moved away from her and sat at the back of the Court until she had finished the business of feeding her baby. You see, being an African who grew up on that Continent, women breastfeeding openly in Public is an everyday occurrence, and so I was not fazed by seeing a woman's breast. In fact, in many places in Africa, women go round bare breasted with no problem from men. It is in the Western World that women's breasts are seen as sexual objects to be hidden under a bra.

In doing interpreting one has to sit very close to the Appellant so as to translate as the other person is speaking. In doing so one cannot help smelling the body odour of the person one has to sit close to. Sometimes the smell is pleasant but in many cases, unpleasant, and being refugees or Asylum Seekers they do not wash as often as one would like, and they do not change their clothes as one would like. So they smell. In many cases one has to put up with bad breath which can be unpleasant. If the case went on for an hour or two, or sometimes three, one had to put up with it.

I did not realize that TB is rife amongst such people until one of my colleague Interpreters complained, when he had to sit next to an Appellant with TB for a case that went on for three hours. Naturally he was very worried about catching the Disease. He complained to the Authorities and they had to issue a Health Awareness Directive from the Health and Safety Office of the Court Service. In the Directive it was stated that although TB was an issue, yet most people would have been vaccinated against it during their time at School, but if one was unsure about this, a visit to the Doctor was recommended for a simple Skin Sensitivity Test, which will show if one is protected or not.

The Directive went on to say that the risk of catching TB in the UK is not high, and even direct conversational contact with a Carrier does not mean that one will become infected. TB, the Directive went on, is usually passed from one person to another through prolonged close contact though it is, in theory, possible to pass the infection by coughing in the face of another person. The Directive stated that Interpreters whose immune system may be compromised by another Condition such as Diabetes, Alcoholism, HIV or those taking Steroids or other immune suppressive therapy should be vigilant. Interpreters should not touch clients or take actions such as sharing eating utensils. In general, Interpreters should take care not

Reflection on my life

to put themselves at risk. The Directive ended with these words 'If you are concerned that, in the course of your Job you are at risk of exposure of TB, talk to your Manager and take prescriptions described above.' Fat lot of good that.

Chapter 39
A TEST CASE

I find it sometimes difficult to be kind to the Home Office Representatives because of the questions they ask. They show such ignorance of life outside the United Kingdom that it is impossible to like them, and they make doing my work difficult. In one case I worked on, involving a very illiterate woman in her late seventies, the outcome of her claim to stay in the country hung on her relationship with her nephew, with whom she was staying. In her interview, when she first asked for Leave to Remain, she was asked whether she would agree to a DNA Test to prove that she was indeed related to him. Her reply then was no, she wouldn't. At her Appeal she was asked why she had refused to take the DNA Test. She looked blank when I interpreted the question to her. Because we are supposed to interpret word for word, I used the word DNA as asked by the Home Office Representative. It was obvious she did not know what DNA meant, so she replied that she had not been asked that Question. 'But' said the Home Office Representative 'it is stated in the Transcript of your Interview that when you were asked the question, you said you would not agree to the Test. But now you say you were never asked the Question.. Which is the truth?'

Luckily for the old lady, she was in front of a very sympathetic Adjudicator who interjected by saying that perhaps she did not know what DNA was. He then asked me to explain to her what it meant. I then told her that this was a Medical Test which would involve taking a sample of her blood or saliva and matching it with that of her Nephew to find out whether they were blood relatives.. When she understood what it was all about, she readily agreed to take the Test. And in fact when the Nephew was asked whether he

Reflection on my life

would agree to a DNA test, he also readily agreed. But then he was educated, had lived in the UK for ten years and knew what DNA was. But after all this, it was not necessary for the Test to be carried out as the Adjudicator said he was not sure that the Test would prove that there was a link between an Aunt and Nephew. Between siblings and between parents and children, yes, but not between extended families.

I just give this example to show that if she had not come before an understanding Adjudicator I am sure her Application would have been turned down just because someone was not thinking enough to find out whether the old lady understood what she was being asked.

Sometimes again the Adjudicator can be a pain in the neck, asking the Interpreter to speak up, look at them when speaking, keep close to the Appellant etc, etc. We have to comply with their requests. But sometimes it is difficult to do what they want. I try to sit as close to the Appellant as much as possible, but it is difficult to do so if the Appellant smells of body odour or has bad breath. In that case I try to keep as far away as possible, but it is not always possible to do so. I just grin and bear it and hope the Case will not take too long.

Chapter 40
THE WHISTLEBLOWER

The facilities vary at the various AIT centres in which Immigration Cases are conducted. Some are good, some so so and some awful. In some, we Interpreters are looked after and treated very well. But in others we are not treated so well. Take the main London Centre, Taylor House in Central London with several Courts, and which makes use of more Interpreters than any other. When I first started working there, the Interpreters' Room was large, with enough chairs to accommodate the number of people there at one time. There was a water cooler and Coffee, Tea and Biscuits provided, for which we have to make a small contribution. Gradually the Tea, Coffee and Biscuits disappeared (people did not always pay the voluntary small contribution, they said). Then one day we turned up to find that the Room had been reduced in size, to make more room for the Centre's Staff. This left us with very cramped accommodation and not enough seats when the place was full. Complaints about the inadequate space for Interpreters fell on deaf ears.

They also brought in more stringent Security measures. This meant that everyone entering the building had to go through one of those Scanner machines, requiring taking everything out of one's pockets....mobile phone, money, keys... before going through the scanner. Bags also had to be opened and searched. There were only two Guards on Duty to process a queue that sometimes stretched round the Building. It sometimes took so long to process all the Appellants and Relatives, their Representatives and Interpreters that by the time the Cases started many people were still outside the

Reflection on my life

Building waiting to get in, and holding up the Proceedings of the Court. Requests by Interpreters to be treated like the Staff who had their own separate entrances and gained access by showing their Security Passes fell on deaf ears. As all Interpreters carry Identity Cards this could have made our lives easier, but it was not to be. There was a short-lived suggestion that we should Sign In at the Reception before coming up to the first floor, but there was so much confusion over this that it was soon abandoned. The List we had to sign never seemed to be there and the Security Guards were too busy to find out where it could be.

Chapter 41

KRIO, JAMAICAN PATOIS AND THOSE JUDGES AND COURTS

Sometime private Interpreting Agencies ring up from time to time, to book me to do some work for them, and if I am free I accept the Booking. But some of them do not understand the difference between the Krio language, which I speak and which is spoken in Sierra Leone where I come from, and Creole which is spoken in places such as Mauritius, which is on the other side of Africa. They do not understand that the Patois spoken in Jamaica is also different from Krio.

I found this out to my cost when I accepted a Booking to interpret in a court in Coventry. It was the first time I had worked for the Agency, and, in fact, it was my first Case in a proper Court rather than in an Immigration Court setting. I was a greenhorn at the time, and got myself into a tangle. In the first place, it was Winter and the day was cold with lots of Snow on the ground. When I arrived at the Station there were no taxis as most of them had got stuck in traffic and Snow drifts. I was told the Court was within walking distance and so set out in the Snow to walk. After about twenty minutes and with lots of slipping and sliding on wet Snow I reached the Court. It was when I was introduced to the Client by his Solicitor, before the Case started, that I realised that the young man in question spoke Jamaican Patois rather than Krio.

Lucky for me I have a good ear and after listening to him for about fifteen minutes I got the hang of his speech pattern. I asked him to speak slowly and was able to go through the whole process of interpreting his answers to the questions put by his Solicitor without too many mistakes. But I was dreading doing the interpreting inside the Court especially in front of a Judge in his Red Robe and Wig. Luckily the Client pleaded Guilty as soon as the Case started, was

Reflection on my life

sentenced, after an Admonition by the Judge and the case was over without me having to utter a word.

After that Case I realised that I could interpret the Jamaican Patois, and started to take on more such cases.

It is sometimes difficult when interpreting to get the correct words as I have found out to my cost several times. In one case the young man stated that he had his index finger broken and what he called one of his Balls crushed. In my haste I translated this as one of his Scrotum crushed. The Adjudicator corrected me that it must have been one of his Testicles and not Scrotum that was crushed. I hung my head in shame.

I have been asked why is it that people from a Country like Sierra Leone, where most people understand some form of English, will come to the UK and pretend that they cannot understand the language, and an Interpreter will have to be provided for them. My feeling is that many of them think that if they say that, then the Interview would not take place and they would be given the benefit of the doubt and allowed to stay. You can see the look on their faces when they are told not to worry as an Interpreter will be provided for them free of charge.

And sometimes they are caught out. Many a times I have turned up to do interpreting to find the client speaks and understand English, and did not need interpreting. In that case, the Adjudicator would ask me to sit by him/her and help to explain something or words that need explaining. One such was when a lady was adamant that she spoke good English and did not need an Interpreter. Just as well that I stayed with her, because she did not know or understand the word Sibling.

As I turn eighty, my Journey is coming to an end, because I have to slow down and take things easy. But the Journey is not yet over, because as my mother used to say, what is left of my life is not as much as what has gone before. But I am not yet ready to kick the bucket, that is, not until I have completed all, or some of the things on my *Bucket List*. And what is on my *Bucket List*? That is another Story.

The End

Reflection on my life

BOOKS WRITTEN BY MICHAEL CROWDER

PAGANS AND POLITICIANS, Published by Hutchinsons of London.

WEST AFRICA UNDER COLONIAL RULE, Published by Hutchinsons of London

THE STORY OF NIGERIA. Published by Hutchinsons of London

SENERAL – A STUDY OF FRENCH ASSIMILATION POLICY, Published by Hutchinsons of London

WEST AFRICAN RESISTANCE: MILITARY ESPONSE TO COLONIAL OCCUPATION

COLONIAL WEST AFRICA: COLLECTED ESSAYS WEST AFRICA: AN INTRODUCTIONTO ITS HISTORY

WITH JOINT AUTHORS

EZERE GOES TO SCHOOL

NIGERIA; A MODERN HISTORY FOR SCHOOLS with Rex Akpofure

HISTORY OF WEST AFRICA: AD. 1000 TO THE PRESENT. With Guda Abdullahi

ARNOLD AWOONOR-GORDON

Reflection on my life

Printed in Great Britain
by Amazon